CREATIVE
HOMEOWNER®

MOST-POPULAR
1-STORY
HOME PLANS

CREATIVE HOMEOWNER®, Upper Saddle River, New Jersey

COPYRIGHT © 2004

CRE**A**TIVE
HOMEOWNER®

A Division of Federal Marketing Corp.
Upper Saddle River, NJ

VP/Publisher: Brian H. Toolan
VP/Editorial Director: Timothy O. Bakke
Production Manager: Kimberly H. Vivas

Home Plans Editor: Kenneth D. Stuts
Home Plans Designer Liaison: Maureen L. Mulligan

Design and Layout: Arrowhead Direct (David Kroha, Cindy DiPierdomenico, Judith Kroha)

Cover Design: David Geer

Manufactured in the United States of America

Current Printing (last digit)
10

Most-Popular 1-Story Home Plans
Library of Congress Control Number: 2003112507
ISBN: 1-58011-184-X

CREATIVE HOMEOWNER®
A Division of Federal Marketing Corp.
24 Park Way
Upper Saddle River, NJ 07458
www.creativehomeowner.com

Note: The homes as shown in the photographs and renderings in this book may differ from the actual blueprints. When studying the house of your choice, please check the floor plans carefully.

PHOTO CREDITS

page 5 courtesy of Western Wood Products
page 6 *top* Freeze Frame Studio/CH; *bottom* courtesy of Trus Joist MacMillan
page 7 Timothy O. Bakke/CH
page 68 courtesy of Merillat Industries
page 69 courtesy of Kraftmaid Cabinetry
pages 70 and 71 *left* courtesy of Kraftmaid Cabinetry; *center* courtesy of Jenn-Air; right courtesy of Wood-Mode Cabinetry
page 72 *top* courtesy of Kohler; bottom right courtesy of Ann Sacks Tile; *bottom left* courtesy of Wilsonart International
page 73 *top row* courtesy of Kraftmaid Cabinetry; bottom courtesy of Armstrong Floors
page 134 courtesy of Mannington Floors
page 135 courtesy of Congoleum
page 136 *top* courtesy of Congoleum; *bottom* courtesy of Mannington Floors **page 137** courtesy of Dal-Tile
page 138 *left* courtesy of Mannington Floors; *right* courtesy of Congoleum
page 139 left courtesy of Mannington Floors; *right* courtesy of Dal-Tile
page 202 *top* courtesy of Trex Decks; *bottom* courtesy of the Hickson Corp.
page 203 courtesy of Arch Wood Protection
page 204 both courtesy of the California Redwood Association
page 205 courtesy of Trex Decks
pages 270 and 271 both George Ross/CH
page 272 Christine Elasigue/CH **page 273** *top* George Ross/CH; *bottom all* Christine Elasigue/CH
page 274 *left* George Ross/CH; *right (top to bottom)* Christine Elasigue/CH
pages 275–277 all Christine Elasigue/CH

Contents

Getting Started

Maybe you can't wait to bang the first nail. Or you may be just as happy leaving town until the windows are cleaned. The extent of your involvement with the construction phase is up to you. Your time, interests, and abilities can help you decide how to get the project from lines on paper to reality. But building a house requires more than putting pieces together. Whoever is in charge of the process must competently manage people as well as supplies, materials, and construction. He or she will have to

■ Make a project schedule to plan the orderly progress of the work. This can be a bar chart that shows the time period of activity by each trade.

■ Establish a budget for each category of work, such as foundation, framing, and finish carpentry.

■ Arrange for a source of construction financing.

■ Get a building permit and post it conspicuously at the construction site.

■ Line up supply sources and order materials.

■ Find subcontractors and negotiate their contracts.

■ Coordinate the work so that it progresses smoothly with the fewest conflicts.

■ Notify inspectors at the appropriate milestones.

■ Make payments to suppliers and subcontractors.

You as the Builder

You'll have to take care of every logistical detail yourself if you decide to act as your own builder or general contractor. But along with the responsibilities of managing the project, you gain the flexibility to do as much of your own work as you want and subcontract out the rest. Before taking this path, however, be sure you have the time and capabilities. Do you also have the

time and ability to schedule the work, hire and coordinate subs, order materials, and keep ahead of the accounting required to manage the project successfully? If you do, you stand to save the amount that a general contractor would charge to take on these responsibilities, normally 15 to 30 percent of the construction cost. If you take this responsibility on but mismanage the project, the potential savings will erode and may even cost you more than if you had hired a builder in the first place. A subcontractor might charge extra for hav-

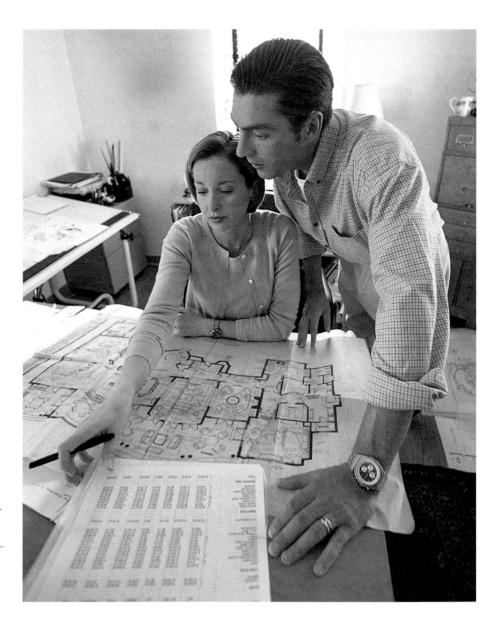

Acting as the builder, above, requires the ability to hire and manage subcontractors.

Building a home, opposite, includes the need to schedule building inspections at the appropriate milestones.

ing to return to the site to complete work that was originally scheduled for an earlier date. Or perhaps because you didn't order the windows at the beginning, you now have to pay for a recent cost increase. (If you had hired a builder in the first place he or she would absorb the increase.)

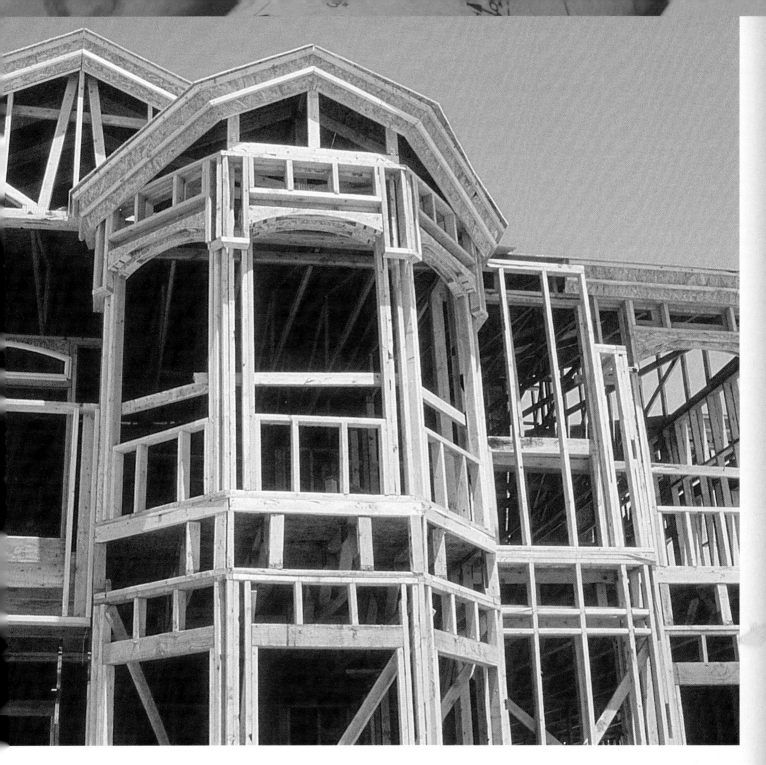

Hiring a Builder to Handle Construction

A builder or general contractor will manage every aspect of the construction process. Your role after signing the construction contract will be to make regular progress payments and ensure that the work for which you are paying has been completed. You will also consult with the builder and agree to any changes that may have to be made along the way.

Leads for finding builders might come from friends or neighbors who have had contractors build, remodel, or add to their homes. Real-estate agents and bankers may have some names handy but are more likely familiar with the builder's ability to complete projects on time and budget than the quality of the work itself.

The next step is to narrow your list of candidates to three or four who you think can do a quality job and work harmoniously with you. Phone each builder to see whether he or she is interested in being considered for your project. If so, invite the builder to an interview at your home. The meeting will serve two purposes. You'll be able to ask the candidate about his or her experience, and you'll be able to see whether or not your personalities are compatible. Go over the plans with the builder to make certain that he or she understands the scope of the project. Ask if they have constructed similar houses. Get references, and check the builder's standing with the Better Business Bureau. Develop a short list of builders, say three, and ask them to submit bids for the project.

Contracts

Lump-Sum Contracts

A lump-sum, or fixed-fee, contract lets you know from the beginning just what the project will cost, barring any changes made because of your requests or unforeseen conditions. This form works well for projects that promise few surprises and are well defined from the outset by a complete set of contract documents. You can enter into a fixed-price contract by negotiating with a single builder on your short list or by obtaining bids from three or four builders. If you go the latter route, give each bidder a set of documents and allow at least two weeks for them to submit their bids. When you get the bids, decide who you want and call the others to thank them for their efforts. You don't have to accept the lowest bid, but it probably makes sense to do so since you have already honed the list to builders you trust. Inform this builder of your intentions to finalize a contract.

Cost-Plus-Fee Contracts

Under a cost-plus-fee contract, you agree to pay the builder for the costs of labor and materials, as verified by receipts, plus a fee that represents the builder's overhead and profit. This arrangement is sometimes referred to as "time and materials." The fee can range between 15 and 30 percent of the incurred costs. Because you ultimately pick up the tab—whatever the costs—the contractor is never at risk, as he is with a lump-sum contract. You won't know the final total cost of a cost-plus-fee contract until the project is built and paid for. If you can live with that uncertainty, there are offsetting advantages. First, this form allows you to accommodate unknown conditions much more easily than does a lump-sum contract. And rather than being tied down by the project documents, you will be free to make changes at any point along the way. This can be a trap, though. Watching the project take shape will spark the desire to add something or do something differently. Each change costs more, and the accumulation can easily exceed your budget. Because of the uncertainty of the final tab and the built-in advantage to the contractor, you should think twice before entering into this form of contract.

Contract Content

The conditions of your agreement should be spelled out thoroughly in writing and signed by both parties, whatever contractual arrangement you make with your builder. Your contract should include provisions for the following:

- The names and addresses of the owner and builder.
- A description of the work to be included ("As described in the plans and specifications dated . . .").
- The date that the work will be completed if time is of the essence.
- The contract price for lump-sum contracts and the builder's allowed profit and overhead costs for changes.
- The builder's fee for cost-plus-fee contracts and the method of accounting and requesting payment.
- The criteria for progress payments (monthly, by project milestones) and the conditions of final payment.
- A list of each drawing and specification section that is to be included as part of the contract.
- Requirements for guarantees. (One year is the standard period for which contractors guarantee the entire project, but you may require specific guarantees on

When submitting bids, all of the builders should base their estimates on the same specifications. Once the work begins, communicate with your builder to keep the work proceeding smoothly.

Inspect your newly built home, if possible, before the builder closes it up and finishes it.

certain parts of the project, such as a 20-year guarantee on the roofing.)
- Provisions for insurance.
- A description of how changes in the work orders will be handled.

The builder may have a standard contract that you can tailor to the specifics of your project. These contain complete specific conditions with blanks that you can fill in to fit your project and a set of "general conditions" that cover a host of issues from insurance to termination provisions. It's always a good idea to have an attorney review the draft of your completed contract before signing it.

Working with Your Builder

The construction phase officially begins when you have a signed copy of the contract and copies of any insurance required from the builder. It's not unheard of for a builder to request an initial payment of 10 to 20 percent of the total cost to cover mobilization costs, those costs associated with obtaining permits and getting set up to begin the actual construction. If you agree to this, keep a careful eye on the progress of the work to ensure that the total paid out at any one time doesn't get too far out of sync with the actual work completed.

What about changes? From here on, it's up to you and your builder to proceed in good faith and to keep the channels of communication open. Even so, changes of one sort or another beset every project, and they usually add to its cost.

Light at the End of the Tunnel.

The builder's request for a final inspection marks the end of the construction phase—almost. At the final inspection meeting, you and the builder will inspect the work, noting any defects or incomplete items on a "punch list." When the builder tidies up the punch list items, you should reinspect. Sometimes, builders go on to another job and take forever to clean up the last few details, so only after all items on the list have been completed satisfactorily should you release the final payment, which often accounts for the builder's profit.

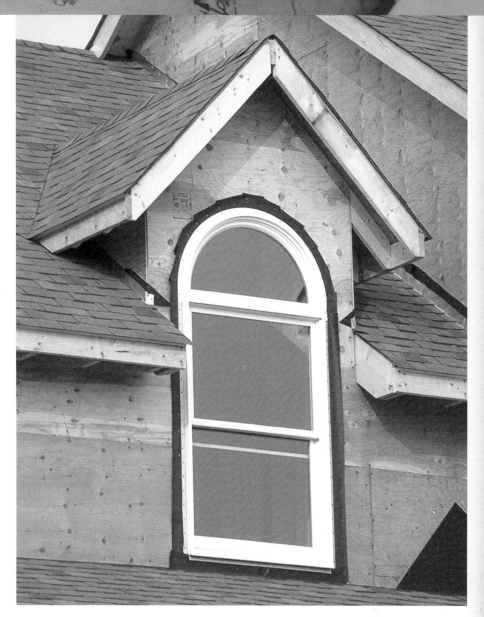

Some Final Words

Having a positive attitude is important when undertaking a project as large as building a home. A positive attitude can help you ride out the rigors and stress of the construction process.

Stay Flexible. Expect problems, because they certainly will occur. Weather can upset the schedule you have established for subcontractors. A supplier may get behind on deliveries, which also affects the schedule. An unexpected pipe may surprise you during excavation. Just as certain, every problem that comes along has a solution if you are open to it.

Be Patient. The extra days it may take to resolve a construction problem will be forgotten once the project is completed.

Express Yourself. If what you see isn't exactly what you thought you were getting, don't be afraid to look into changing it. Or you may spot an unforeseen opportunity for an improvement. Changes usually cost more money, though, so don't make frivolous decisions.

Finally, watching your home go up is exciting, so stay upbeat. Get away from your project from time to time. Dine out. Take time to relax. A positive attitude will make for smoother relations with your builder. An optimistic outlook will yield better-quality work if you are doing your own construction. And though the project might seem endless while it is under way, keep in mind that all the planning and construction will fade to a faint memory at some time in the future, and you will be getting a lifetime of pleasure from a home that is just right for you.

Living Room

Plan #111004

Dimensions: 76' W x 85' D
Levels: 1
Square Footage: 2,968
Bedrooms: 4
Full Bathrooms: 3½
Foundation: Slab
Crawl space available for an extra fee
Materials List Available: No
Price Category: F

If you've been looking for a home that includes a special master suite, this one could be the answer to your dreams.

Features:

• **Living Room:** Make a sitting area around the fireplace here so that the whole family can enjoy the warmth on chilly days and winter evenings. A door from this room leads to the rear covered porch, making this room the heart of your home.

• **Kitchen:** An island with a cooktop makes cooking a pleasure in this well-designed kitchen, and the breakfast bar invites visitors at all times of day.

• **Utility Room:** A sink and a built-in ironing board make this room totally practical.

• **Master Suite:** A private fireplace in the corner sets a romantic tone for this bedroom, and the door to the covered porch allows you to sit outside on warm summer nights. The bath has two vanities, a divided walk-in closet, a standing shower, and a deluxe corner bathtub.

Wood Deck

Covered Porch

Master Bedroom 16'9"x21'5"

Master Bath

WIC

Breakfast 14'x12'1"

Living 24'8"x19'3"

Bedroom 12'4"x12'1"

Kitchen 18'4"x14'10"

Dining 13'1"x14'7"

Foyer

Bedroom 13'x12'

Bedroom 12'1"x13'

Utility

Porch

Garage 21'2"x27'2"

Kitchen

Dining Room

Master Bath

Master Bath

SMARTtip®

How to Quit Smoking — Lighting Your Fireplace

Before attempting to light a wood fire, make certain that the damper is open all the way. This allows a good draft (flow of air up the chimney) to prevent smoke from blowing back into the room. To ensure a good draft—particularly if your home is well insulated—open a window a bit when lighting a fire.

The opposite of draft is downdraft, which occurs when cold air flows down the chimney and into the room. If the fireplace is properly designed and maintained, the smoke shelf will prevent backpuffing from downdraft most of the time by redirecting cold air currents back up the chimney. The open damper also helps prevent backpuffing.

Also, build a fire slowly to let the chimney liner heat up, which will create a good draft and minimize the chances of downdraft.

Don't wait until fall to inspect the chimney. Do this job, or call a chimney sweep, when the weather is mild. Because some repairs take a while to make, it's best to have them done when the fireplace is not normally in use. If you do the inspection yourself, wear old clothes, eye goggles, and a mask.

Illustration provided by designer/architect.

Copyright by designer/architect.

Plan #211017

Dimensions: 60' W x 31' D
Levels: 1
Square Footage: 1,212
Bedrooms: 3
Bathrooms: 2
Foundation: Slab
Materials List Available: No
Price Category: B

SMARTtip®

Adding Trim Accessories

Consider adding plinth and corner blocks to door and window casings. These relatively inexpensive elements add a decorative flourish to wall openings, bringing depth and richness to an interior space.

Illustration provided by designer/architect.

Copyright by designer/architect.

Plan #211018

Dimensions: 40' W x 64' D
Levels: 1
Square Footage: 1,266
Bedrooms: 3
Bathrooms: 2
Foundation: Crawl space
Materials List Available: Yes
Price Category: B

Plan #121056

Dimensions: 48' W x 50' D

Levels: 1

Square Footage: 1,479

Bedrooms: 2

Bathrooms: 2

Foundation: Basement

Materials List Available: Yes

Price Category: B

Photo provided by designer/architect.

Copyright by designer/architect.

Optional Third Bedroom Floor Plan

Plan #391038

Dimensions: 59' W x 44' D

Levels: 1

Square Footage: 1,642

Bedrooms: 3

Bathrooms: 2

Foundation: Crawl space, slab, and basement

Materials List Available: Yes

Price Category: C

Images provided by designer/architect.

Copyright by designer/architect.

Optional basement stairs

Plan #131005

Dimensions: 70' W x 37'4" D
Levels: 1
Square Footage: 1,595
Bedrooms: 3
Bathrooms: 2
Foundation: Basement, crawl space, or slab
Materials List Available: Yes
Price Category: C

Photos provided by designer/architect.

SMARTtip®

Create a Courtyard

Create a private walled-garden retreat with fences covered by climbing vines. Add height with trellises, and divide spaces with clipped boxwood hedges. Include an (almost) instant patio by digging away an area of sod and then covering it with a layer of sand and landscaping mesh to discourage weeds. Then cover it with pea gravel, and add a garden bench, statuary, and perhaps an antique or two. The result? European ambiance for even the most nondescript suburban yard.

With the finest features of an open design in the main living areas, this home gives privacy where you need it. Best of all, it's wheelchair accessible.

Features:

• Foyer: A high ceiling gives this area real presence and serves to blend it seamlessly with the great room and the dining room.

• Great Room: The open design allows you to use this room as an extension of the dining room or, if you wish, furnish it to create a private reading nook or visually separate media center.

• Breakfast Room: Both this room and the adjacent well-appointed kitchen flow into the rest of the living area. However, access to the rear porch, where you can sit out and enjoy the weather while you eat, distinguishes this room.

• Master Suite: Located in the same wing as the other bedrooms, this suite has a separate entrance and features a vaulted ceiling, three closets, and a compartmented bath.

Copyright by designer/architect.

Foyer

Dining Room

Living Room

Great Room

SMARTtip®

Natural Trellis

Create a natural rustic trellis that might even, if growing conditions are right, produce its own pretty blooms. Cut and place saplings in the ground as uprights. Then weave old grapevines with smaller saplings for the lattice.

Plan #161013

Dimensions: 59'4" W x 46'4" D

Levels: 1

Square Footage: 1,509

Bedrooms: 3

Bathrooms: 2

Foundation: Poured

Materials List Available: Yes

Price Category: C

Illustration provided by designer/architect.

Copyright by designer/architect.

Rear Elevation

Plan #161014

Dimensions: 51'8" W x 49'8" D

Levels: 1

Square Footage: 1,698

Bedrooms: 3

Bathrooms: 2

Foundation: Poured

Materials List Available: Yes

Price Category: C

Illustration provided by designer/architect.

Copyright by designer/architect.

Rear Elevation

Copyright by designer/architect.

Plan #321010

Dimensions: 59' W x 37'8" D
Levels: 1
Square Footage: 1,787
Bedrooms: 3
Bathrooms: 2
Foundation: Basement
Materials List Available: Yes
Price Category: C

Illustration provided by designer/architect.

SMARTtip®

Country Décor in Your Bathroom

Collections are often part of a country decor, even in the bathroom. All you need is three or more of anything that have size, shape, or color in common. You can mass them on walls, on shelves, on the windowsills, or even along the edge of the tub.

Copyright by designer/architect.

Plan #321013

Dimensions: 68' W x 30' D
Levels: 1
Square Footage: 1,360
Bedrooms: 3
Bathrooms: 2
Foundation: Basement
Materials List Available: Yes
Price Category: B

Illustration provided by designer/architect.

SMARTtip®

Glass Doors and Fire Safety

Professionals recommend keeping glass doors open while a fire is burning. When the doors are left completely open, the burning flame has a more realistic appearance and the glass doesn't become soiled by swirling ashes. When the doors are closed, heat from a large hot fire can break the glass.

Plan #221002

Dimensions: 52' W x 46' D

Levels: 1

Square Footage: 1,508

Bedrooms: 3

Bathrooms: 2

Foundation: Basement

Materials List Available: No

Price Category: C

Illustration provided by designer/architect.

The classic brick-and-siding exterior of this ranch allows you to choose landscaping plants of any size, shape, or color.

Features:

- Ceiling Height: 8 ft.

- Entry: A vaulted ceiling announces the distinction of this design.

- Living Room: Also with a vaulted ceiling for a feeling of spaciousness, this living room features well-positioned windows that look out to the backyard.

- Dining Room: Sliding glass doors in this room open to the outside.

- Kitchen: This thoughtfully designed kitchen will please even the most discerning cook. For serving ease, the bright and cheery room is open to the dining room.

- Master Bedroom: You can look out to the backyard from the windows in this private retreat or relax in the charming, fully equipped bath.

Rear Elevation

Copyright by designer/architect.

Plan #101002

Dimensions: 46' W x 42' D

Levels: 1

Square Footage: 1,296

Bedrooms: 3

Bathrooms: 2

Foundation: Crawl space, slab, basement

Materials List Available: No

Price Category: B

Illustration provided by designer/architect.

This affordable compact home is also strikingly attractive.

Features:

- Ceiling Height: 8 ft.

- Foyer: Beveled glass front provides a luxurious entry.

- Family Room: This spacious 16-ft. x 20-ft. room has a vaulted ceiling.

- Laundry Room: Here is ample space to fold clothes—and a convenient sink.

- Master Bedroom Suite: Split from other bedrooms, this suite has many his and her features.

- Kitchen: This galley kitchen offers open traffic patterns with a breakfast bar.

- Breakfast Eating Area: A growing family will find additional seating space that leads to a covered porch providing a pleasant retreat

Copyright by designer/architect.

SMARTtip®

Preparing Walls for Paint

Poor surface preparation is the number-one cause of paint failure. Preparing surfaces properly—including removing loose paint and thoroughly sanding—may be tedious, but it's important for a good-looking and long-lasting finish.

Plan #211013

Dimensions: 48' W x 29' D

Levels: 1

Square Footage: 998

Bedrooms: 3

Bathrooms: 1

Foundation: Slab, optional crawl space, or basement

Materials List Available: Yes

Price Category: A

If you're looking for a well-designed, space-efficient small home, you'll love this traditional beauty.

Features:

• Ceiling Height: 8 ft.

• Living Room: Large enough to make entertaining easy, this room is positioned so that friends and family will naturally gather here.

• Kitchen: This galley kitchen streamlines your work patterns and provides good storage areas as well as counter space.

• Patio: Walk from the kitchen straight onto this patio in the morning to enjoy your breakfast in the sunshine or in the afternoon and evening when you're entertaining guests or grilling for the family.

• Master Bedroom: A large walk-in closet gives good storage space here, and direct access to the bathroom adds convenience.

Illustration provided by designer/architect.

Copyright by designer/architect.

SMARTtip®

Mixing Patterns

A trick for mixing patterns is to provide links of scale, motif, and color. The regularity of checks, stripes, textural looks, and geometrics, particularly if small-scale and low-contrast, tends to make them easy-to-mix "neutral" patterns. A small floral can play off a thin ticking stripe, while a cabbage-rose chintz may require a bolder stripe as a same-scale foil. Use the same or similar patterns in varying sizes, or develop them by focusing on florals, geometric, or ethnic prints.

Plan #301002

Dimensions: 57'2" W x 54'10" D

Levels: 1

Square Footage: 1,845

Bedrooms: 3

Bathrooms: 2½

Foundation: Crawl space, slab

Materials List Available: Yes

Price Category: D

Illustration provided by designer/architect.

Although compact, this home is filled with surprisingly luxurious features.

Features:

- Ceiling Height: 8 ft. unless otherwise noted.

- Front Porch: Guests will be sheltered from the rain by this lovely little porch.

- Foyer: This elegant foyer features a 10-ft. ceiling and is open to the dining room and the rear great room.

- Dining Room: The 10-ft. ceiling from the foyer continues into this spacious dining room.

- Family Room: This family room features a vaulted ceiling and a fireplace with built-in bookcases.

- Kitchen: This kitchen boasts a pantry and plenty of storage and counter space.

- Master Bedroom: This master bedroom includes a cathedral ceiling and two walk-in closets. The master bath has two vanities, a corner spa, and a walk-in closet.

-Copyright by designer/architect.

Plan #161002

Dimensions: 64'2" W x 44'2" D

Levels: 1

Square Footage: 1,860

Bedrooms: 3

Bathrooms: 2

Foundation: Poured basement

Materials List Available: Yes

Price Category: D

Photos and illustrations provided by designer/architect.

The brick, stone, and cedar shake facade provides color and texture to the exterior, while the unique nooks and angles inside this delightful one-level home give it character.

Features:

- **Great Room/Dining Room:** This spacious great room is furnished with a wood-burning fireplace, a high ceiling, and French doors. Wide entrances to the breakfast room and dining room expand its space to comfortably hold large gatherings.

- **Kitchen:** The breakfast bar offers additional seating. The covered porch lets you enjoy a view of the landscape and is conveniently located for outdoor meals off this kitchen and breakfast area.

- **Master Bedroom:** The master bedroom is a private retreat. An alcove creates a comfortable sitting area, and an angled entry leads to the bath with whirlpool and a double-bowl vanity.

Left Side Elevation

Rear Elevation

Right Side Elevation

Copyright by designer/architect.

Dining Room

Living Room / Dining Room

Great Room/Breakfast Area

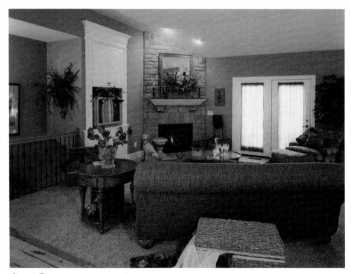

Great Room

SMARTtip®

Installing Rods and Poles

The way to install a rod or pole depends on the type it is, the brackets that will hold it, the weight of the window treatment, and the surface to which it is being fastened. Given below are some general guidelines, but for specific installation procedures, refer to the instructions that accompany the rod or pole.

- Use a stepladder to reach high places.

- Use the proper tools.

- Take accurate measurements.

- Work with a helper.

- If attaching a bracket to wood, first drill small pilot holes to avoid splitting the wood.

- Consider using wall anchors, particularly for the heavier window treatments.

- Use a level as needed to help you position the brackets for the pole or rod.

- Take care not to drill or hammer into any pipes or electrical wiring.

Because they're designed to stand out, decorative poles and their finials require more room for installation than conventional drapery rods. Finials add inches to the ends of a window treatment, so make sure you have enough wall room to display your hardware to its full advantage. And because decorative rods are often heavy, be certain your window frames and walls can support the weight.

Plan #241001

Dimensions: 65' W x 56'3" D

Levels: 1

Square Footage: 2,350

Bedrooms: 3

Bathrooms: 2½

Foundation: Slab

Materials List Available: No

Price Category: E

Illustration provided by designer/architect.

Classic, traditional rooflines combine with arched windows to draw immediate attention to this lovely three-bedroom home.

Features:

• **Great Room:** The foyer introduces you to this impressive great room, with its grand 10-ft. ceiling and handsome fireplace.

• **Kitchen:** Certain to become the hub of such a family-oriented home, this spacious kitchen, which adjoins the breakfast area and a delightful sunroom, features an abundance of counter space, a pantry, and a convenient eating bar.

• **Master Suite:** You will enjoy the privacy and comfort of this master suite, which features a whirlpool tub, split vanities, and a separate shower.

• **Study:** Adjourn to the front of the house, and enjoy the quiet confines of this private study with built-in bookshelves to work, read, or just relax.

Copyright by designer/architect.

SMARTtip®

Kitchen Counters

Make use of counter inserts to help with the cooking chores. For example, ceramic tiles inlaid in a laminate counter create a heat-proof landing zone near the range. A marble or granite insert is tailor-made for pastry chefs. And a butcher-block inlay is a great addition to the food prep area.

Plan #391019

Dimensions: 56' W x 32' D
Levels: 1
Square Footage: 1,792
Bedrooms: 3
Bathrooms: 1¾
Foundation: Basement
Materials List Available: Yes
Price Category: C

Images provided by designer/architect.

This southern-style cottage with sociable porch fits in almost anywhere, from a leafy lane to hillside or curbside and renders a lot of living space and hospitality.

Features:

• **Family Room:** This room features a central stone fireplace, plus two walls of windows to usher in the light. Sloping ceilings and decorative beams boost its rustic charm. An enormously generous space, it opens wide to the corner kitchen.

• **Dining Room:** This room has its own level of sophistication, including entry outside to the deck.

• **Utility Areas:** The family-sized pantry and laundry area are set off by themselves to avoid interference with everyday living.

• **Master Suite:** A leisurely hall leads to the master bedroom and private full bath, wide walk-in closets, and a trio of windows.

• **Bedrooms:** Across the hall the two secondary bedrooms share a roomy bath and a view of the front porch.

Copyright by designer/architect.

SMARTtip®

Electrical Safety in the Kitchen

Sometimes the special needs of the disabled may seem to conflict with those of the very young. A case in point is accessible switch placement, which is lower on a wall. The NKBA recommends locating outlets and switches inside the front of an adult-accessible tilt-down drawer to conceal them from children. Alternatively, an outlet strip can be kept out of a child's reach and at a convenient adult location while lessening the reach to outlets and switches installed in the backsplash.

Plan #221001

Dimensions: 87' W x 60' D
Levels: 1
Square Footage: 2,600
Bedrooms: 3
Bathrooms: 2½
Foundation: Basement
Materials List Available: No
Price Category: F

You'll love this traditional ranch for its unusual spaciousness and many comfortable amenities.

Features:

- **Great Room:** As you enter the home, you'll have a clear view all the way to the backyard through the many windows in this huge room. Built-ins here provide a practical touch, and the fireplace makes this room cozy when the weather's cool.

- **Kitchen:** This large kitchen has been thoughtfully designed to make cooking a pleasure. It flows into a lovely dining nook, so it's also a great place to entertain.

- **Master Suite:** Relaxing will come naturally in this lovely suite, with its two walk-in closets, private sitting area, and large, sumptuous bathroom that features a Jacuzzi tub.

- **Additional Bedrooms:** Located on the opposite side of the house from the master

suite, these bedrooms are both convenient to a full bath. You can use one room as a den if you wish.

Copyright by designer/architect.

Rear Elevation

Kitchen

Illustration provided by designer/architect.

Plan #251005

Dimensions: 50' W x 44'2" D
Levels: 1
Square Footage: 1,631
Bedrooms: 3
Bathrooms: 2
Foundation: Basement
Materials List Available: Yes
Price Category: C

This elegant home features hip roof lines that will add appeal in any neighborhood.

Features:

- Ceiling Height: 9 ft.
- Front Porch: The porch stretches across the entire front of the home, offering plenty of space to sit and enjoy evening breezes.
- Family Room: This family room features a handsome fireplace and has plenty of room for all kinds of family activities.

- Dining Room: This dining room has plenty of room for dinner parties. After dinner, guests can step through French doors onto the rear deck.
- Kitchen: This kitchen is a pleasure in which to work. It features an angled snack bar with plenty of room for informal family meals.
- Master Bedroom: You'll enjoy retiring at day's end to this master bedroom, with its large walk-in closet.
- Master Bath. This master bath features a double vanity, a deluxe tub, and a walk-in shower.

Copyright by designer/architect.

SMARTtip®

Victorian Style

Victorian, today, is a very romantic look. To underscore this, add the scent of lavender or some other dried flower to the room or use potpourri, which you can keep in a bowl on the vanity. Hang a fragrant pomander on a hook, display lavender soaps on a wall shelf, or tuck sachets between towels on a shelf. For an authentic touch, display a Victorian favorite, the spider plant.

Plan #321001

Dimensions: 83' W x 42' D

Levels: 1

Square Footage: 1,721

Bedrooms: 3

Bathrooms: 2

Foundation: Basement, crawl space, or slab

Materials List Available: Yes

Price Category: C

Illustration provided by designer/architect.

Rear View

You'll love the atrium that creates a warm, naturally lit space inside this gracious home, as well as the roof dormers that give it wonderful curb appeal from the outside.

Features:

- **Great Room:** Bathed in light from the atrium window wall, this room, with its vaulted ceiling, will be the hub of your family life.

- **Dining Room:** This room also has a vaulted ceiling and is lit by the atrium, but you can draw drapes at night to create a cozy, warm feeling.

- **Kitchen:** Designed for functionality, this step-saving kitchen is easy to organize and makes cooking a pleasure.

- **Breakfast Room:** For convenience, this room is located between the kitchen and the rear covered porch.

- **Master Suite:** Retire with pleasure to this lovely retreat, with its luxurious bath.

Copyright by designer/architect.

Plan #131009

Dimensions: 64'10" W x 57'8" D
Levels: 1
Square Footage: 2,018
Bedrooms: 3
Bathrooms: 2
Foundation: Basement, crawl space, or slab
Materials List Available: Yes
Price Category: E

Illustration provided by designer/architect.

The pavilion-styled great room at the heart of this H-shaped ranch gives it an unusual elegance that you're sure to enjoy.

Features:

- Great Room: The tray ceiling sets off this room, and a fireplace warms it on chilly nights and cool days. Two sets of sliding glass doors leading to the backyard terrace let in natural light and create an efficient traffic flow.

- Kitchen: Designed for a gourmet cook, this kitchen features a snack bar that everyone will enjoy and easy access to the breakfast room.

- Breakfast Room: Open to the columned rear porch, this breakfast room is an ideal spot for company or family brunches.

- Master Suite: A sitting area and access to the porch make the bedroom luxurious, while the private bath featuring a whirlpool tub creates a spa atmosphere.

Great Room

Copyright by designer/architect.

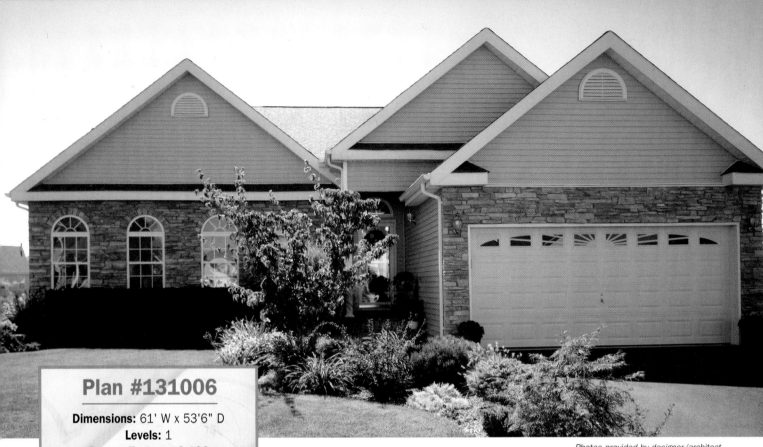

Plan #131006

Dimensions: 61' W x 53'6" D
Levels: 1
Square Footage: 2,193
Bedrooms: 3
Bathrooms: 2
Foundation: Basement, crawl space, or slab
Materials List Available: Yes
Price Category: E

Photos provided by designer/architect.

This compact home is perfect for a small lot, but even so, has all the features of a much larger home, thanks to its space-saving interior design that lets one area flow into the next.

Features:

- Great Room: This wonderful room is sure to be the heart of your home. Visually, it flows from the foyer and dining room to the rear of the house, giving you enough space to create a private nook or two in it or treat it as a single, large room.

- Dining Room: Emphasize the formality of this room by decorating with subdued colors and sumptuous fabrics.

- Kitchen: Designed for efficiency, this kitchen features ample counter space and cabinets in a layout guaranteed to please you.

- Master Suite: You'll love the amenities in this private master suite, with its lovely bedroom and a bath filled with contemporary fixtures.

Rear View

TRAY CEIL
DEN
16'-4" x 15'-6"

FIREPLACE

SL GL DRS

9' CLG
BKFST RM
21'-4" x 13'-0"

KIT

VAULTED
GREAT RM
15'-0" x 23'-0"

STEPPED CLG
MSTR BEDRM
15'-0" x 16'-4"

REF

CL

WICL

BATH

LIN

CL

9' CLG
BEDRM #2
11'-0" x 13'-0"

9' CLG
DINING RM
12'-4" x 15'-4"

FOY.

W D

LAUN RM

CL

LIN

UTIL

MSTR BATH

LOCATION OF OPT BSMT STAIR

TWO CAR GARAGE
18'-4" x 20'-0"

COV. PORCH

9' CLG
BEDRM #3
16'-4" x 13'-4"

9' CLG
BKFST RM
21'-4" x 13'-0"

BUILT-IN

FIREPLACE

VAULTED
GREAT RM
15'-0" x 23'-0"

REF

CL

KIT

CL

BATH

LIN

Foyer / Dining Room

Kitchen

Great Room

Plan #141004

Dimensions: 37' W x 61' D

Levels: 1

Square Footage: 1,514

Bedrooms: 3

Bathrooms: 2

Foundation: Slab, basement

Materials List Available: No

Price Category: C

Designed for the narrow lot, this cottage-style home features Craftsman-style exterior columns.

Features:

- Ceiling Height: 8 ft. unless otherwise noted.

- Entry: There's no defined foyer, so you enter immediately into the living area, with its vaulted ceiling that flattens over the dining area at a soaring 14 ft.

- Living/Dining Areas: The see-through fireplace flanked by bookcases is a main focal point of the home. It serves as the divider between the living room and dining room.

- Kitchen: This kitchen shares the vaulted ceiling with the dining room and living room. A plant shelf over the cabinets facing the dining room defines the space without obstructing the view of the fireplace.

- Master Suite: This private retreat has its own entrance away from the other bedrooms and boasts a cathedral ceiling over both bedroom and bath.

Copyright by designer/architect.

Plan #311002

Dimensions: 56'6" W x 82' D

Levels: 1

Square Footage: 2,402

Bedrooms: 4

Bathrooms: 2½

Foundation: Crawl space, slab

Materials List Available: Yes

Price Category: E

Illustrations provided by designer/architect.

This lovely home has an open floor plan in the main living area but privacy in the bedrooms.

Features:

• Foyer: With an 11-ft. ceiling, this foyer opens to both the great room and the dining room.

• Great Room: A 10-ft. ceiling and handsome fireplace highlight this spacious room, which is open to both the kitchen and breakfast room.

• Dining Room: A butler's pantry and built-in china closet spell convenience in this lovely room.

• Breakfast Room: Bask in the sunshine flowing through the bay windows in this room, which opens to the rear porch.

• Kitchen: Designed for efficiency, this kitchen will charm all the cooks in the family.

• Master Suite: It's easy to feel pampered by the huge closet and bath with corner tub and two vanities.

Plan #151037

Dimensions: 50' W x 56' D

Levels: 1

Square Footage: 1,538

Bedrooms: 3

Bathrooms: 2

Foundation: Crawl space, slab, or basement

Materials List Available: No

Price Category: C

Images provided by designer/architect.

You'll love this traditional-looking home, with its covered porch and interesting front windows.

Features:

- Ceiling Height: 8 ft.

- Great Room: This large room has a boxed window that emphasizes its dimensions and a fireplace where everyone will gather on chilly evenings. A door opens to the backyard.

- Dining Room: A bay window overlooking the front porch makes this room easy to decorate.

- Kitchen: This well-planned kitchen features ample counter space, a full pantry, and an eating bar that it shares with the dining room.

- Master Suite: A pan ceiling in this lovely room gives an elegant touch. The huge private bath includes two walk-in closets, a whirlpool tub, a dual-sink vanity, and a skylight in the ceiling.

- Additional Bedrooms: On the opposite side of the house, these bedrooms share a large bath, and both feature excellent closet space.

Copyright by designer/architect.

Plan #161003

Dimensions: 60' W x 47' D

Levels: 1

Square Footage: 1,508

Bedrooms: 3

Bathrooms: 2

Foundation: Basement

Materials List Available: Yes

Price Category: C

Multiple gables and a cozy front porch invite you to this enchanting one-story home.

Features:

• Great Room: This bright and cheery room features a sloped ceiling and fireplace. The great room is designed for convenience, with easy access to the foyer and dining area, creating the look and feel of a home much larger than its actual size.

• Dining Area: Adjacent to the great room, this dining area has multiple windows and angles that add light and dimension.

• Kitchen: This spacious kitchen is designed for easy work patterns with an abundance of counter and cabinet space. It also features a snack bar.

• Master Bedroom: Designed for step-saving convenience, this master bedroom includes a compartmented bath, double-bowl vanity, and large walk-in closet.

Images provided by designer/architect.

Copyright by designer/architect.

Rear Elevation

Plan #291002

Dimensions: 63' W x 37' D

Levels: 1

Square Footage: 1,550

Bedrooms: 3

Bathrooms: 2

Foundation: Basement

Materials List Available: No

Price Category: C

Images provided by designer/architect.

This comfortable Southwestern-style ranch house will fit perfectly into any setting.

Features:

- Ceiling Height: 8 ft. unless otherwise noted.

- Front Porch: This scalloped front porch offers plenty of room for enjoying a cool summer breeze.

- Foyer: Upon entering this impressive foyer you'll be greeted by a soaring space encompassing the living room and dining room.

- Living/Dining Area: This combined living room and dining room has a handsome fireplace as its focal point. When dinner is served, guests will flow casually into the dining area.

- Kitchen: Take your cooking up a notch in this terrific kitchen. It features a 42-in.-high counter that will do double-duty as a snack bar for family meals and a wet bar for entertaining.

- Master Suite: This master retreat is separated from the other bedrooms and features an elegant vaulted ceiling. The dressing area has a compartmentalized bath and a walk-in closet.

Rear View

Copyright by designer/architect.

order direct: 1-800-523-6789

Plan #171013

Dimensions: 74' W x 72' D
Levels: 1
Square Footage: 3,084
Bedrooms: 4
Bathrooms: 3½
Foundation: Slab, crawl space
Materials List Available: Yes
Price Category: G

Impressive porch columns add to the country charm of this amenity-filled family home.

Features:

- Ceiling Height: 10 ft.

- Foyer: The sense of style continues from the front porch into this foyer, which opens to the formal dining room and the living room.

- Dining Room: Two handsome support columns accentuate the elegance of this dining room.

- Living Room: This living room features a cozy corner fireplace and plenty of room for the entire family to gather and relax.

- Kitchen: You'll be inspired to new culinary heights in this kitchen, which offers plenty of counter space, a snack bar, a built-in pantry, and a china closet.

- Master Suite: The bedroom of this master suite has a fireplace and overlooks a rear courtyard. The bath has two vanities a large walk-in closet, a deluxe tub, a walk-in shower, and a skylight.

Bonus Room

Plan #211003

Dimensions: 62' W x 64'8" D
Levels: 1
Square Footage: 1,865
Bedrooms: 3
Bathrooms: 2
Foundation: Slab
Materials List Available: Yes
Price Category: D

SMARTtip

Fire Extinguishers

The word PASS is an easy way to remember the proper way to use a fire extinguisher.

Pull the pin at the top of the extinguisher that keeps the handle from being accidentally pressed.

Aim the nozzle of the extinguisher toward the base of the fire.

Squeeze the handle to discharge the extinguisher. Stand approximately 8 feet away from the fire.

Sweep the nozzle back and forth at the base of the fire. After the fire appears to be out, watch it carefully because it may reignite!

The traditional style of this home is blended with all the amenities required for today's lifestyle.

Features:

• Ceiling Height: 8 ft. unless otherwise noted.

• Front Porch: Guests will feel welcome arriving at the front door under this sheltering front porch.

• Dining Room: This large room will accommodate dinner parties of all sizes, from large formal gatherings to more intimate family get-togethers.

• Living Room: Guests and family alike will feel right at home in this inviting room. Sunlight streaming through the skylights in the 12-ft. ceiling, combined with the handsome fireplace, makes the space both airy and warm.

• Back Patio: When warm weather comes around, step out the sliding glass doors in the living room to enjoy entertaining or just relaxing on this patio.

• Kitchen: A cathedral ceiling soars over this efficient modern kitchen. It includes an eating area that is perfect for informal family meals.

Copyright by designer/architect.

Plan #111006

Dimensions: 56' W x 67' D

Levels: 1

Square Footage: 2,241

Bedrooms: 4

Bathrooms: 2½

Foundation: Slab

Materials List Available: No

Price Category: E

Images provided by designer/architect.

You'll love this plan if you're looking for a home with fantastic curb appeal on the outside and comfortable amenities on the inside.

Features:

- **Foyer:** This lovely foyer opens to both the living and dining rooms.

- **Dining Room:** Three columns in this room accentuate both its large dimensions and its slightly formal air.

- **Living Room:** This room gives an airy feeling, and the fireplace here makes it especially inviting when the weather's cool.

- **Kitchen:** This G-shaped kitchen is designed to save steps while you're working, and the ample counter area adds even more to its convenience. The breakfast bar is a great gathering area.

- **Master Suite:** Two walk-in closets provide storage space, and the bath includes separate vanities, a standing shower, and a deluxe corner bathtub.

Front Elevation

Copyright by designer/architect.

Plan #281011

Dimensions: 50' W x 54' D

Levels: 1

Square Footage: 1,314

Bedrooms: 3

Bathrooms: 2

Foundation: Basement

Materials List Available: Yes

Price Category: B

Images provided by designer/architect.

This attractive ranch home takes advantage of views at both the front and rear.

Features:

- Ceiling Height: 8 ft.

- Porch: This large, inviting porch welcomes your guests and provides shade for the big living-room window on hot summer days.

- Living Room: This large main living area has plenty of room for entertaining and family activities.

- Dining Room: This room can accommodate large dinner parties. It's located near the living room and the kitchen for convenient entertaining.

- Deck: Family and friends will enjoy stepping out on this large covered sun deck that is accessible from the living room, dining room, and kitchen.

- Master Suite: You'll enjoy retiring at the end of the day to this luxurious master suite, which features its own walk-in closet and bathroom.

Copyright by designer/architect.

Rear Elevation

SMARTtip

Rag-Rolling Off

Paint Tip: Work with a partner. One person can roll on the glaze while the other lifts it off with the rag in a rhythmic pattern of even, steady strokes.

Plan #221003

Dimensions: 69' W x 51'4" D

Levels: 1

Square Footage: 1,802

Bedrooms: 3

Bathrooms: 2

Foundation: Basement

Materials List Available: No

Price Category: D

Images provided by designer/architect.

If you'd love to enjoy the evening breeze from a rocker on your own front porch, this stylish ranch design could be the home of your dreams.

Features:

- Ceiling Height: 8 ft.

- Great Room: A cathedral ceiling in this room gives it grandeur as well as a spacious feeling. Large windows that look out to the backyard flank the classic fireplace here.

- Kitchen: This step-saving layout will delight the cooks in the family. Everyone will gather in the dining nook here, and when there's a party, you'll appreciate the open design between the kitchen/nook area and the great room.

- Master Suite: You'll love the storage space in the bedroom's walk-in closet and revel in the luxury of the fully equipped private bath.

- Garage: You can park two cars in this garage and still have room to store a mower, tools and equipment, and even off-season clothing.

Rear Elevation

Copyright by designer/architect.

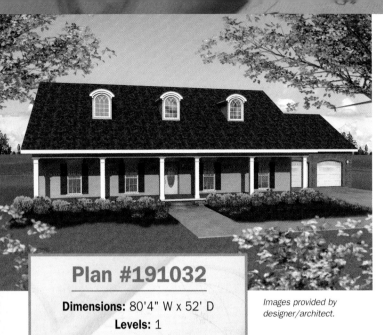

Plan #191032

Dimensions: 80'4" W x 52' D

Levels: 1

Square Footage: 2,091

Bedrooms: 3

Bathrooms: 2

Foundation: Slab

Materials List Available: No

Price Category: D

Images provided by designer/architect.

Copyright by designer/architect.

Plan #101023

Dimensions: 52' W x 42' D

Levels: 1

Square Footage: 1,197

Bedrooms: 3

Bathrooms: 2

Foundation: Crawl space, slab

Materials List Available: No

Price Category: B

Images provided by designer/architect.

Copyright by designer/architect.

Plan #191033

Dimensions: 68'4" W x 80' D
Levels: 1
Square Footage: 2,214
Bedrooms: 3
Bathrooms: 2
Foundation: Crawl space, slab
Materials List Available: No
Price Category: E

The classic good looks of this lovely home's exterior perfectly suit the interior, which is designed for the comfort of your family.

Features:

- Great Room: A fireplace and a door to the rear covered porch make this room a natural gathering spot for the whole family.

- Dining Room: Situated between the foyer and kitchen/breakfast area, this room is ideal for entertaining or serving family meals.

- Kitchen: You'll love the convenient center island with a cooktop and snack bar. An adjacent walk-in pantry, large laundry room, and mudroom add practical touches.

- Breakfast Area: Set a table between the windows to bask in sunny morning light.

- Owner's Suite: This suite features a walk-in closet and a private bath with a large tub, separate shower, and dual vanity.

Copyright by designer/architect.

Rear Elevation

Plan #121001

Dimensions: 56' W x 58' D

Levels: 1

Square Footage: 1,911

Bedrooms: 3

Bathrooms: 2

Foundation: Basement

Materials List Available: Yes

Price Category: D

Images provided by designer/architect.

Detailed, soaring ceilings and top-notch amenities set this distinctive home apart.

Features:

- Ceiling Height: 8 ft. except as noted.

- Great Room: A soaring ceiling and six tall transom-topped windows make this a light and airy spot for entertaining.

- Formal Dining Room: The entry enjoys a pleasing view of this dining room's detailed 12-ft. ceiling and picture window.

- Great Room: At the back of the home, a see-through fireplace in this great room is joined by a built-in entertainment center.

- Hearth Room: This bayed room shares the see-through fireplace with the great room.

- Master Suite: Enjoy the stars and the sun in the private bath's whirlpool and separate shower. The bath features the same decorative ceiling as the dining room.

Copyright by designer/architect.

Plan #131003

Dimensions: 60' W x 39'10" D
Levels: 1
Square Footage: 1,466
Bedrooms: 3
Bathrooms: 2
Foundation: Basement, crawl space, or slab
Materials List Available: Yes
Price Category: B

Images provided by designer/architect.

Victorian styling adds elegance to this compact and easy-to-maintain ranch design.

Features:

- Ceiling Height: 8 ft.

- Foyer: Bridging between the front door and the great room, this foyer is a surprise feature.

- Great Room: A 10-ft. ceiling adds to the spacious feeling of this room, while the corner fireplace gives it an intimate feeling. Sliding glass doors at the rear of the room open to the backyard.

- Dining Room: This formal room adjoins the great room, allowing guests and family to flow between the rooms.

- Breakfast Room: Turrets add a Victorian feeling to this room that's just off the kitchen and overlooks the front porch.

- Master Suite: Privacy is assured in this suite, which is separated from the main part of the house. A compartmented bath and large walk-in closet add convenience to its beauty.

Copyright by designer/architect.

Breakfast Room

Plan #351006

Dimensions: 72'10" W x 41' D

Levels: 1

Square Footage: 1,638

Bedrooms: 3

Bathrooms: 2

Foundation: Basement, crawl space, or slab

Materials List Available: Yes

Price Category: C

Stair Location for Basement Option

Plan #351003

Dimensions: 64' W x 45'10" D

Levels: 1

Square Footage: 1,751

Bedrooms: 3

Bathrooms: 2

Foundation: Basement, crawl space, or slab

Materials List Available: Yes

Price Category: C

Plan #181018

Dimensions: 39' W x 45' D
Levels: 1
Square Footage: 1,231
Bedrooms: 2
Bathrooms: 1
Foundation: Basement
Materials List Available: Yes
Price Category: B

Images provided by designer/architect.

The dramatic double-glass-door arched entry sets the tone for this elegant European beauty.

Features:

- Ceiling Height: 8 ft.
- Family Room: Family and friends will be drawn to the warmth and grace of this room, which is filled with natural light streaming from the spectacular full wall of windows. Warm yourself by the fireplace.

- Kitchen: This kitchen shares the fireplace with the adjoining family room. Cooking will be a pleasure, thanks to plenty of counter space and a double pantry.

- Breakfast Area: This eat-in area off the kitchen offers plenty of room for the whole family to enjoy informal meals.

- Bedrooms: The flexible floor plan offers either one large master suite with a walk-in closet or two nicely sized bedrooms, each with its own closets. Both options include a luxurious full bathroom with a relaxing whirlpool tub.

**Alternate
Floor Plan**

*Copyright by
designer/architect.*

Plan #321002

Dimensions: 72' W x 28' D

Levels: 1

Square Footage: 1,400

Bedrooms: 3

Bathrooms: 2

Foundation: Basement, crawl space

Materials List Available: Yes

Price Category: B

If you're looking for a well-designed compact home with contemporary amenities, this could be the home of your dreams.

Features:

• Porch: Just the right size for some rockers and a swing, this porch could become your outdoor living area when the weather is fine.

• Living Room: A vaulted ceiling adds to the spacious feeling in this room, where friends and family are sure to gather.

• Kitchen: This space-saving design, in combination with the ample counter and cabinet space, makes cooking a pleasure.

• Utility Room: This large room is fitted with cabinets for extra storage space. You'll find storage space in the large garage, too.

• Master Bedroom: This room is somewhat secluded for privacy, making it an ideal place for some quiet time at the end of the day.

Images provided by designer/architect.

Copyright by designer/architect.

SMARTtip

Fabric Draping Ability

Test a fabric's draping ability by looking at a large piece in a fabric store. Gather at least two to three yards of material, holding one end in your hand. Check how it drapes. Does it fall into folds easily? Also look at the pattern when it is gathered. Does the design become lost in the folds? Ask a salesclerk or a friend to hold the fabric, and look at it from a few feet away.

Plan #131010

Dimensions: 70' W x 34'4" D
Levels: 1
Square Footage: 1,667
Bedrooms: 3
Bathrooms: 2
Foundation: Basement, crawl space, or slab
Materials List Available: Yes
Price Category: D

Images provided by designer/architect.

You'll love this affordable ranch house, with its open floor plan that gives so much usable space, and its graceful layout.

Features:

- **Living Room:** Adjacent to the dining room, this living room features a pass-through fireplace that is open to the family room beyond.

- **Family Room:** A vaulted ceiling with a sky light gives character to this room, where everyone will gather on weekend afternoons and in the evening, to relax.

- **Kitchen:** Also lit from above by a skylight, this kitchen features an island work space.

- **Breakfast Room:** Just off the kitchen, this breakfast room is sure to be a popular spot at any time of day.

- **Master Bedroom:** Get away from it all in this lovely room, with space to spread out and relax in private.

Copyright by designer/architect.

Family Room / Kitchen
Living Room

LAUNDRY ROOM WITH
BASEMENT PLAN

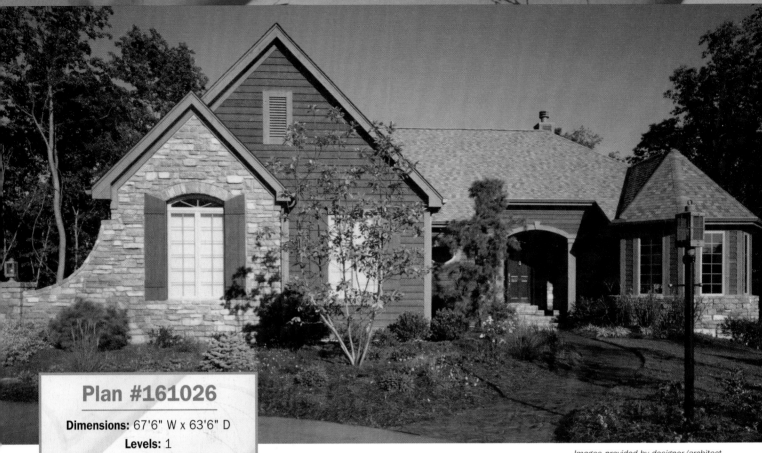

Plan #161026

Dimensions: 67'6" W x 63'6" D
Levels: 1
Square Footage: 2,041
Bedrooms: 3
Bathrooms: 2
Foundation: Basement
Materials List Available: No
Price Category: D

Images provided by designer/architect.

You'll love the special features of this home, which has been designed for efficiency and comfort.

Features:

- Foyer: This raised foyer offers a view through the great room and beyond it to the covered deck.

- Great Room: Elegant windows allow versatility — decorate casually or more formally.

- Kitchen: You'll find ample counter space and cabinets in this spacious room, which adjoins the dining room and opens onto the rear yard.

- Library: Curl up on the window seat that wraps around the tower in this quiet spot.

- Laundry Room: A tub makes this large room practical for crafts as well as laundry.

- Master Suite: A vaulted ceiling gives grace to the sitting area, and the garden bath with a walk-in closet and whirlpool tub adds luxury.

Rear Elevation

Main Level Floor Plan

Basement Level Floor Plan

Copyright by designer/architect.

Left Side Elevation

Right Side Elevation

Front View

Living Room

Plan #311001

Dimensions: 65'11" W x 67'9" D

Levels: 1

Square Footage: 2,085

Bedrooms: 3

Bathrooms: 2½

Foundation: Crawl space, slab

Materials List Available: No

Price Category: D

Images provided by designer/architect.

Rear View

Copyright by designer/architect.

Optional Bonus Area

Plan #311004

Dimensions: 68'2" W x 57'4" D

Levels: 1

Square Footage: 2,046

Bedrooms: 3

Bathrooms: 2½

Foundation: Basement, crawl space, or slab

Materials List Available: Yes

Price Category: D

Images provided by designer/architect.

Copyright by designer/architect.

Rear View

Plan #151040

Dimensions: 70' W x 51'10" D

Levels: 1

Square Footage: 2,444

Bedrooms: 4

Bathrooms: 2½

Foundation: Crawl space, slab (basement option for fee)

Materials List Available: No

Price Category: E

Images provided by designer/architect.

Copyright by designer/architect.

Plan #171008

Dimensions: 72' W x 40' D

Levels: 1

Square Footage: 1,652

Bedrooms: 3

Bathrooms: 2

Foundation: Slab, crawl space

Materials List Available: Yes

Price Category: C

Images provided by designer/architect.

Copyright by designer/architect.

SMARTtip

Lighting for Decorative Shadows

Use lighting to create decorative shadows. For interesting, undefined shadows, set lights at ground level aiming upward in front of a shrub or tree that is close to a wall. For silhouetting, place lights directly behind a plant or garden statue that is near a wall. In both cases, using a wide beam will increase the effect.

Plan #231006

Dimensions: 66' W x 80' D

Levels: 1

Square Footage: 1,961

Bedrooms: 3

Bathrooms: 2

Foundation: Crawl space

Materials List Available: No

Price Category: D

Images provided by designer/architect.

Copyright by designer/architect.

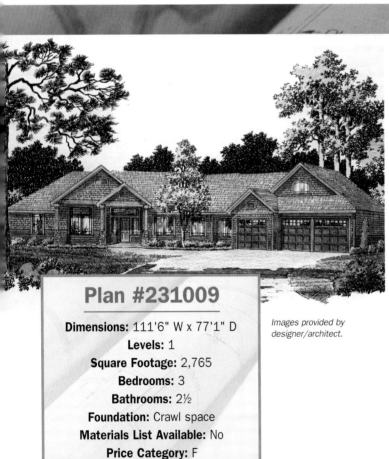

Plan #231009

Dimensions: 111'6" W x 77'1" D

Levels: 1

Square Footage: 2,765

Bedrooms: 3

Bathrooms: 2½

Foundation: Crawl space

Materials List Available: No

Price Category: F

Images provided by designer/architect.

Copyright by designer/architect.

Optional Bonus Area

Plan #341036

Dimensions: 51'6" W x 34' D

Levels: 1

Square Footage: 1,134

Bedrooms: 3

Bathrooms: 2

Foundation: Crawl space, slab (basement option for fee)

Materials List Available: Yes

Price Category: B

Images provided by designer/architect.

Copyright by designer/architect.

PATIO

BEDROOM 1
12'-0" X 13'-2"

BATH 1

KITCHEN
8'-3" X 9'-9"

SINK DW

RANGE

REF

DINING AREA
10'-9" X 13'-7"

GARAGE
13'-7" X 23'-3"

CLOSET

WASH DRY

COATS

34'-0"

BATH 2

LINENS

CLOSET

BEDROOM 3
10'-0" X 10'-0"

FAMILY ROOM
12'-9" X 13'-8"

BEDROOM 2
10'-9" X 10'-0"

CLOSET

PORCH

51'-6"

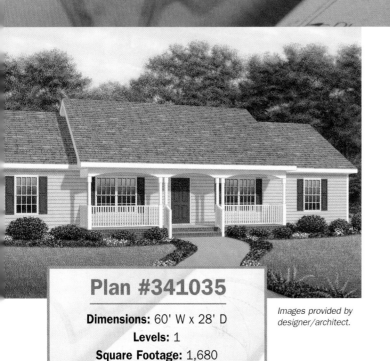

Plan #341035

Dimensions: 60' W x 28' D

Levels: 1

Square Footage: 1,680

Bedrooms: 4

Bathrooms: 2

Foundation: Crawl space, slab (basement option for fee)

Materials List Available: Yes

Price Category: C

Images provided by designer/architect.

Copyright by designer/architect.

DECK
12'-0" X 10'-0"

GARDEN TUB

BATH 1

CLOSET

KITCHEN
13'-1" X 13'-5"

SINK DW

RANGE

DRY WASH

BEDROOM 2
10'-6" X 13'-5"

BATH 2

BEDROOM 3
10'-6" X 10'-11"

REF

ISLAND

PANTRY

CLOSET

LIN

SHWR

LINENS

CLOSET

CLOSET

28'-0"

BEDROOM 1
13'-11" X 13'-5"

DINING ROOM
12'-4" X 13'-5"

LIVING ROOM
18'-10" X 13'-5"

PREFAB VENTLESS GAS LOG FIREPLACE

COAT

SHELVES

BEDROOM 4
10'-6" X 10'-11"

PORCH

60'-0"

Plan #141005

Dimensions: 38' W x 66' D

Levels: 1

Square Footage: 1,532

Bedrooms: 3

Bathrooms: 2

Foundation: Slab, basement

Materials List Available: No

Price Category: C

Images provided by designer/architect.

Board and batten combine with shake siding to give this cottage an appealing Tudor style.

Features:

- Ceiling Height: 8 ft. unless otherwise noted.

- Entry: This front entry is highlighted by a dormer that opens to the cathedral ceiling of the spacious open great room.

- Open Floor Plan: The living room, dining areas, and kitchen all flow together to create the feeling of a much larger home.

- Kitchen: This kitchen is defined by a curved bar, which can house a bench seat to service a small cafe-style table.

- Master Suite: This private suite is separated from the rest of the bedrooms. It features a volume ceiling and separate sitting area.

- Basement Option: The house is designed primarily for a slab on a narrow lot but can also be built over a basement.

Copyright by designer/architect.

Plan #151050

Dimensions: 69'2" W x 74'10" D

Levels: 1

Square Footage: 2,096

Bedrooms: 3

Bathrooms: 2½

Foundation: Crawl space, slab, or basement

Materials List Available: No

Price Category: D

You'll love this spacious home for both its elegance and its convenient design.

Features:

- Ceiling Height: 8 ft.

- Great Room: A 9-ft. boxed ceiling complements this large room, which sits just beyond the front gallery. A fireplace and door to the rear porch make it a natural gathering spot.

- Kitchen: This well-designed kitchen includes a central work island and shares an angled eating bar with the adjacent breakfast room.

- Breakfast Room: This room's bay window is gorgeous, and the door to the garage is practical.

- Master Suite: You'll love the 9-ft. boxed ceiling in the bedroom and the vaulted ceiling in the bath, which also includes two walk-in closets, a corner whirlpool tub, split vanities, a shower, and a compartmentalized toilet.

- Workshop: A huge workshop with half-bath is ideal for anyone who loves to build or repair.

Plan #271075

Dimensions: 80' W x 52' D

Levels: 1

Square Footage: 2,233

Bedrooms: 2-4

Bathrooms: 1½-3½

Foundation: Basement

Materials List Available: No

Price Category: E

Images provided by designer/architect.

Optional Basement Level Floor Plan

Copyright by designer/architect.

Plan #271076

Dimensions: 69' W x 57' D

Levels: 1

Square Footage: 2,188

Bedrooms: 2-4

Bathrooms: 1½-2½

Foundation: Daylight basement

Materials List Available: No

Price Category: D

Images provided by designer/architect.

Optional Basement Level Floor Plan

Copyright by designer/architect.

Plan #271077

Dimensions: 70' W x 53' D

Levels: 1

Square Footage: 1,786

Bedrooms: 1-4

Bathrooms: 1½-2½

Foundation: Daylight basement

Materials List Available: No

Price Category: C

Images provided by designer/architect.

Optional Basement Level Floor Plan

Copyright by designer/architect.

Plan #271061

Dimensions: 68' W x 52' D

Levels: 1

Square Footage: 1,750

Bedrooms: 1-3

Bathrooms: 1½-2½

Foundation: Daylight basement

Materials List Available: No

Price Category: C

Images provided by designer/architect.

Copyright by designer/architect.

Optional Basement Level Floor Plan

Images provided by designer/architect.

Plan #121058

Dimensions: 50' W x 52'8" D

Levels: 1

Square Footage: 1,554

Bedrooms: 2

Bathrooms: 2

Foundation: Basement

Materials List Available: Yes

Price Category: C

Copyright by designer/architect.

Images provided by designer/architect.

Plan #121059

Dimensions: 52' W x 59'4" D

Levels: 1

Square Footage: 1,782

Bedrooms: 3

Bathrooms: 2

Foundation: Basement

Materials List Available: Yes

Price Category: C

Copyright by designer/architect.

Plan #321024

Dimensions: 47' W x 32' D

Levels: 1

Square Footage: 1,403

Bedrooms: 3

Bathrooms: 1-2

Foundation: Daylight basement

Materials List Available: Yes

Price Category: B

Images provided by designer/architect.

Copyright by designer/architect.

Optional Basement Level Floor Plan

Plan #291003

Dimensions: 42'4" W x 73'4" D

Levels: 1

Square Footage: 1,890

Bedrooms: 3

Bathrooms: 2

Foundation: Crawl space

Materials List Available: No

Price Category: D

Images provided by designer/architect.

Copyright by designer/architect.

Plan #211020

Dimensions: 54' W x 44'6" D

Levels: 1

Square Footage: 1,346

Bedrooms: 3

Bathrooms: 2

Foundation: Slab

Materials List Available: Yes

Price Category: B

Images provided by designer/architect.

Copyright by designer/architect.

Plan #211021

Dimensions: 61' W x 35' D

Levels: 1

Square Footage: 1,375

Bedrooms: 3

Bathrooms: 2

Foundation: Slab

Materials List Available: Yes

Price Category: B

Images provided by designer/architect.

Copyright by designer/architect.

SMARTtip

Creating Built-up Cornices

Combine various base, crown, and cove moldings to create an elaborate cornice that is both imaginative and tasteful. Use the pattern throughout your home to establish a unique architectural element having the appearance of being professionally designed.

Plan #321011

Dimensions: 83' W x 50'4" D
Levels: 1
Square Footage: 2,874
Bedrooms: 4
Bathrooms: 2½
Foundation: Basement
Materials List Available: Yes
Price Category: F

Images provided by designer/architect.

SMARTtip

Drilling for Kitchen Plumbing

Drill holes for plumbing and waste lines before installing the cabinets. It is easier to work when the cabinets are out in the middle of the floor, and there is no danger of knocking them out of alignment when creating the holes if they are not screwed to the wall studs or one another yet.

Plan #321012

Dimensions: 58'8" W x 51'2" D
Levels: 1
Square Footage: 1,882
Bedrooms: 3
Bathrooms: 2
Foundation: Basement
Materials List Available: Yes
Price Category: D

Images provided by designer/architect.

Plan #221004

Dimensions: 67'8" W x 43' D

Levels: 1

Square Footage: 1,763

Bedrooms: 3

Bathrooms: 2

Foundation: Basement

Materials List Available: No

Price Category: C

Images provided by designer/architect.

Rear Elevation

You'll love the spacious feeling provided by the open design of this traditional ranch.

Features:

• Ceiling Height: 8 ft.

• Dining Room: This formal room is perfect for entertaining groups both large and small, and the open design makes it easy to serve.

• Living Room: The vaulted ceiling here and in the dining room adds to the elegance of these rooms. Use window treatments that emphasize these ceilings for a truly sumptuous look.

• Kitchen: Designed for practicality and efficiency, this kitchen will thrill all the cooks in the family. An attached dining nook makes a natural gathering place for friends and family.

• Master Suite: The private bath in this suite features a double vanity and whirlpool tub. You'll find a walk-in closet in the bedroom.

• Garage: You'll love the extra storage space in this two-car garage.

Copyright by designer/architect.

Plan #101004

Dimensions: 55'8" W x 56'6" D

Levels: 1

Square Footage: 1,787

Bedrooms: 3

Bathrooms: 2

Foundation: Slab, crawl space, or basement

Materials List Available: No

Price Category: C

Images provided by designer/architect.

This carefully designed ranch provides the feel and features of a much larger home.

Features:

- Ceiling Height: 9 ft. unless otherwise noted.

- Foyer: Guests will step up onto the inviting front porch and into this foyer, with its impressive 11-ft. ceiling.

- Dining Room: Open to the entry and to its left is this elegant dining room, perfect for entertaining or informal family gatherings.

- Family Room: This family gathering place features an 11-ft. ceiling to enhance its sense of spaciousness.

- Kitchen: This intelligently designed kitchen has an open plan. A breakfast bar and a serving bar are features that add to its convenience.

- Master Suite: This suite is loaded with amenities, including a double-step tray ceiling, direct access to the screened porch, a sitting room, deluxe bath, and his and her walk-in closets.

Copyright by designer/architect.

Plan #211033

Dimensions: 46' W x 66' D
Levels: 1
Square Footage: 1,732
Bedrooms: 3
Bathrooms: 2
Foundation: Slab
Materials List Available: Yes
Price Category: C

Images provided by designer/architect.

You'll love the good taste with which this home was designed, as well as the versatility its mixture of formal and informal areas affords.

Features:

• Ceiling Height: 9-ft. ceilings.

• Living Room: The dimensions of this room make it easy to decorate for either formal or informal occasions and entertaining.

• Dining Room: Close to the kitchen for convenience, this dining room is also versatile

enough to be appropriate for any sort of entertaining.

• Kitchen: The practical design here allows you to work without needlessly wasting precious time or energy, and the location of this kitchen means that serving and clearing-up chores are eased.

• Master Suite: Retreat to this area after a long, stressful day so that you can recharge your batteries—either by resting or showering.

Copyright by designer/architect.

SMARTtip

Types of Paintbrush Bristles

Nylon Bristles. Bristles made of nylon are most suitable for latex paint, although they can also be used with solvent-based paint.

Natural Bristles. Also called "China bristle," natural bristle brushes are preferred for use with solvent-based paints and varnishes because they tend to hold more paint and generally brush out to a smoother looking finish. Natural bristle brushes should not be used with latex paint. The water in the paint will cause the bristles to expand and ruin the brush.

Choosing Brushes. When buying a brush, check for thick, resilient bristles that are firmly held in place. Be sure, also, to get the proper type brush for the job.

Plan #241003

Dimensions: 60' W x 58' D

Levels: 1

Square Footage: 2,080

Bedrooms: 3

Bathrooms: 2

Foundation: Slab

Materials List Available: No

Price Category: D

Striking rooflines combine with a stone-and-shingle exterior to give this lovely country home immediate appeal.

Features:

• Great Room: Certain to become a favorite gathering place for friends and family, this great room features a fireplace, bookshelves, and an entertainment center.

• Kitchen: This well-designed kitchen—with ample counter space and cabinets—features a pantry, island, and large breakfast area. It also includes a convenient computer nook, well suited for managing today's complexities.

• Master Suite: Separated for privacy, this master suite features his and her vanities, a corner tub, a separate shower, a large walk-in closet, and a delightful window seat for your relaxing pleasure.

• Garage: Use the extra space in this garage for storage.

Images provided by designer/architect.

Copyright by designer/architect.

SMARTtip

Color Basics for Kids' Rooms

Use color effectively to enhance the perception of the space itself. Make a large room feel cozy with warm colors, which tend to advance. Conversely, open up a small room with cool colors or neutrals, which tend to recede. The less-intense version of a color will generally reduce its tendency to advance or recede, as well. Other tricks: Sharp contrasts often have the same impact as a dark color, reducing perceived space. Monochromatic schemes enlarge space. Neutrals of similar value make walls appear to retreat.

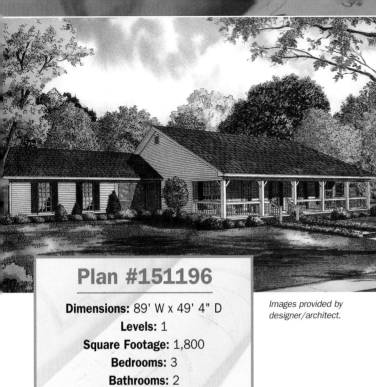

Plan #151196

Dimensions: 89' W x 49' 4" D
Levels: 1
Square Footage: 1,800
Bedrooms: 3
Bathrooms: 2
Foundation: Crawl space, slab
Materials List Available: No
Price Category: D

Images provided by designer/architect.

Copyright by designer/architect.

Plan #391005

Dimensions: 60' W x 40'4" D
Levels: 1
Square Footage: 1,575
Bedrooms: 3
Bathrooms: 2
Foundation: Crawl space, basement, slab
Materials List Available: Yes
Price Category: C

Images provided by designer/architect.

SMARTtip

Kitchen Cabinet Styles

You may not need to purchase expensive kitchen cabinetry to get fine-furniture quality details. Try adding crown molding to the top of basic cabinets and replacing the hardware with reproduction polished-brass door and drawer pulls to achieve a traditional look.

Copyright by designer/architect.

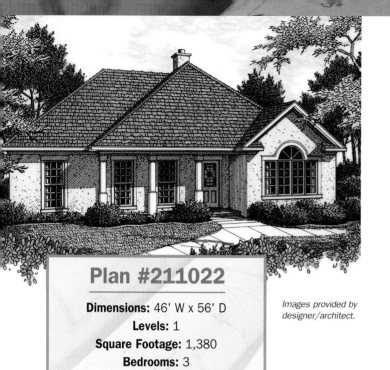

Plan #211022

Dimensions: 46' W x 56' D

Levels: 1

Square Footage: 1,380

Bedrooms: 3

Bathrooms: 2

Foundation: Slab

Materials List Available: Yes

Price Category: B

Images provided by designer/architect.

Copyright by designer/architect.

Plan #361004

Dimensions: 77' W x 81' D

Levels: 1

Square Footage: 2,191

Bedrooms: 3

Bathrooms: 2

Foundation: Crawl space

Materials List Available: No

Price Category: D

Images provided by designer/architect.

Copyright by designer/architect.

Creating a Stylish Kitchen

Style meets state of the art in the kitchen. If you need inspiration when the time comes to make decorating decisions about your new kitchen, think about some of today's popular decorating styles: country, contemporary, cottage, French country, Shaker, and Arts and Crafts. Which one says the most about you and your lifestyle? You might try starting with the cabinets, which will have the most impact on how your kitchen will look because they will be the largest element in the space. The key is to build a room around a theme while incorporating your personality into it. A favorite color is one way to do this; another way is a repeated pattern or theme.

For inspiration, visit showrooms and read magazines. Is there someone you know who has a kitchen that you've particularly admired? Was it a painted finish on the cabinetry? The color or pattern of the wallpaper or window treatment? A handsome wood floor? A pretty collection displayed in a hutch or on a wall? How did the room make you feel? Cheerful? Relaxed? Animated? Nostalgic? This is the kind of thinking that will help you to zero in on a design that will have staying power.

In addition, look for clues in the details you are planning for the rest your house. What is the intended architectural style?

Will there be elaborate trimwork, or will the walls, doors, and windows be streamlined and spare? Even if the rest of the house will be plain, you can introduce a period flavor in the kitchen with reproduction cabinets and fixtures, window treatments, wallpaper, and accessories.

Do you like antiques or modern art? Are you a collector or someone who prefers pared-down space? You can build on these

Today's traditional styles, below, are updated with fresh finishes and details.

Moldings and raised-panel doors, opposite, dress up any style of cabinetry.

preferences or depart from them entirely. If your kitchen will be open to other areas, such as the family room, link the two spaces with color or related materials.

Whatever you do, your approach to decorating the new kitchen should be deliberate. Let it evolve over time; don't rush your choices. Live with paint, tile, and wallpaper samples for a while.

You might start with some of the ideas that are discussed here. They are just suggestions, however. Let your own preferences be your ultimate guide. If you're not sure about something, don't do it right away or just keep your decorating simple until you're ready to add the details.

Traditional Style

Today's traditional style incorporates elements of English and American eighteenth- and early nineteenth-century design. Marked by symmetry and balance and enhanced by the look of fine-crafted details, it is dignified, rich, and formal.

Choose wood cabinetry finished with a cherry or mahogany stain or painted white, with details such as fluted panels, bull's-eye corner blocks, and dentil and crown molding. For the door style, a raised cathedral panel (top slightly arched) is typical. On the countertop, use marble or a laminate faux version, and install tiles on the back-

splash. Polished brass hardware and fittings add a refined touch.

Colors to consider include classic Wedgwood blue or deep rich tones. Windows and French doors with true divided lights or double-hung units with pop-in muntins have great traditional-style appeal. Dress them with formal curtain panels or swags. Botanical-inspired patterns, formal stripes, or tapestry fabrics are perfect for window treatments or for chair cushions and table linens.

Furnish the kitchen with an antique or reproduction hutch, where you can display formal china, and a table and chairs in traditional Windsor or Queen Anne style.

Contemporary Style

What's referred to as "contemporary" style evokes images of clean architectural lines; an absence of decoration and color; and materials such as stainless steel, chrome, glass, and stone. Indeed, its roots are at the turn of the last century, when architects and designers flatly rejected the exaggerated artificial embellishments of the Victorians by turning to natural products and pared-down forms. Various modern movements, evolving over the course of the industrialized twentieth century, gradually incorporated new man-made materials into their streamlined forms. Hence the high-tech look popularized in the 1970s and 1980s.

Today, contemporary style is taking a softer turn, even in the kitchen, a place where hard edges, cool reflective surfaces, and cutting-edge technology abound. It's not unusual to see updated versions of tra-

Color finishes on cabinets, below, can be combined with artful wall treatments.

Furniture-like pieces, right, make a kitchen less utilitarian looking.

Reproduction light fixtures, opposite, capture a mood or period style.

ditional fixtures and fittings or new uses for natural materials in a contemporary kitchen, especially as improved finishes make these products more durable and easier to maintain.

Although a contemporary room is often monochromatic or neutral, don't be afraid to use color or to mix several materials. Combinations of wood and various metals—stainless steel, chrome, copper, brass, and pewter on surfaces like cabinet doors, countertops, and floors—make strong statements, as do stone and glass.

Country Style

Country cabinets are typically made of wood with framed or raised-panel doors. Beadboard cabinets are a typical American country choice. Or leave the doors off, allowing colorful dishes and canned and boxed goods to create a fun display. For the countertop, install butcher block or hand-painted or silk-screened tiles. Another option is a colorful or patterned countertop fabricated from inlaid solid-surfacing material. A working fireplace will definitely add charm to your country kitchen, but a simple potted herb garden on the windowsill will, too.

Wood floors are a natural choice in this setting. For a custom touch, add a stenciled backsplash or wall border. Or try a faux finish like sponging, ragging, or combing. These techniques are fun and easy, and they add texture to your walls.

Install double-hung windows. (Standard casement windows look too contemporary in this setting.) Finish them with full trim, and dress them with simple curtains.

The Cottage Look

This vintage look, inspired by quaint English-country style, is appealing in the kitchen because it's cozy, casual, and warm. Framed wood cabinets with an unfitted or unmatched appearance provide a good starting point for building on this theme, especially in a finish such as a honey maple paired with a color stain that looks properly distressed but not shabby. Muntin-glass doors, plate or pot racks, and open shelves should be part of the cabinetry's design. Milk- or clear-glass knobs and pulls complement cottage cabinets. But you could also mix a couple of different styles for mismatched chic.

Beadboard on the walls or ceiling always looks at home in this style kitchen, as does brick. Use brick as a backsplash or as a surround at the cooker. An English import, the AGA cooker, is a great way to

bring the old-time European look of a cast-iron stove into the room while providing all the modern-day conveniences. Install an exposed-apron (farmhouse-style) sink with a reproduction chrome-and-porcelain faucet set to add more charm. On the floor, use wide wood planks or stone with a colorful hand-painted floorcloth on top. Bring more color into the room with blue-green surfaces accented in varying shades of rose and cream.

A double-hung window lends a traditional note, but if you can make the style work with the exterior of your house, a Gothic-inspired architectural design would tie it all together. Accent with lighting fixtures that resemble old-fashioned Victorian gas lamps.

For furniture, include a good-size farmhouse table in your plan, as well as a Welsh dresser and plate rack for displaying a pretty collection of transferware.

French Country Style

To create the rustic charm of a French-country farmhouse, whitewash the walls or apply a subtle glaze finish in an earth tone, such as rose ocher or sienna. Install wood ceiling beams with an aged or distressed look. Use limestone tile or clay pavers, which also have a warm, earthy appeal, on the floor. For the appearance of a hearth, design a cooking alcove to house the range or cooktop. Accent it with colorful tiles or brick. Create a focal point at the cooking area with a handsome copper range hood. Hang a rack for copper pots and pans. Pair an exposed apron sink with a high-arc spout.

Use unfitted cabinetry, open shelves, or a baker's rack for storage. Decorate with provincial mini-prints in mustard yellow, clay red, and deep blue. Dress windows with lace café curtains, and stencil a pretty fleur de lis border around the trim.

Add details such as flavored oils and vinegars displayed in pretty glass bottles, fresh herbs growing from racks in sunny windows, and blue and white tiles.

An exposed-apron sink, left, comes in many finishes and colors.

A stone look, below left, can be reproduced in solid-surfacing material.

A high-arc faucet, below, captures nostalgic styles and practicality.

Cabinet Door Style Choices

Shaker Style

The Shakers' plain, practical designs featured dovetailed joints and hand-planed tops, plain panels on doors, and legs tapered almost to a pencil point. The finishes on original Shaker cabinets were always dyes and oils, never varnishes, to enhance the wood.

Accent woodwork in colors inspired by natural dyes—terra cotta, yellow ochre, olive green, green-blue, and denim. Ceramic tile installed in a quiltlike pattern on the countertop or backsplash or as a mural above the cooktop can add more color accents and a reasonable amount of decoration, unless you're a purist at heart. The fixtures could be white, bisque, or black, with plain fittings in a brushed chrome or pewter finish. Trim kits, available from appliance and cabinet manufacturers, can camouflage modern-day appliances that the Shakers eschewed.

A traditional double-hung window, with or without muntins, fits in fine with the Shaker theme. Install plain wood shutters and panel-style curtains with simple cotton tab tops.

Shaker-inspired furniture is widely available today. Tall ladder-back chairs with tape-woven seats look at home around a simple trestle table. A pegged chair rail is a Shaker classic. Installed high on the wall, it can be a display for a collection of hand-woven baskets, dried flowers, tapered candles, or even small wooden chairs.

Many period looks include wood floors, which can be impractical in a kitchen. A laminate look-alike is a good substitute.

Arts & Crafts Style

Styles that are related to or part of the Arts and Crafts movement include Mission, Craftsman, and Prairie, the signature style of the architect Frank Lloyd Wright. Start with plain oak cabinets with a handcrafted appearance. Several manufacturers make reproduction wood cabinets, metal hardware, and period wallpaper and lighting fixtures today.

Decorate with colors that reflect natural hues, such as brown, green, blue, and orange. Accessorize with organically shaped pottery in these colors, too. Pull it all together by incorporating Native American textiles, such as a rug, into this room. Design a custom-tiled backsplash with matte or "art pottery" glazed tiles.

Plain windows should be curtained very simply—if at all—in an Arts and Crafts-style room, using natural fabrics such as linen or muslin with an embroidered border. Typical motifs include ginkgo leaves and poppy seeds. Instead of traditional treatments, use stained-glass or art-glass windows. To complete the look, furnish the kitchen in period style with a Mission table and chairs and a hutch, if there is room for one.

Plan #131007

Dimensions: 59'10" W x 47'8" D
Levels: 1
Square Footage: 1,595
Bedrooms: 3
Bathrooms: 2
Foundation: Crawl space, slab, basement, or walkout
Materials List Available: Yes
Price Category: D

Imagine living in this home, with its traditional country comfort and individual brand of charm.

Features:

- Exterior elements: The mixture of a front porch with a cameo front door, decorative posts, bay windows, and dormers will delight you.

- Great Room: A tray ceiling gives distinction to this large room, and a wet bar eases entertaining.

- Screened Porch: At dusk and dawn, this porch is sure to be your favorite outdoor spot.

- Kitchen: Eat any meal in this large kitchen for a touch of homey charm.

- Dining Room: Perfect for hosting a formal dinner, this bayed dining room can increase your enjoyment of simple family meals.

- Master Bedroom: For the sake of privacy, this room is somewhat secluded. Decorate to emphasize the elegant tray ceiling.

SCREENED PORCH 13'-4" x 12'-8"

BEDRM #3 13'-4" x 11'-0"

BATH

BEDRM #2 11'-0" x 14'-0"

FOY

GREAT RM 14'-0" x 22'-8" — TRAY CEIL

WET BAR

DINING RM 10'-0" x 13'-0"

KITCHEN 10'-0" x 11'-0"

COV. PORCH

MSTR BEDRM 12'-0" x 18'-0" — TRAY CEIL

WICL

DRSG

MSTR BATH

W D

STOR

UTIL

LOCATION OF OPT BSMT STAIR

TWO CAR GARAGE 20'-0" x 21'-4"

Copyright by designer/architect.

Rear Elevation

Alternate Front View

Foyer / Dining Room

Great Room

SMARTtip

Add the Extras

Simple or plain, it's the little conveniences and miscellaneous touches that push the dining experience to perfection. Here are some extra things to think about.

- You can never have too many serving trays when you entertain outside. For carrying food or drinks from the kitchen or the grill, trays are indispensable.

- A serving cart on wheels makes a perfect movable outdoor bar and provides an additional serving surface. Look for one at yard sales or buy one new.

- Chances are you won't have a sideboard, but a few small tables to hold excess items are great substitutes for one. They're also easier to position in the different places where you need them.

- For cooler weather or even a summer's evening with a bit of nip in the air, nothing beats an outdoor fireplace for comfort. You could build one into the house, but various types of stand-alone units are sold in home centers. To add a Southwest ambiance, consider a chiminea, a clay fireplace. Try burning some piñon pine, and you'll feel as if you're in Santa Fe. Be sure to follow manufacturers' instructions when using these fireplaces. You might also have to store them during the winter.

- Pots of fragrant plants—lavender, scented geraniums, flowering tobacco, or jasmine—provide a sensual aroma. Flowers such as roses climbing up an arbor or trellis are beautiful, evoke a romantic feeling, and lend a delicate scent to the atmosphere as well.

Nothing adds romance and intrigue to an evening soiree as candlelight does. Include just a few candles for an intimate dinner. Use more for a larger gathering, placing one or more on each table. Scatter luminaries around the yard. As the beautiful evening dusk begins, light candles, a few at a time, so your eyes can adjust to the dimming light. Not only do the candles illuminate the night in a magical way but they can also keep bugs at bay.

Plan #321003

Dimensions: 67'4" W x 48' D
Levels: 1
Square Footage: 1,791
Bedrooms: 4
Bathrooms: 2
Foundation: Basement
Materials List Available: Yes
Price Category: C

Images provided by designer/architect.

The traditional good looks of the exterior of this home are complemented by the stunning contemporary design of the interior.

Features:

- Great Room: With a vaulted ceiling to highlight its spacious dimensions, this room is certain to be the central gathering spot for friends and family.

- Dining Room: Also with a vaulted ceiling, this room has an octagonal shape for added interest. Windows here and in the great room look out to the covered patio.

- Kitchen: A center island gives a convenient work space in this well-designed kitchen, which features a pass-through to the dining room for easy serving, and large, walk-in pantry for storage.

- Breakfast Room: A bay window lets sunshine pour in to start your morning with a smile.

- Master Bedroom: A vaulted ceiling and a sitting area make you feel truly pampered in this room.

Copyright by designer/architect.

SMARTtip

Bay & Bow Windows

Occasionally too little room exists between the window frame (if there is one) and the ceiling. In this situation you might be able to use ceiling-mounted hardware. Alternatively, a cornice across the top and a rod mounted inside the cornice will give you the dual benefit of visually lowering the top of the window and concealing the hardware.

Plan #131011

Dimensions: 75'2" W x 60'9" D
Levels: 1
Square Footage: 1,897
Bedrooms: 4
Bathrooms: 2
Foundation: Basement, crawl space, or slab
Materials List Available: Yes
Price Category: E

Images provided by designer/architect.

You'll love this home if you're looking for a plan for a sloping lot or flat one or if you want to orient the rear porch to face into or away from the sun.

Features:

• Ceiling Height: 8 ft.

• Living Area: The whole family will find it easy to congregate in this lovely room.

• Kitchen: The angle of this home makes the kitchen especially convenient while also giving it an unusual amount of character.

• Study: Located near the front door, this room can serve as a home office or fourth bedroom as easily as it does a private study.

• Master Suite: Located at the opposite end of the home from the other two bedrooms, this master suite offers privacy and quiet.

• Additional Bedrooms: These two bedrooms share a distinctive hall bathroom.

Copyright by designer/architect.

Rear View

Images provided by designer/architect.

Plan #141006

Dimensions: 64' W x 52' D
Levels: 1
Square Footage: 1,787
Bedrooms: 3
Bathrooms: 2½
Foundation: Basement
Materials List Available: No
Price Category: C

This stately and traditional ranch has a well-designed floor plan that makes it seem larger.

Features:

- Ceiling Height: 9 ft. unless otherwise noted:

- Tall Main Ceilings: The main part of the house has an elegant look, with 12-ft. ceilings in the foyer, living area, and dining room. The taller windows allow room for transom windows that fill the rooms with sunlight.

- Fireplace: The handsome fireplace is designed to vent directly to the outside. Without the need for a chimney, a television niche can be installed above the fireplace, maximizing the use of space in the room.

- Kitchen: This kitchen gains light from the breakfast room and the living area. The sink is angled to allow the cook to participate in living-area conversation.

- Master Suite: This elegant private suite has its own access off the rear entry hall.

Master Bdrm. 13⁶ x 15⁰ Tray Ceil.

Sundeck

Brkfst. 9⁴ x 9⁴

Bdrm.3 11⁶ x 11⁶

M Bath Vaulted

Plant Shelf Above

Kit. 11⁴ x 12²

Living Area 17¹⁰ x 15⁶ 12' High Ceil.

Dbl. Garage 19⁸ x 21⁸

Dining 11⁴ x 13⁶

Foyer 6⁰ x 8⁰ 12' High Ceil.

Bdrm.2 11⁶ x 13⁶

Bth.2

Copyright by designer/architect.

SMARTtip

Arts and Crafts Style in Your Kitchen

The heart of this style lies in its earthy connection. The more you can bring nature into it, the more authentic it will appear. An easy way to do this is with plants. Open the space up to nature with glass doors that provide a view to a green garden.

Plan #391008

Dimensions: 50' W x 40' D
Levels: 1
Square Footage: 1,312
Bedrooms: 3
Bathrooms: 2
Foundation: Slab, basement, crawl space
Materials List Available: Yes
Price Category: B

Images provided by designer/architect.

Copyright by designer/architect.

Here's the sum of brains and beauty, which will please all types of families, from starters and nearly empty nesters to those going golden.

Features:

• **Entry:** This restful fresh-air porch and formal foyer bring you graciously toward the great room, with its fireplace and vaulted ceiling.

• **Dining Room:** This adjacent dining room features sliding doors to the deck and smooth open access to the U-shaped kitchen.

• **Laundry Room:** The laundry area has its own separate landing from the garage, so it's conveniently out of the way.

• **Master Suite:** This master suite with tray ceilings features nearly "limitless" closet space, a private bath, and large hall linen closet.

• **Bedrooms:** The two secondary bedrooms, also with roomy closets, share a full bath. Bedroom 3 easily becomes a home office with direct foyer access and a window overlooking the porch.

Option

Plan #391020

Dimensions: 54' W x 50' D

Levels: 1

Square Footage: 2,387

Bedrooms: 3

Bathrooms: 2½

Foundation: Basement

Materials List Available: Yes

Price Category: E

Images provided by designer/architect.

This bi-level home transforms 2387 sq. ft. so families can make the most of both formal and relaxed living. Vaulted ceilings soar above most rooms including the living and bedrooms.

Features:

- Kitchen: This room features a peninsula counter which feeds into the dining room and living room on one side. On the other side, it nurtures a breakfast nook with deck access.

- Bedrooms: Secondary bedrooms share a full bath and a front yard view.

- Master Suite: A dreamy window seat that overlooks the backyard and a spa-style private bath featuring double vanity sinks. A U-shaped walk-in closet provides storage for two.

- Family Room: Step down in modern style to a great-sized room where built-in bookshelves border the fireplace and a walk-out leads to the outdoor deck.

Copyright by designer/architect.

Plan #281012

Dimensions: 46' W x 54' D

Levels: 1

Square Footage: 1,368

Bedrooms: 3

Bathrooms: 2

Foundation: Daylight basement

Materials List Available: Yes

Price Category: B

Images provided by designer/architect.

Copyright by designer/architect.

Rear Elevation

Plan #281013

Dimensions: 64' W x 39'4" D

Levels: 1

Square Footage: 1,407

Bedrooms: 3

Bathrooms: 2

Foundation: Daylight basement

Materials List Available: Yes

Price Category: B

Images provided by designer/architect.

Copyright by designer/architect.

Rear Elevation

Images provided by designer/architect.

Plan #211026

Dimensions: 56' W x 50' D

Levels: 1

Square Footage: 1,415

Bedrooms: 3

Bathrooms: 2

Foundation: Slab

Materials List Available: Yes

Price Category: B

Copyright by designer/architect.

Images provided by designer/architect.

Plan #211029

Dimensions: 68' W x 60' D

Levels: 1

Square Footage: 1,672

Bedrooms: 3

Bathrooms: 2

Foundation: Crawl space

Materials List Available: Yes

Price Category: C

Copyright by designer/architect.

SMARTtip

Ponds

If a pond or small body of water already exists on your property, arrange your garden elements to take advantage of it. Build a bridge over it to connect it to other areas of the garden. If there's a dock already in place, make use of it for an instant midday picnic for one.

Plan #321014

Dimensions: 64' W x 43'8" D
Levels: 1
Square Footage: 1,676
Bedrooms: 3
Bathrooms: 2
Foundation: Basement
Materials List Available: Yes
Price Category: C

Copyright by
designer/architect.

SMARTtip

Blending Architecture

An easy way to blend the new deck with the architecture of a house is with railings. Precut railings and caps come in many styles and sizes.

Plan #321015

Dimensions: 48' W x 64' D
Levels: 1
Square Footage: 1,501
Bedrooms: 3
Bathrooms: 2
Foundation: Basement
Materials List Available: Yes
Price Category: C

Copyright by designer/architect.

Plan #221007

Dimensions: 48' W x 56'4" D

Levels: 1

Square Footage: 1,472

Bedrooms: 3

Bathrooms: 2

Foundation: Basement

Materials List Available: No

Price Category: B

Illustration provided by designer/architect.

Rear Elevation

If you're looking for a compact home with a floor plan that makes every square inch count, you'll love this design.

Features:

- Ceiling Height: 8 ft.

- Great Room: A cathedral ceiling gives stature to this room and the corner fireplace creates a cozy nook where everyone will gather.

- Dining Room: A cathedral ceiling adds an elegant touch, and the door to the screened-in porch makes outdoor entertaining easy.

- Kitchen: This well-planned kitchen is adjacent to the dining room for serving ease and includes a breakfast bar for casual snacking.

- Master Suite: A huge walk-in closet gives a practical touch to this luxurious area, which includes a door to the screened-in porch. The bath includes a whirlpool tub and standing shower.

- Secondary Bedrooms: Both rooms feature large closets and share a full bath.

Copyright by designer/architect.

Plan #101005

Dimensions: 63' W x 57'2" D

Levels: 1

Square Footage: 1,992

Bedrooms: 3

Bathrooms: 2½

Foundation: Slab, crawl space, or basement

Materials List Available: Yes

Price Category: D

Images provided by designer/architect.

This midsized ranch is accented with Palladian windows and inviting front porch.

Features:

- Ceiling Height: 9 ft. unless otherwise noted.

- Special Ceilings: Tray or vaulted ceilings adorn the living room, family room, dining room, and master suite.

- Kitchen: This bright and airy kitchen is designed to be a pleasure in which to work. It shares a big bay window with the contiguous breakfast room.

- Breakfast Room: The light streaming in from the bay window makes this the perfect place to linger with coffee and the Sunday paper.

- Master Suite: This exceptional suite has a sitting area and direct access to the deck, as well as a sitting area, full-featured bath, and spacious walk-in closet.

- Secondary Bedrooms: The other bedrooms each measure about 13 ft. x 11 ft. They have walk-in closets and share a "Jack-and-Jill" bath.

Rear View

Copyright by designer/architect.

Plan #211038

Dimensions: 72' W x 42' D
Levels: 1
Square Footage: 1,898
Bedrooms: 3
Bathrooms: 2
Foundation: Slab
Materials List Available: Yes
Price Category: D

Images provided by designer/architect.

A railed front porch, a charming cupola, and stylish shutters add classic flair to this home.

Features:

- Ceiling Height: 8 ft. unless otherwise noted.

- Family Room: The welcoming entry flows into this attractive family gathering area. The room features a handsome fireplace and a 14-ft. vaulted ceiling with exposed beams. French doors lead to a backyard patio.

- Formal Dining Room: This elegant room adjoins the living room. You'll usher your guests through a half-wall with decorative spindles.

- Kitchen: Food preparation will be a pleasure working at the wraparound counter.

- Eating Nook: Modern life includes lots of quick, informal meals, and this is the spot to enjoy them. The nook includes a laundry closet, so you can change loads while cooking.

- Master Suite: This private retreat boasts a private bath with a separate dressing area and a roomy walk-in closet.

Copyright by designer/architect.

SMARTtip

Efficient Kitchen Appliances

Appliances that carry the **Energy Star** label — a program of the Department of Energy — are significantly more energy efficient than most other appliances. Dishwashers, for example, must be 25 percent more energy efficient than models that meet minimum federal energy requirements. Energy Star refrigerators must be 10 percent more efficient than the newest standards.

Plan #241005

Dimensions: 53' W x 55'9" D
Levels: 1
Square Footage: 1,670
Bedrooms: 3
Bathrooms: 2
Foundation: Slab, crawl space,
(basement available for extra fee)
Materials List Available: No
Price Category: C

This charming starter home, in split-bedroom format, combines big-house features in a compact design.

Features:

- **Great Room:** With easy access to the formal dining room, kitchen, and breakfast area, this great room features a cozy fireplace.

- **Kitchen:** This big kitchen, with easy access to a walk-in pantry, features an island for added work space and a lovely plant shelf that separates it from the great room.

- **Master Suite:** Separated for privacy, this master suite offers a roomy bath with whirlpool tub, dual vanities, a separate shower, and a large walk-in closet.

- **Additional Rooms:** Additional rooms include a laundry/utility room—with space for a washer, dryer, and freezer—a large area above the garage, well-suited for a media or game room, and two secondary bedrooms.

Images provided by designer/architect.

Copyright by
designer/architect.

Plan #321004

Dimensions: 91'8" W x 62'4" D
Levels: 1
Square Footage: 2,808
Bedrooms: 3
Bathrooms: 2½
Foundation: Basement
Materials List Available: Yes
Price Category: F

You'll love the sophistication of this design, with its three porches and elegance at every turn.

Features:

- **Entry:** This impressive space welcomes guests into the living room on one side and the dining room on the other.

- **Living Room:** This spacious room will be a family favorite, especially in warm weather when you can use the adjoining porch as an outdoor extension of this area.

- **Dining Room:** Decorate this room to highlight its slightly formal feeling or to create a more casual ambiance for large family dinners.

- **Kitchen:** The family cooks will appreciate the thought that went into designing the convenient counter space and generous storage areas here.

- **Master Suite:** A vaulted ceiling, bath with a corner tub, double vanities, walk-in closet, and secluded screened porch make this area a joy.

Images provided by designer/architect.

Copyright by designer/architect.

SMARTtip

Ornaments in a Garden

Placement is everything with ornaments in a garden. Some elements are best sitting by themselves. Others are better when they are part of a cohesive whole, perhaps placed in the greenery at a corner or flanking a structure.

Plan #131012

Dimensions: 71'4" W x 35'10" D
Levels: 1
Square Footage: 1,366
Bedrooms: 3
Bathrooms: 2
Foundation: Basement, crawl space, or slab
Materials List Available: Yes
Price Category: C

Images provided by designer/architect.

You're sure to love this home, with its covered front porch and gabled roofline.

Features:

- **Entry:** The 11-ft. ceiling height makes an impressive entryway.

- **Living Room:** A pair of French doors frames the fireplace in this room, and a central sky light provides natural lighting during the day and drama at night.

- **Dining Room:** Open to the living room, this area also features an 11-ft.-high ceiling.

- **Kitchen:** A laundry closet, ample counter space, and dinette opening to the expansive backyard terrace add up to convenience in this room.

- **Master Suite:** Enjoy the dressing area, two closets, and bath with whirlpool tub and shower.

- **Additional Bedrooms:** An arched window and 11-ft. ceiling mark the larger of these two rooms.

Living Room

Plan #141007

Dimensions: 65' W x 56'5" D
Levels: 1
Square Footage: 1,854
Bedrooms: 3
Bathrooms: 2½
Foundation: Basement
Materials List Available: No
Price Category: D

Images provided by designer/architect.

This home offers a spacious layout, all on one level for convenient modern living.

Features:

• Ceiling Height: 8 ft. unless otherwise noted.

• Dining Room: The 12-ft. ceiling makes this the perfect dining room for the most elegant of dinner parties.

• Living Room: The elegant 12-ft. ceiling continues into this living room. Its handsome fireplace will make it the focal point for all gatherings.

• Kitchen: This well-designed kitchen will make cooking a pleasure. It features a pantry and an island for food preparation.

• Breakfast Area: The breakfast area is just off the kitchen. Measuring 11 ft. x 11 ft., it offers plenty of room for the whole family to enjoy informal meals.

• Master Suite: Located away from the other bedrooms, this luxurious retreat has a tray ceiling. The master bath has separate vanities, a jet tub, and a separate shower.

Copyright by designer/architect.

SMARTtip

Painting Walls

Paint won't hide imperfections. Rather, it will make them stand out. So shine a bright light at a low angle across the surface to spot problem areas before painting.

Plan #161005

Dimensions: 60' W x 48'10" D

Levels: 1

Square Footage: 1,593

Bedrooms: 3

Bathrooms: 2

Foundation: Basement

Materials List Available: Yes

Price Category: C

Images provided by designer/architect.

Rear Elevation

This delightful ranch home includes many thoughtful conveniences and a full basement to expand your living enjoyment.

Features:

- **Great Room:** Take pleasure in welcoming guests through a spacious foyer into the warm and friendly confines of this great room with corner fireplace, sloped ceiling, and view to the rear yard.

- **Kitchen:** Experience the convenience of enjoying meals while seated at the large island that separates the dining area from this well-designed kitchen. Also included is an over-sized pantry with an abundance of storage.

- **Master Suite:** This master suite features a compartmented bath, large walk-in closet, and master bedroom that has a tray ceiling with 9-ft. center height.

- **Porch:** Retreat to this delightful rear porch to enjoy a relaxing evening.

Copyright by designer/architect.

Plan #311005

Dimensions: 87' W x 57'3" D
Levels: 1
Square Footage: 2,497
Bedrooms: 3
Bathrooms: 3½
Foundation: Crawl space, slab
Materials List Available: Yes
Price Category: E

You'll love this home, which mixes practical features with a gracious appearance.

Features:

- Great Room: A handsome fireplace and flanking windows that give a view of the back patio are the highlights of this gracious room.

- Kitchen: A curved bar defines the perimeter of this well-planned kitchen.

- Breakfast Room: Open to both the great room and the kitchen, this sunny spot leads to the rear porch, which in turn, leads to the patio beyond.

- Master Suite: Vaulted ceilings, a huge walk-in closet, and deluxe bath create luxury here.

- Bonus Room: Finish this 966-sq.-ft. area as a huge game room, or divide it into a game room, study, and sewing or craft room.

- Additional Bedrooms: Each bedroom has a private bath and good closet space.

Images provided by designer/architect.

Main Level Floor Plan

Patio 18-0x14-6

Porch 13-0x8-0

Breakfast 11-6x12-7

Master Bedroom 16-0x21-0

Bath

Bedroom 11-0x14-3

Greatroom 18-0x21-1

Kitchen 11-10x15-6

1/2 Bath

Laun.

Stor.

M.Bath

Bedroom 12-9x10-10

Foyer

Dining 17-1x13-2

Garage 21-8x23-3

Porch 43-0x7-0

Copyright by designer/architect.

Bonus Area Floor Plan

Future 17-5x20-4

Future 12-9x18-4

6-8x8-11 (Raised)

Future 16-4x18-4

SMARTtip

Front Porch

A front porch proclaims you to the outside world, so furnish it in a way that expresses what you want the world to know about you. Use the walls of your porch to hang interesting items such as sundials or old shutters. Set a mirror into an old window to reflect a portion of the garden.

Images provided by designer/architect.

Copyright by designer/architect.

Plan #271001

Dimensions: 52'8" W x 35'4" D
Levels: 1
Square Footage: 1,400
Bedrooms: 3
Bathrooms: 2
Foundation: Basement
Materials List Available: Yes
Price Category: B

This contemporary design builds on the basics, creating a comfortable home that offers possibilities for entertaining or quiet downtime.

Features:

- Great room: The heart of the home, this massive gathering room features a handsome fireplace and a handy wet bar, and flows into the dining space. Sliding glass doors between the two spaces lead to a deck.

- Kitchen/Breakfast: This combination space uses available space efficiently and comfortably.

- Master Suite: The inviting master bedroom includes a private bath.

SMARTtip

Candid Camera for Your Landscaping

To see your home and yard as others see them, take some camera shots. Seeing your house and landscaping on film will create an opportunity for objectivity. Problems will become more obvious, and you will then be better able to prioritize your home improvements, as well as your landscaping plan.

Plan #221008

Dimensions: 60'4" W x 46' D

Levels: 1

Square Footage: 1,540

Bedrooms: 3

Bathrooms: 2

Foundation: Basement

Materials List Available: Yes

Price Category: C

Images provided by designer/architect.

Rear Elevation

You'll love the well-designed interior of this traditional-looking ranch.

Features:

- Ceiling Height: 9 ft.

- Entry: This vaulted entry leads to the living room and includes a coat closet for convenience.

- Living Room: The highlights of this spacious room are the direct-vent gas fireplace in the corner and the large windows looking out to the backyard.

- Dining Room: Adjacent to the kitchen, this lovely room opens to a large screened porch where you'll love to entertain.

- Kitchen: A corner sink gives this well-designed kitchen a nice touch, and the breakfast bar it shares with the dining room adds convenience.

- Master Suite: A large walk-in closet and windows looking into the backyard give practicality to the bedroom, and the full private bath adds a note of luxury.

Copyright by designer/architect.

Plan #101006

Dimensions: 63' W x 58' D

Levels: 1

Square Footage: 1,982

Bedrooms: 3

Bathrooms: 2½

Foundation: Slab, crawl space, or basement

Materials List Available: Yes

Price Category: D

Radius-top windows and siding accented with wood shingles give this home a distinctive look.

Features:

- Ceiling Height: 9 ft. unless otherwise noted.

- Family Room: This room is perfect for all kinds of informal family activities. A vaulted ceiling adds to its sense of spaciousness.

- Dining Room: This room, with its tray ceiling, is designed for elegant dining.

- Porch: When the weather gets warm, you'll enjoy stepping out onto this large screened porch to catch a breeze.

- Master Suite: You'll love ending your day and getting up in the morning to this exquisite master suite, with its vaulted ceiling, sitting area, and large walk-in closet.

- Bonus Room: Just off the kitchen are stairs leading to this enormous bonus room, offering more than 330 sq. ft. of future expansion space.

Images provided by designer/architect.

Copyright by designer/architect.

SMARTtip

Art in Pools

The tiled walls and floor of a pool make great canvases for art, so incorporate a serious or whimsical design. Also, make the stairs wide and shallow to form a wading area for kids.

Plan #211044

Dimensions: 70' W x 48' D
Levels: 1
Square Footage: 1,997
Bedrooms: 4
Bathrooms: 2½
Foundation: Slab
Materials List Available: Yes
Price Category: D

Images provided by designer/architect.

Interior angles add a touch of architectural excitement to this traditional home.

Features:

• Ceiling Height: 8 ft. unless otherwise noted.

• Wood-and-Stone Facade: This pleasantly charming exterior combines wood siding with stone to give the home a solid, comfortable look that fits into any neighborhood.

• Foyer: This entry is flanked by a formal living room and formal dining room.

• Dining Room: This formal room is designed to accommodate dinner parties of all sizes.

• Family Room: Accessible from the entry, this large living room will become the focal point of all informal gatherings. The 19-ft. vaulted ceiling adds plenty of drama, while the handsome fireplace and built-in bookshelves ensure that the room is still warm and cozy.

Copyright by designer/architect.

SMARTtip

Lubricating Window Tracks and Hinges

No one appreciates windows and doors that stick, especially in the winter, when energy losses from a window that won't shut properly can become expensive quickly. Use a lubricant on all hinges and window tracks to keep them operating smoothly and efficiently all year long.

Plan #241006

Dimensions: 51' W x 53' D

Levels: 1

Square Footage: 1,744

Bedrooms: 3

Bathrooms: 2

Foundation: Slab

Materials List Available: No

Price Category: C

The striking rooflines and arched window of this split-bedroom home will captivate onlookers and guests.

Features:

- **Great Room:** A spacious foyer introduces this great room, which features a cozy corner fireplace. Guests will enjoy a natural flow through a columned entry to the formal dining room or through a French door to the rear yard.

- **Kitchen:** Designed for total convenience, this kitchen features ample counter space, an eating bar, a pantry, and a roomy breakfast area. A 42-in.-high wall separating it from the dining room maximizes the openness of the kitchen.

- **Master Suite:** You will enjoy the comfort and privacy of this master suite, which features a whirlpool tub, dual vanities, a corner glass shower, and a large walk-in closet.

- **Additional Bedrooms:** Two secondary bedrooms share a common bath.

Plan #321005

Dimensions: 69' W x 53'8" D
Levels: 1
Square Footage: 2,483
Bedrooms: 4
Bathrooms: 2
Foundation: Basement
Materials List Available: Yes
Price Category: E

You'll love the grand feeling of this home, which combines with the very practical features that make living in it a pleasure.

Features:

- **Porch:** The open brick arches and Palladian door set the tone for this magnificent home.

- **Great Room:** An alcove for the entertainment center and vaulted ceiling show the care that went into designing this room.

- **Dining Room:** A tray ceiling sets off the formality of this large room.

- **Kitchen:** The layout in this room is designed to make your work patterns more efficient and to save you steps and time.

- **Study:** This quiet room can be a wonderful refuge, or you can use it for a fourth bedroom if you wish.

- **Master Suite:** Made for relaxing at the end of the day, this suite will pamper you with luxuries.

Images provided by designer/architect.

Copyright by designer/architect.

SMARTtip

Art in Pools

The tiled walls and floor of a pool make great canvases for art, so incorporate a serious or whimsical design. Also, make the stairs wide and shallow to form a wading area for kids.

Plan #131014

Dimensions: 48' W x 43'4" D
Levels: 1
Square Footage: 1,380
Bedrooms: 3
Bathrooms: 2
Foundation: Basement, crawl space, or slab
Materials List Available: Yes
Price Category: B

Images provided by designer/architect.

The exterior of this home looks formal, thanks to its twin dormers, gables, and the bay windows that flank the columned porch, but the inside is contemporary in both design and features.

Features:

- Great Room: Centrally located, this great room has a 10-ft. ceiling. A fireplace, built-in cabinets, and windows that overlook the rear covered porch make it as practical as it is attractive.

- Dining Room: A bay window adds to the charm of this versatile room.

- Kitchen: This U-shaped room is designed to make cooking and cleaning jobs efficient.

- Master Suite: With a bay window, a walk-in closet, and a private bath with an oval tub, the master suite may be your favorite area.

- Additional Bedrooms: Located on the opposite side of the house from the master suite, these rooms share a full bath in the hall.

Copyright by designer/architect.

Bonus Room

Great Room

Rear Elevation

Plan #141011

Dimensions: 54' W x 60'6" D

Levels: 1

Square Footage: 1,869

Bedrooms: 3

Bathrooms: 2

Foundation: Basement, crawl space, or slab

Materials List Available: Yes

Price Category: D

The blending of brick and stone on this plan gives the home an old-world appeal.

Features:

• Ceiling Height: 8 ft. unless otherwise noted.

• Tall Ceilings: The main living areas feature dramatic 12-ft. ceilings.

• Open Plan: This home's open floor plan maximizes the use of space and makes it flexible. This main living area has plenty of room for large gatherings.

• Kitchen: The kitchen is integrated into the main living area. It features a breakfast room that is ideal for informal family meals.

• Master Suite: You'll enjoy unwinding at the end of the day in this luxurious space. It's located away from the rest of the house for maximum privacy.

• Secondary Bedrooms: You have the option of adding extra style to the secondary bedrooms by including volume ceilings.

Images provided by designer/architect.

Copyright by designer/architect.

Plan #391034

Dimensions: 72'4" W x 43' D
Levels: 1
Square Footage: 1,737
Bedrooms: 3
Bathrooms: 2
Foundation: Basement, crawl space, slab
Materials List Available: Yes
Price Category: C

Images provided by designer/architect.

This lovely home brings together traditional single-level architectural elements, current features, and just the right amount of living space.

Features:

• Entry: A demure covered porch and well-mannered foyer deliver all the important rooms.

• Dining Room: This formal room features exquisite vaulted ceilings.

• Kitchen: This close-knit kitchen with pantry embraces a cheerful breakfast nook with sliding doors to the deck.

• Master Suite: This suite is a visual treat, with its own vaulted ceiling as well as a skylight over the master bathtub and shower area.

• Bedrooms: The two secondary bedrooms are pampered with good closeting, proximity to a shared bath with double sink vanities, and wonderful windows that enhance the spacious atmosphere.

Copyright by designer/architect.

Plan #151005

Dimensions: 58' W x 54'10" D
Levels: 1
Square Footage: 1,940
Bedrooms: 4
Bathrooms: 2
Foundation: Basement, crawl space, or slab
Materials List Available: No
Price Category: D

Images provided by designer/architect.

A covered front porch with stately 10-in. round columns and a classically-styled foyer invite family and guests into this well-designed, traditional 4-bedroom home.

Features:

- Great Room: The 9-ft. boxed-ceiling, radiant fireplace, and built-in shelving add up to create a cozy and practical room where friends and family will love to gather.

- Dining Room: Open access from this dining room to the kitchen, and from there to the breakfast room, makes this room an ideal place for entertaining.

- Master Suite: This luxuriously appointed suite, with a 9-ft. pan ceiling in the bedroom, is located just of the breakfast room. The spectacular bath is fitted with a whirlpool tub, separate shower, and double vanities.

- Bedrooms 2 and 3: Large walk-in closets make these rooms easy to organize and keep tidy.

Copyright by designer/architect.

Plan #211008

Dimensions: 56' W x 93' D

Levels: 1

Square Footage: 2,259

Bedrooms: 3

Bathrooms: 2½

Foundation: Slab

Materials List Available: Yes

Price Category: E

Images provided by designer/architect.

If you're looking for a design that suits a narrow building lot, you'll love this home, with its exterior that resembles an old European cottage.

Features:

- Ceiling Height: 10-ft. except as noted.

- Courtyards: Use formal gardens full of easy-care plants to make the most of the lovely courtyards.

- Living Room: The massive glass wall in this room with 16-ft. ceilings looks out to the entry courtyard. In cool weather you'll love the fireplace, which is flanked by lovely built-ins that can hold everything from books to collectables.

- Kitchen: With a contemporary layout and up-to-date conveniences, this kitchen is as convenient as it is attractive.

- Master Suite: Relax beside the bedroom fireplace, or luxuriate in the bath, with its two walk-in closets, soaking tub, shower, two vanities, linen closet, and private room for toilet and bidet.

Copyright by designer/architect.

Plan #221009

Dimensions: 68' W x 59' D

Levels: 1

Square Footage: 1,795

Bedrooms: 3

Bathrooms: 2

Foundation: Basement

Materials List Available: No

Price Category: C

Images provided by designer/architect.

If your family likes the spaciousness and convenience of an open floor plan, they'll love this ranch-style home.

Features:

- Ceiling Height: 9 ft.

- Entry: From this lovely entryway, with its convenient coat closet, openings into both the great room and the dining room give you a glimpse of the home's open design.

- Living Room: A fireplace in this living room is flanked by windows that look out to the back.

- Dining Room: The highlight of this area is the door to the screened-in porch, where you'll love to serve meals in fine weather.

- Kitchen: Merging with the dining room, this well-designed kitchen is a delight for any cook. An island provides extra counter space, and you'll have the corner pantry for a generous storage area.

- Master Suite: Enjoy the walk-in closet and the bath with whirlpool tub and double sinks.

Rear Elevation

Copyright by designer/architect.

Plan #101008

Dimensions: 67'8" W x 52'6" D

Levels: 1

Square Footage: 2,088

Bedrooms: 3

Bathrooms: 2½

Foundation: Slab, crawl space, or basement

Materials List Available: Yes

Price Category: D

This ranch sports an attractive brick-and-stucco exterior accented with quoins and layered trim.

Features:

- Ceiling Height: 11 ft. unless otherwise noted.

- Kitchen: You'll love cooking in this bright, airy kitchen, which is lit by an abundance of windows.

- Breakfast room: Off the kitchen is this breakfast room, the perfect spot for informal family meals.

- Master Suite: You'll look forward to retiring at the end of the day to this truly exceptional master suite, with its grand bath, spacious walk-in closet, and direct access to the porch.

- Morning Porch: Greet the day with your first cup of coffee on this porch, which is accessible from the master suite.

- Secondary Bedrooms: These bedrooms measure a generous 11 ft. x 14 ft. They share a compartmented bath.

Images provided by designer/architect.

Copyright by designer/architect.

SMARTtip

Accentuating Your Bathroom with Details

No matter how big or small the room, details will pull the style together. Some of the best details that you can include are the smallest—drawer pulls from an antique store or shells in a glass jar or just left on the countertop. Add period flavor with crown molding, or dress up contemporary fixtures with polished stone fittings.

Plan #211054

Dimensions: 80' W x 62' D
Levels: 1
Square Footage: 2,358
Bedrooms: 3
Bathrooms: 2½
Foundation: Slab
Materials List Available: Yes
Price Category: E

Images provided by designer/architect.

This ranch has a low-maintenance exterior of brick combined with board-and-batten siding.

Features:

• Ceiling Height: 8 ft. unless otherwise noted.

• Foyer: Guests will be greeted by a view of the living room when they step into this inviting entry area.

• Living Room: There's plenty of room for all kinds of entertaining in this generously sized living room. The room seems even more spacious, thanks to the vaulted and beamed ceiling and the built-ins, which maximize the use of floor space. When you entertain, you can gather around the handsome brick fireplace and fix your guests a drink from the small wet bar that is tucked behind the bi-fold doors.

• Game Room: The kids will love this super-sized game room located just behind the living room. It features a volume ceiling and lots of built-ins.

• Garage: In addition to parking for two cars, you will find lots of extra storage space in this attached garage.

Copyright by designer/architect.

SMARTtip

Dressing Up a Simple Fireplace

Painting a wood surround with a faux marble or faux bois (wood) is inexpensive. Adding a simple, prefabricated wooden shelf mantel can add lots of architectural character.

Plan #241008

Dimensions: 65' W x 56'8" D

Levels: 1

Square Footage: 2,526

Bedrooms: 4

Bathrooms: 3

Foundation: Slab

Materials List Available: No

Price Category: E

A covered back porch—with access from the master suite and the breakfast area—makes this traditional home ideal for siting near a golf course or with a backyard pool.

Features:

- **Great Room:** From the foyer, guests enter this spacious and comfortable great room, which features a handsome fireplace.

- **Kitchen:** This kitchen—the hub of this family-oriented home—is a joy in which to work, thanks to abundant counter space, a pantry, a convenient eating bar, and an adjoining breakfast area and sunroom.

- **Master Suite:** Enjoy the quiet comfort of this coffered-ceiling master suite, which features dual vanities and separate walk-in closets.

- **Additional Bedrooms:** Two secondary bedrooms, which share a full bath, are located at the opposite end of the house from the master suite. Bedroom 4—in front of the house—can be converted into a study.

Images provided by designer/architect.

Copyright by designer/architect.

SMARTtip

Traditional-Style Kitchen Cabinetry

You can modify stock kitchen cabinetry to enjoy fine furniture-quality details. Prefabricated trims may be purchased at local lumber mills and home centers. For example, crown molding, applied to the top of stock cabinetry and stained or painted to match the door style, may be all you need. Likewise, you can replace hardware with reproduction polished-brass door and drawer knobs or pulls for a finishing touch.

Covered Patio
20' x 10'

Bedroom
12'2" x 11'

Nook
12'6" x 11'8"

Vaulted
Master Suite
18'2" x 14'8"

Vaulted
Great Room
17'2" x 19'4"

Kitchen
12'6" x 12'

Bedroom
11' x 11'8"

Up

Dn

Bonus
Room
13' x 23'

Bedroom
12'2" x 11'

Vaulted
Entry

Dining
13' x 11'

Utility

Covered Porch
20'6" x 8'

Garage
31'4" x 23'2"

Images provided by designer/architect.

Plan #361005

Dimensions: 68' W x 71' D

Levels: 1

Square Footage: 2,759

Bedrooms: 4

Bathrooms: 2½

Foundation: Crawl space

Materials List Available: No

Price Category: F

Copyright by designer/architect.

Patio

Covered Patio

Living

Vaulted
Great Room
37'8" x 15'2"

Dining

Master Suite
19' x 16'

Bedroom
15' x 11'4"

Kitchen

12'
Ceiling
Entry

Media/
Study
11'4" x 13'

Utility

Vaulted
Bedroom
12'8" x 13'6"

Porch

Garage
33'4" x 29'4"

Garage

Alternate Basement Stairs

Dn

Images provided by designer/architect.

Plan #361006

Dimensions: 70' W x 62' D

Levels: 1

Square Footage: 2,274

Bedrooms: 3

Bathrooms: 2½

Foundation: Crawl space, basement

Materials List Available: No

Price Category: E

Copyright by designer/architect.

Utility Dn

Alternate Basement Stairs

Deck

Master Suite
14'6" x 14'

Vaulted
Family
14'2" x 18'2"

Vaulted
Nook
12' x 10'

Utility

Kitchen

Garage
19'8" x 19'10"

Bedroom
11'8" x 11'4"

Living
14' x 13'8"

Vaulted
Entry

Bedroom
11'8" x 10'6"

Covered Porch

Images provided by designer/architect.

Copyright by designer/architect.

Plan #361002

Dimensions: 62' W x 50' D
Levels: 1
Square Footage: 1,794
Bedrooms: 3
Bathrooms: 2
Foundation: Crawl space, basement
Materials List Available: No
Price Category: C

Plan #211037

Dimensions: 66' W x 60' D
Levels: 1
Square Footage: 1,800
Bedrooms: 3
Bathrooms: 2
Foundation: Crawl space, basement
(slab available for an extra fee)
Materials List Available: Yes
Price Category: D

Images provided by designer/architect.

Copyright by designer/architect.

mbr
15 x 14

sto
6 x 4

sto
10x6

util 9x6

eating
10 x 8

porch
15 x 12

br 3
12 x 11

garage
25 x 22

kit
13 x 11

living
18 x 16

skylight

br 2
14 x 11

dining
14 x 12

entry 11x4

porch 44 x 6

SMARTtip

Reflected Light in the Bathroom

The addition of a large mirror can bring reflected light into a small bathroom, adding the illusion of space without the expense of renovation.

Rear View

Plan #321017

Dimensions: 77' W x 36'8" D

Levels: 1

Square Footage: 2,531

Bedrooms: 1-4

Bathrooms: 1-2½

Foundation: Daylight basement

Materials List Available: Yes

Price Category: E

Images provided by designer/architect.

Optional Basement Level Floor Plan

Copyright by designer/architect.

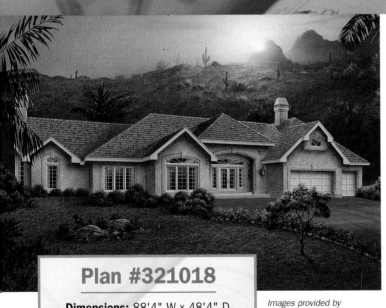

Plan #321018

Dimensions: 88'4" W x 48'4" D

Levels: 1

Square Footage: 2,523

Bedrooms: 3

Bathrooms: 2

Foundation: Basement

Materials List Available: Yes

Price Category: E

Images provided by designer/architect.

Copyright by designer/architect.

SMARTtip

Tiebacks

You don't have to limit yourself to tiebacks made from matching or contrasting fabric. Achieve creative custom looks by making tiebacks from unexpected items. Some materials to consider are old cotton bandannas or silk scarves, strings of beads, lengths of leather, or old belts and chains.

Plan #201016

Dimensions: 51'10" W x 40'4" D

Levels: 1

Square Footage: 1,293

Bedrooms: 3

Bathrooms: 2

Foundation: Crawl space, slab, or basement

Materials List Available: Yes

Price Category: B

Images provided by designer/architect.

Copyright by designer/architect.

Plan #351004

Dimensions: 78' W x 49'6" D

Levels: 1

Square Footage: 1,852

Bedrooms: 3

Bathrooms: 2½

Foundation: Crawl space, slab, or basement

Materials List Available: Yes

Price Category: D

Images provided by designer/architect.

Copyright by designer/architect.

Rear Elevation

Bonus Room

Plan #321006

Dimensions: 76' W x 45' D

Levels: 1, optional lower

Square Footage: 1,977

Optional Basement Level Sq. Ft.: 1,416

Bedrooms: 4

Bathrooms: 2½

Foundation: Basement

Materials List Available: Yes

Price Category: D

This design is ideal if you're looking for a home with space to finish as your family and your budget grow.

Features:

- **Great Room:** A vaulted ceiling in this room sets an elegant tone that the gorgeous atrium windows pick up and amplify.

- **Atrium:** Elegance marks the staircase here that leads to the optional lower level.

- **Kitchen:** Both experienced cooks and beginners will appreciate the care that went into the design of this step-saving kitchen, with its ample counter space and generous cabinets.

- **Master Suite:** Enjoy the luxuries you'll find in this suite, and revel in the quiet that the bedroom can provide.

- **Lower Level:** Finish the 1,416 sq. ft. here to create a family room, two bedrooms, two bathrooms, and a study.

Images provided by designer/architect.

Optional Basement Level Floor Plan

Copyright by designer/architect.

Plan #131018

Dimensions: 66'4" W x 30'4" D
Levels: 1
Square Footage: 1,243
Bedrooms: 3
Bathrooms: 2
Foundation: Basement, crawl space, or slab
Materials List Available: Yes
Price Category: C

Images provided by designer/architect.

If you're looking for an easy-care home that makes your family and your guests feel welcome, this charming ranch will delight you.

Features:

- **Living Room:** Everyone will gravitate to this central area, not only because of its location but also because it forms the hub of this home.

- **Dining Room:** Flowing from the living room, this dining room is large enough for a crowd but cozy enough for intimate dinners.

- **Kitchen:** This well-designed kitchen is a pleasure in which to work, thanks to the ample counter area and good-sized cabinets. It's also large enough that so you can use it as a second eating area.

- **Laundry Room:** Having a separate space for laundry simplifies this chore.

- **Patio:** Enjoy the large backyard patio at any time of year, but make it a special place to entertain during the warm months.

Copyright by designer/architect.

SMARTtip

Fabric for Outdoor Use

For outdoor furnishings, pick a fabric that contains a fade-resistant coating, particularly if you are using dark colors. Sunlight also weakens fibers, so look for sun-resistant coatings as well. But don't be surprised if outdoor fabrics wear faster than those indoors.

Plan #121002

Dimensions: 42' W x 54' D
Levels: 1
Square Footage: 1,347
Bedrooms: 3
Bathrooms: 2
Foundation: Basement
Materials List Available: Yes
Price Category: B

Images provided by designer/architect.

This home's convenient single level and luxury amenities are a recipe for gracious living.

Features:

- Ceiling Height: 8 ft. except as noted.

- Great Room: The entry enjoys a long view into this great room where a pair of transom-topped windows flanks the fireplace and a 10-ft. ceiling visually expands the space.

- Snack Bar: This special feature adjoins the great room, making it a real plus for informal entertaining, as well as the perfect spot for family get-togethers.

- Kitchen: An island is the centerpiece of this well-designed convenient kitchen that features an island, a door to the backyard, a pantry, and convenient access to the laundry room.

- Master Suite: Located at the back of the home for extra privacy, the master suite feels like its own world. It features a tiered ceiling and sunlit corner whirlpool.

Copyright by designer/architect.

Plan #271002

Dimensions: 44'8" W x 50'8" D

Levels: 1

Square Footage: 1,252

Bedrooms: 3

Bathrooms: 2

Foundation: Basement

Materials List Available: Yes

Price Category: B

Images provided by designer/architect.

This traditional home combines a modest square footage with stylish extras.

Features:

- Living Room: Spacious and inviting, this gathering spot is brightened by a Palladian window arrangement, warmed by a fireplace, and topped by a vaulted ceiling.

- Dining Room: The vaulted ceiling also crowns this room, which shares the living room's fireplace. Sliding doors lead to a backyard deck.

- Kitchen: Smart design ensures a place for everything.

- Master Suite: The master bedroom boasts a vaulted ceiling, cheery windows, and a private bath.

Copyright by designer/architect.

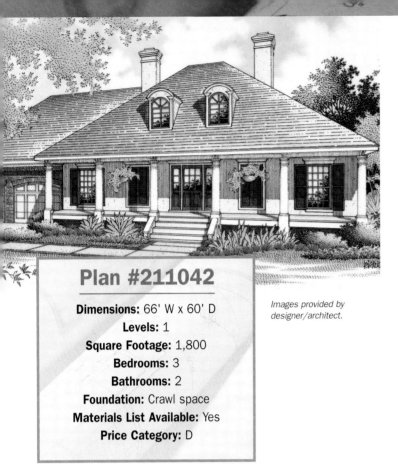

Plan #211042

Dimensions: 66' W x 60' D

Levels: 1

Square Footage: 1,800

Bedrooms: 3

Bathrooms: 2

Foundation: Crawl space

Materials List Available: Yes

Price Category: D

Images provided by designer/architect.

Copyright by designer/architect.

Plan #211046

Dimensions: 62' W x 68' D

Levels: 1

Square Footage: 1,936

Bedrooms: 3

Bathrooms: 2

Foundation: Crawl space

Materials List Available: Yes

Price Category: D

Images provided by designer/architect.

Copyright by designer/architect.

Plan #321020

Dimensions: 58' W x 47'6" D

Levels: 1

Square Footage: 1,882

Bedrooms: 4

Bathrooms: 2

Foundation: Basement

Materials List Available: Yes

Price Category: D

Images provided by designer/architect.

Copyright by designer/architect.

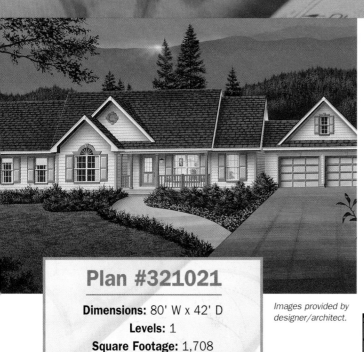

Plan #321021

Dimensions: 80' W x 42' D

Levels: 1

Square Footage: 1,708

Bedrooms: 3

Bathrooms: 2

Foundation: Basement

Materials List Available: Yes

Price Category: C

Images provided by designer/architect.

Copyright by designer/architect.

SMARTtip

Planning a Safe Children's Room

Keep safety in mind when planning a child's room. Make sure that there are covers on electrical outlets, guard rails on high windows, sturdy screens in front of radiators, and gates blocking any steps. Other suggestions include safety hinges for chests and nonskid backing for rugs.

Copyright by designer/architect.

Plan #201023

Images provided by designer/architect.

Dimensions: 67'4" W x 32'10" D

Levels: 1

Square Footage: 1,390

Bedrooms: 3

Bathrooms: 2

Foundation: Crawl space, slab

Materials List Available: Yes

Price Category: B

Plan #201024

Images provided by designer/architect.

Dimensions: 50'10" W x 38'10" D

Levels: 1

Square Footage: 1,324

Bedrooms: 3

Bathrooms: 2

Foundation: Crawl space, slab

Materials List Available: Yes

Price Category: B

Copyright by designer/architect.

Plan #211047

Dimensions: 74'6" W x 50' D

Levels: 1

Square Footage: 2,009

Bedrooms: 3

Bathrooms: 2

Foundation: Slab

Materials List Available: Yes

Price Category: D

Images provided by designer/architect.

Copyright by designer/architect.

SMARTtip

Saw Setup

If you're using a new saw, it's tempting to plug it in and start cutting. But you should take the time to read the owner's manual, including the safety precautions.

Plan #211051

Dimensions: 58' W x 71' D

Levels: 1

Square Footage: 2,123

Bedrooms: 3

Bathrooms: 2½

Foundation: Crawl space

Materials List Available: Yes

Price Category: D

Images provided by designer/architect.

Copyright by designer/architect.

Bonus Area

Plan #161007

Dimensions: 66'4" W x 43'10" D
Levels: 1
Square Footage: 1,611
Bedrooms: 3
Bathrooms: 2
Foundation: Basement
Materials List Available: Yes
Price Category: C

A lovely front porch and an entry with side-lights invite you to experience the impressive amenities offered in this exceptional ranch home.

Features:

• Great Room: Grand openings, featuring columns from the foyer to this great room and continuing to the bayed dining area, convey an open, spacious feel. The fireplace and matching windows on the rear wall of the great room enhance this effect.

• Kitchen: This well-designed kitchen offers convenient access to the laundry and garage. It also features an angled counter with ample space and an abundance of cabinets.

• Master Suite: This deluxe master suite contains many exciting amenities, including a lavishly appointed dressing room and a large walk-in closet.

• Porch: Sliding doors lead to this delightful screened porch for relaxing summer interludes.

Images provided by designer/architect.

Copyright by designer/architect.

Rear Elevation

Plan #221010

Dimensions: 73' W x 58'8" D

Levels: 1

Square Footage: 2,196

Bedrooms: 3

Bathrooms: 2½

Foundation: Basement

Materials List Available: Yes

Price Category: D

Images provided by designer/architect.

If you've been looking for a plan that combines traditional good looks with contemporary comforts, you'll love this home.

Features:

- Ceiling Height: 8 ft.

- Great Room: A vaulted ceiling speaks elegance, and the handsome fireplace with flanking windows adds warmth and light.

- Dining Room: Near the kitchen, this room is ideal for family meals or formal dining.

- Kitchen: Ample counter and cabinet space will steal the family chef's heart, and the large nook with a door to the huge screened porch will be everybody's favorite gathering spot.

- Master Suite: You'll love the walk-in closet and the luxurious private bath with its whirlpool tub.

- Garage: This three-car garage has plenty of extra space for storage.

- Laundry Room: You'll find everything you'll need in this work space.

Rear Elevation

Copyright by designer/architect.

Plan #101009

Dimensions: 70'2" W x 59' D

Levels: 1

Square Footage: 2,097

Bedrooms: 3

Bathrooms: 3

Foundation: Slab

Materials List Available: No

Price Category: D

Round columns enhance this country porch design, which will nestle into any neighborhood.

Features:

- Ceiling Height: 9 ft. unless otherwise noted.

- Family Room: This large family room seems even more spacious, thanks to the vaulted ceiling. It's the perfect spot for all kinds of family activities.

- Dining Room: This elegant dining room is adorned with a decorative round column and a tray ceiling.

- Kitchen: You'll love the convenience of this enormous 14-ft.-3-in. x 22-ft.-6-in. country kitchen, which is open to the living room.

- Screened Porch: A French door leads to this breezy porch, with its vaulted ceiling.

- Master Suite: This sumptuous suite includes a double tray ceiling, a sitting area, a large walk-in closet, and a luxurious bath.

- Patio or Deck: This area is accessible from both the screened porch and master bedroom.

SMARTtip

Single-Level Decks

A single-level deck can use a strong vertical element, such as a pergola or a gazebo, to make it interesting. A simple and less-expensive option is a potted conical shrub or a clematis growing on a trellis.

Plan #211055

Dimensions: 88' W x 64' D

Levels: 1

Square Footage: 2,394

Bedrooms: 3

Bathrooms: 2

Foundation: Crawl space

Materials List Available: Yes

Price Category: E

Images provided by designer/architect.

Except for the porch areas, this traditional design is finished with a no-maintenance brick veneer.

Features:

- Ceiling Height: 8 ft.

- Living Room: There is plenty of space for entertaining and family activities in this well-designed open living room.

- Formal Parlor: This traditional parlor is open to the living area, or alternately, it can be used as a bedroom by relocating the door to the hall.

- Kitchen: This smartly designed kitchen is set at an angle to take advantage of the rear views. It's open to the bay eating area and the living room, so the cook won't be isolated from the festivities.

- Eating Area: This eating area is perfect for entertaining and family meals.

- Master Suite: Featuring private access to the rear porch, this luxurious retreat has its own sitting area and a plush bath with twin giant walk-in closets and a quarter-circle whirlpool.

Copyright by designer/architect.

Plan #321007

Dimensions: 76' W x 55'2" D
Levels: 1
Square Footage: 2,695
Bedrooms: 3
Bathrooms: 2½
Foundation: Basement
Materials List Available: Yes
Price Category: F

Images provided by designer/architect.

You'll love the way this spacious ranch reminds you of a French country home.

Features:

- **Foyer:** Come into this lovely home's foyer, and be greeted with a view of the gracious staircase and the great room just beyond.

- **Great Room:** Settle down by the cozy fireplace in cool weather, and reach for a book on the built-in shelves that surround it.

- **Kitchen:** Designed for efficient work patterns, this large kitchen is open to the great room.

- **Breakfast Room:** Just off the kitchen, this sunny room will be a family favorite all through the day.

- **Master Suite:** A bay window, walk-in closet, and shower built for two are highlights of this area.

- **Additional Bedrooms:** These large bedrooms both have walk-in closets and share a Jack-and-Jill bath for total convenience.

SMARTtip

Decorative Poles

Drapery poles are supported by the brackets fastened to the window frame or wall. The brackets that are provided with the poles generally coordinate and blend in with the pole finish. Brackets can be simple but also decorative. If you opt for a spectacular, attention-grabbing bracket, consider choosing less showy finials for the ends of the pole.

Plan #131019

Dimensions: 83'6" W x 53'4" D
Levels: 1
Square Footage: 2,243
Bedrooms: 3
Bathrooms: 2½
Foundation: Basement, crawl space, or slab
Materials List Available: Yes
Price Category: F

Images provided by designer/architect.

Drama marks this contemporary, angled ranch-style home which can be placed to suit any site, even the most difficult.

Features:

- **Great Room:** Imagine having an octagonal great room! The shape alone makes it spectacular, but the view to the backyard from its four exterior sides adds to the impression it creates, and you'll love its 16-ft. tray ceiling, fireplace, and wall designed to fit a large entertainment center.

- **Kitchen:** This room is adjacent to and visually connected to the great room but has excellent features of its own that make it an easy place to cook or clean.

- **Master Suite:** Separated from the other bedrooms, this suite is planned for privacy. You'll love the bath here and look forward to the quiet you can find at the end of the day.

- **Additional Bedrooms:** In a wing of their own, the other two bedrooms share a bath.

Rear Elevation

Copyright by designer/architect.

Plan #321022

Dimensions: 44' W x 27' D

Levels: 1

Square Footage: 1,140

Bedrooms: 3

Bathrooms: 2

Foundation: Basement

Materials List Available: Yes

Price Category: B

Images provided by designer/architect.

SMARTtip

Basement Moldings

Keep moldings simple in a basement with lower ceilings. Elaborate moldings around the ceiling or floor can shorten the height of the room.

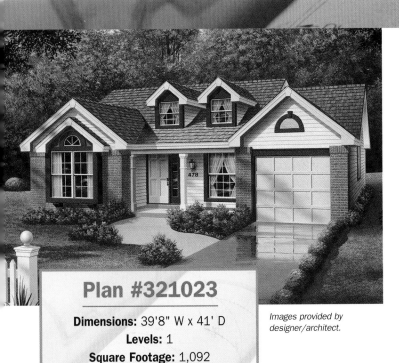

Plan #321023

Dimensions: 39'8" W x 41' D

Levels: 1

Square Footage: 1,092

Bedrooms: 3

Bathrooms: 1½

Foundation: Basement

Materials List Available: Yes

Price Category: B

Images provided by designer/architect.

Plan #351002

Dimensions: 64' W x 45'10" D

Levels: 1

Square Footage: 1,751

Bedrooms: 3

Bathrooms: 2

Foundation: Basement, crawl space, or slab

Materials List Available: Yes

Price Category: C

Plan #351007

Dimensions: 73'8" W x 53'2" D

Levels: 1

Square Footage: 2,251

Bedrooms: 3

Bathrooms: 2½

Foundation: Basement, crawl space, or slab

Materials List Available: Yes

Price Category: E

Bonus Room

Plan #211057

Dimensions: 50' W x 86' D
Levels: 1
Square Footage: 2,366
Bedrooms: 4
Bathrooms: 3
Foundation: Slab
Materials List Available: No
Price Category: E

Images provided by designer/architect.

Plan #211064

Dimensions: 83' W x 78' D
Levels: 1
Square Footage: 2,936
Bedrooms: 4
Bathrooms: 2½
Foundation: Crawl space
Materials List Available: No
Price Category: F

Images provided by designer/architect.

Copyright by designer/architect.

Plan #321027

Dimensions: 72' W x 68' D

Levels: 1

Square Footage: 2,758

Bedrooms: 4

Bathrooms: 2½

Foundation: Basement

Materials List Available: Yes

Price Category: F

Images provided by designer/architect.

Copyright by designer/architect.

Plan #321028

Dimensions: 79' W x 64'2" D

Levels: 1

Square Footage: 2,723

Bedrooms: 3

Bathrooms: 2½

Foundation: Basement

Materials List Available: Yes

Price Category: F

Images provided by designer/architect.

Copyright by designer/architect.

Plan #161008

Dimensions: 64'2" W x 46'6" D
Levels: 1
Square Footage: 1,860
Bedrooms: 3
Bathrooms: 2
Foundation: Slab
Materials List Available: No
Price Category: D

If you enjoy casual living and formal entertaining, this delightful floor plan will attract your eye.

Features:

• Great Room: A sloped ceiling and corner fireplace combine to provide this great room with an open and cozy atmosphere, perfect for relaxing evenings.

• Kitchen: This kitchen offers ample counter and cabinet space. A convenient snack bar provides a view to the breakfast area and great room

• Master Suite: Enjoy the elegance and style of this master suite, with its deluxe bath, large walk-in closet, and secluded alcove.

• Laundry Room: You will appreciate the ample counter space in this large laundry room with utility closet.

• Porch: From the breakfast area, enjoy a relaxed meal on this rear covered porch in warm weather.

Images provided by designer/architect.

Copyright by designer/architect.

SMARTtip
Espaliered Fruit Trees

Try a technique used by the royal gardeners at Versailles— espalier. They trained the fruit trees to grow flat against the walls, creating patterns. It's not difficult, especially if you go to a reputable nursery and purchase an apple or pear tree that has already been espaliered. Plant it against a flat surface that's in a sunny spot.

Plan #221011

Dimensions: 59' W x 58' D

Levels: 1

Square Footage: 1,756

Bedrooms: 3

Bathrooms: 2

Foundation: Basement

Materials List Available: No

Price Category: C

Images provided by designer/architect.

You'll love this design if you've been looking for a compact design with a spacious, open feeling.

Features:

• Ceiling Height: 8 ft.

• Entry: A vaulted ceiling here sets a luxurious tone for the whole house.

• Family Room: Also with a vaulted ceiling, this room features a handsome fireplace that's flanked on either side by windows looking out to the backyard.

• Dining Room: Open to the family room, this large room has large, well-placed windows that flood the room with natural light.

• Kitchen: The eating bar that divides this room from the dining room gives family members a great place to perch while they chat with the cook or do their homework.

• Master Suite: Located just off the kitchen for privacy, this suite includes a walk-in closet and a full bath with its own linen closet.

Rear Elevation

Copyright by designer/architect.

Plan #151009

Dimensions: 44' W x 86'2" D

Levels: 1

Square Footage: 1,601

Bedrooms: 3

Bathrooms: 2

Foundation: Crawl, slab

Materials List Available: No

Price Category: C

This can be the perfect home for a site with views you can enjoy in all seasons and at all times.

Features:

- Porches: Enjoy the front porch with its 10-ft. ceiling and the more private back porch where you can set up a grill or just get away from it all.

- Foyer: With a 10-ft. ceiling, this foyer opens to the great room for a warm welcome.

- Great Room: Your family will love the media center and the easy access to the rear porch.

- Kitchen: This well-designed kitchen is open to the dining room and the breakfast nook, which also opens to the rear porch.

- Master Suite: The bedroom has a 10-ft. boxed ceiling and a door to the rear. The bath includes a corner whirlpool tub with glass block windows.

- Bedrooms: Bedroom 2 has a vaulted ceiling, while bedroom 3 features a built-in desk.

SMARTtip
Fertilizing Your Grass

Fertilizers contain nutrients balanced for different kinds of growth. The ratio of nutrients is indicated on the package by three numbers (for example, 10-10-10). The first specifies nitrogen content; the second, phosphorus; and the third, potash.

Nitrogen helps grass blades to grow and improves the quality and thickness of the turf. Fertilizers contain up to 30 percent nitrogen.

Phosphorus helps grass to develop a healthy root system. It also speeds up the maturation process of the plant.

Potash helps grass stay healthy by providing amino acids and proteins to the plants.

Plan #121005

Dimensions: 48' W x 52' D

Levels: 1

Square Footage: 1,496

Bedrooms: 3

Bathrooms: 2

Foundation: Basement

Materials List Available: Yes

Price Category: B

Images provided by designer/architect.

A beautiful starter or retirement home with all the amenities you'd expect in a much bigger house.

Features:

- Ceiling Height: 8 ft.

- Great Room: A cathedral ceiling visually expands the great room making it the perfect place for family gatherings or formal entertaining.

- Formal Dining Room: This elegant room is ideal for entertaining dinner guests. It conveniently shares a wet bar and service counter with a bayed breakfast area next door.

- Breakfast Area: In addition to the service area shared with the dining room, this cozy area features a snack bar, pantry, and desk that's perfect for household paperwork.

- Master Suite: The master bedroom features special ceiling details. It's joined by a private bath with a whirlpool, shower, and spacious walk-in closet.

- Garage: The two-bay garage offers plenty of storage space.

Optional Den

Copyright by designer/architect.

Flooring

Selecting a flooring material is one of the most important decisions you will make when decorating a room. The right material can enhance the color scheme and the overall look of the room, and flooring provides a unique tactile component to the design.

If you are are acting as your own designer, one of the first things you should do is learn about the various types of flooring—from wood to stone to vinyl—on today's market. The choices are myriad and innovations in technology have widened the range of finishes.

Choices in Wood

In bygone eras, a wood floor was simply one that was created by laying wide wood planks side by side. Later, as the milling of lumber improved, homeowners were able to choose narrower planks that look more refined than rustic. Parquet floors were created by woodcrafters with a flair for the dramatic and an appreciation of the artistic richness of wood grains set in nonlinear patterns.

Today's manufacturers have made it possible to have it all. The wood floor, factory- or custom-stained to suit a particular style or mood in a room, is still a traditional favorite. It's readily available in strips of 1 to 2¼ inches wide, or in country-style planks of 3 to 8 inches wide. The formal, sophisticated look of a parquet floor is unparalleled for richness of visual texture.

Types of Wood Flooring

Wood varieties available as a surface material are vast, and cost varies widely, depending on the type and grade of wood and on the choice of design.

Softwoods, like pine and fir, are often used to make simple tongue-and-groove floorboards. These floors are less expen-

sive than hardwoods but also less durable. The hardwoods—maple, birch, oak, ash—are far less likely to mar with normal use. A hardwood floor is not indestructible; however, it will stand up to demanding use.

Both hardwoods and softwoods are graded according to their color, grain, and imperfections. The top of the line is known as clear, followed by select, No. 1 common, and No. 2 common. In addition to budget considerations, the decision whether to pay top dollar for clear wood or to economize with a lesser grade depends on use factors and on the design objectives. For example, if you plan to install a wood floor in a small room and then cover most of it with an area rug, the No. 2 common grade may be a good

choice; lesser grades are also fine for informal rooms where a few defects just enhance a lived-in look. If your design calls for larger areas of rich wood grain that will be exposed, with scatter rugs used for color accents, a clear or select grade will make an attractive choice.

Finishing Options

Color stains—reds, blues, and greens—may work in settings where a casual or rustic feeling is desired. This, however, is a departure from the traditional use of

Wood flooring, below, fits well in both formal and informal spaces.

Laminate flooring, opposite, can mimic the look of real wood or natural stone.

Laminate Flooring

Laminate flooring is the great pretender among flooring materials. When your creative side tells you to install wood but your practical side knows it just won't hold up in the traffic-heavy location for which you're considering it, a wood floor look-alike might be just the thing. Faux wood and faux stone laminate floors provide you with the look you want, tempered with physical wear and care properties that you and your family can live with. Laminate is particularly suited to rooms where floors are likely to see heavy duty—kitchens, family rooms, hallways, and children's bedrooms and playrooms—anywhere stain and scratch resistance and easy cleanup count. Prolonged exposure to moisture will damage some laminate products, but many can now be used in wet areas. Manufacturers of laminate offer warranties against staining, scratching, cracking, and peeling for up to 25 years.

Laminate is made from paper impregnated with melamine, an organic resin, and bonded to a core of particleboard, fiberboard, or other wood byproducts. It can be laid over virtually any subflooring surface, including wood and concrete. It can also be applied on top of an existing wood, ceramic, or vinyl tile, as well as vinyl or other sheet flooring. You can even install it over certain types of carpeting, but check the manufacturer's guidelines before doing so.

Installation and Care

The installation of laminate flooring is a reasonably quick and relatively easy do-it-yourself project. It requires sheets of a special foam underlayment followed by the careful placement, cutting, and gluing of the laminate.

Laminate is available in sheets that are ideal when your design calls for a uniform look, such as monotone stone, or a linear design that mimics strip or plank wood flooring. Laminate planks, squares, and blocks offer added design flexibility: with them, you can design your own tile patterns, lay strips of wood-look planks with alternating "stain" finishes, or border your floor with a contrasting color.

wood. Wood is not typically used to deliver color impact; instead it blends with and subtly enhances its surroundings. Natural wood stains range from light ash tones to deep, coffee-like colors. Generally, lighter stains make a room feel less formal, and darker, richer stains suggest a stately atmosphere. As with lighter colors, lighter stains create a feeling of openness; darker stains foster a more intimate feeling and can reduce the visual vastness of a large space.

Installation

If the design plan calls for the laying of unfinished wood strips, factor the cost of hiring a skilled professional into your budget. Many manufacturers offer products with installation kits that make wood flooring a do-it-yourself option for those whose skills are good but don't necessarily approach a professional carpenter's level. Some make strips or planks already finished and sealed. Most parquet tiles come finished and sealed as well.

Vinyl Sheet & Tile Flooring

Like laminate, resilient flooring is also available in design-friendly sheet or tile form. Resilient floors can be made from a variety of materials, including linoleum, asphalt, cork, or rubber. However, the most commonly used material in manufacturing today's resilient floors for homes is vinyl.

Price, durability, and easy maintenance make resilient flooring an attractive and popular choice. Do-it-yourself installation, an option even for those who are not particularly skilled, can mean further savings.

Sheet versus Tiles

Resilient flooring comes in an enormous array of colors and patterns, plus many of the flooring styles have a textured surface. With the tiles, you can combine color and pattern in limitless ways. Even the sheet form of resilient flooring can be customized with inlay strips.

Cushioned sheet vinyl offers the most resilience. It provides excellent stain resistance; it's comfortable and quiet underfoot and easy to maintain, with no-wax and never-wax finishes often available. These features make the floor especially attractive for areas with lots of kid traffic. Beware though: only the more expensive grades show an acceptable degree of resistance to nicking and denting. In rooms where furniture is often moved around, this could be a problem. Although the range of colors, patterns, and surface textures is wide, sheet floor-

Vinyl sheet flooring, left, is a good choice for high-traffic areas, such as kitchens, family rooms, and playrooms. Most products have a no-wax finish that is easy to maintain.

Vinyl flooring, above, comes in a variety of styles and colors. Tiles and sheet flooring can look like ceramic tiles and natural stone.

Ceramic tile, opposite, offers a number of possibilities—from simple patterns to more elaborate designs that feature borders and inlays.

ing is not as flexible as vinyl tile when it comes to customizing your look.

Regular sheet vinyl is less expensive than the cushioned types, but it carries the same disadvantages and is slightly less resilient. Except for the availability of no-wax finishes, a vinyl tile floor is as stain resistant and as easy to maintain as the sheet-vinyl products. Increased design possibilities are the trade-off.

Here, as with other flooring materials, one possible way out of the choice maze is to take the unconventional step of mixing flooring materials. For example, use a durable cushioned sheet vinyl in more trafficked areas, but frame it with a pretty vinyl tile or laminate border.

Ceramic Choices

Ceramic tile—actually fired clay—is an excellent choice for areas subject to a lot of traffic and in rooms where resistance to moisture and stains is needed. These features, combined with easy cleanup, have made ceramic tile a centuries-old tradition for flooring, walls, and ceilings in bathrooms and kitchens. Color, texture, and pattern choices available today make ceramic tile the most versatile flooring option in terms of design possibilities.

Tile Options

Some handcrafted ceramic tiles are very costly, but manufacturers have created a market full of design and style options.

Tiles come in a variety of sizes, beginning with 1-inch-square mosaic tiles up to large 16 x 16-inch squares. Other shapes, such as triangles, diamonds, and rectangles, are also available. Tile textures range from shiny to matte-finished and from glass-smooth to ripple-surfaced. Tiles are available either glazed or unglazed. Glazed tiles have a hard, often colored, surface that is applied during the firing process; the resulting finish can range from glossy to matte. Unglazed tiles, such as terra-cotta or quarry tiles, have a matte finish, are porous, and need to be sealed to prevent staining.

Consider using accent borders to create unique designs, such as a faux area rug, that visually separate sections of a room or separate one room from another. When added in a random pattern, embossed accent tiles add interest, variety, and elegance to an expanse of single-colored tiles.

Alas, no surfacing material is perfect. Ceramic tile offers long-lasting beauty, design versatility, and simplicity of maintenance, but it also has some hard-to-live-with features. Tile is cold underfoot, noisy when someone walks across it in hard-soled shoes, and not at all resilient—always expect the worst when something breakable falls on a tile floor. If you have infants and toddlers around, it may be best to wait a few years for your tiled floor.

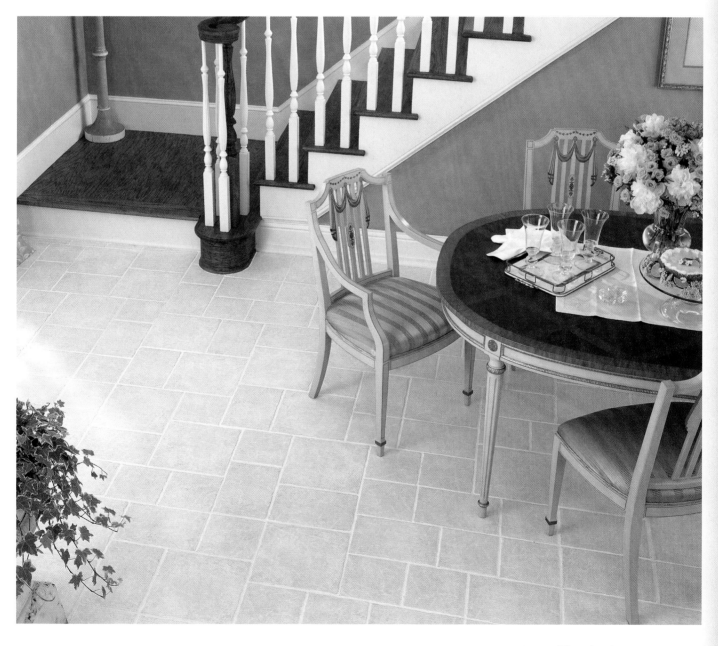

Natural Stone

Like ceramic tile, stone and marble are classified as "non-resilients." Like tile, these materials offer richness of color, durability, moisture and stain resistance, and ease of maintenance. They also share with tile the drawbacks of being cold to the touch, noisy to walk on, and unforgivingly hard.

Stone and marble floors are clearly, unmistakably natural. As remarkably good as some faux surfaces look, no product manufactured today actually matches the rustic irregularity and random color variation of natural stone.

Picking a Flooring Material

Now that you've got the facts about each floor surface option, picking the right one for your design will be much less confusing. The following steps can make it downright simple.

Step 1: Make a "Use/Abuse" Analysis. Begin by asking yourself the most important question: How will this room used? Your answer should tell you just what kind of traffic the future floor surface will endure. With a relatively expensive investment like a floor, it's best not to guess. Instead, use this system to arrive at an accurate use/abuse analysis.

On a piece of paper, make columns headed "Who" and "Activities," and then list who in the family will use the room and what activities will occur there. Will the kids play with toys on the floor? Will they do arts and crafts projects with paint, glue, and glitter? Will the family gather on Saturday afternoons and snack while watching a football game on television? Is it a formal living room where you will entertain your friends and business clients? Is it a busy kitchen? Does the hallway extend from your front entrance or from a busier back door where the kids will drop off their hockey skates?

The answers to these questions will help you to determine how durable and resilient a flooring surface needs to be, whether warmth and softness are requirements, and how much maintenance will be necessary to keep the surface clean.

Step 2: Determine Your Design Objectives. Your choices are limited by the other elements in the room. Your color choices can enhance the color palette you are planning. Because you will be starting from scratch—including walls, furniture, and accessories—you have more flexibility, although your job is a bit more complex and involves more decisions.

Once you've determined your design objectives, compare your use/abuse analysis

High-traffic areas, below left, require flooring that can stand up to abuse.

Laminate flooring, below right, is a good choice for a variety of rooms.

to the types of flooring that meet both your style and use needs. From the list of options that are left, you can narrow down your choices even more.

Step 3: Draw and Use a Floor Plan.

After you have completed the use/abuse analysis and the list of design objectives, draw up a floor plan—a separate one for experimenting with your flooring ideas. Follow these guidelines: measure the length and width of the room, and plot it on graph paper, using a scale of 1 inch to 1 foot. If your room is larger than 8 x 10 feet, you can tape two pieces of 8½- x 11-inch graph paper together. Measure and mark the locations of entryways and any permanent features in the room, such as cabinets, fixtures, or appliances.

Make several photocopies of your floor plan. Reserve one copy as a template. Use the other copies for previewing pattern ideas for flooring that comes in tiles (ceramic, vinyl, or carpeting tiles). Buy

multicolored pencils, and fill in your grid. You'll be able to determine not only how the pattern will look but also how many tiles of various colors you'll need to buy to complete the project. Don't forget to include such items as borders and inlays.

Step 4: Convert Your Overall Budget to Cost per Square Foot.

After you've completed the use/abuse analysis, determined your design objectives, and created a floor plan, the next step is determining cost.

Most flooring is priced in terms of square feet. To determine how many square feet are in your room, round the measurements up to the next foot. Then simply multiply the length by the width. For example, for a room measuring 10 feet 4 inches x 12 feet 6 inches, round the figures to 11 x 13 feet. Multiply 11 x 13 feet (that's 143 square feet). You will end up with extra flooring, but it is better to have more than less.

Some flooring—like carpeting—is priced in terms of square yards. To determine the number of square yards in your room, divide the number of square feet by nine. In our example, there are just under 16 square yards in 143 square feet.

Let's say you have a budget of $850 to purchase tile for your 10-foot-4-inch x 12-foot-6-inch room. For the sake of the illustration, let's assume your subflooring is adequate, you have the tools, and the cost of adhesive and grout for your room is about $75. That leaves you with $775. To determine how much you can spend per tile, divide the remainder by the number of square feet in the room. In our example, $775 divided by 143 square feet equals about $5.40 per square foot of tile.

Light colors, below left, make a room feel more open than darker colors.

Consider the rest of the room, below, when selecting flooring.

Plan #271073

Dimensions: 69' W x 56' D
Levels: 1
Square Footage: 1,920
Bedrooms: 3
Bathrooms: 2
Foundation: Daylight basement
Materials List Available: No
Price Category: B

A great floor plan and plenty of space make this home perfect for people who welcome family members back home to visit.

Features:

• Great Room: This vaulted space shares a see-through fireplace with a cozy hearth room.

• Kitchen: An angled island and a step-in pantry are the highlights of this room.

• Study: Double doors introduce this versatile space, which shows off a nice bay window.

• Master Suite: Double doors lead to the bedroom. The private bath hosts a whirlpool tub and a separate shower.

• Basement: This level contains more bedrooms and family spaces for visiting relatives.

Images provided by designer/architect.

Basement Level Floor Plan

Copyright by designer/architect.

Plan #151034

Dimensions: 58'6" W x 68'4" D

Levels: 1

Square Footage: 2,133

Bedrooms: 3

Bathrooms: 2

Foundation: Crawl space, slab, or basement

Materials List Available: No

Price Category: D

Note: The photographed home has been modified to suit homeowner preferences   Images provided by designer/architect.

You'll love the high ceilings, open floor plan, and contemporary design features in this home.

Features:

- Great Room: A pass-through tiled fireplace between this lovely large room and the adjacent hearth room allows you to notice the mirror effect created by the 10-ft. boxed ceilings in both rooms.

- Dining Room: An 11-ft. ceiling and 8-in. boxed column give formality to this lovely room, where you're certain to entertain.

- Kitchen: If you're a cook, this room may become your favorite spot in the house, thanks to its great design, which includes plenty of work and storage space, and a very practical layout.

- Master Suite: A 10-ft. boxed ceiling gives elegance to this room. A pocket door opens to the private bath, with its huge walk-in closet, glass-blocked whirlpool tub, separate glass shower, and private toilet room.

Copyright by designer/architect.

Rendering reflects floor plan

Images provided by designer/architect.

Plan #101011

Dimensions: 71'2" W x 58'1" D

Levels: 1

Square Footage: 2,184

Bedrooms: 3

Bathrooms: 3

Foundation: Slab, crawl space, or basement

Materials List Available: No

Price Category: D

A classic design and spacious interior add up to a flexible design suitable to any modern lifestyle.

Features:

- Ceiling Height: 9 ft. unless otherwise noted.

- Formal Dining room: A decorative square column and a tray ceiling adorn this elegant dining room.

- Screened Porch: Enjoy summer breezes in style by stepping out of the French doors into this vaulted screened porch.

- Kitchen: Does everyone want to hang out in the kitchen while you are cooking? No problem. True to the home's country style, this huge 14-ft.-3-in. x 22-ft.-6-in. has plenty of room for helpers.

- The kitchen is open to the vaulted family room.

- Patio or Deck: This pleasant outdoor area is accessible from both the screened porch and the master bedroom.

- Master Suite: This luxurious suite includes a double tray ceiling, a sitting area, two walk-in closets, and an exquisite bath.

Copyright by designer/architect.

Plan #211061

Dimensions: 74' W x 78' D

Levels: 1

Square Footage: 2,655

Bedrooms: 3

Bathrooms: 3

Foundation: Slab, crawl space, or basement

Materials List Available: Yes

Price Category: F

Images provided by designer/architect.

The exterior of this home is a replica of an Antebellum home located in Natchez, Mississippi.

Features:

- Ceiling Height: 9 ft. unless otherwise noted.

- Open Plan: The interior living spaces of this home are open and flowing. This makes it the ideal home for entertaining and allows lots of flexibility in the use of space.

- Wet Bar: This triangular wet bar is neatly tucked between the living room and the sunroom. It's also convenient to the kitchen and the eating areas.

- Sunroom: There's nothing quite like enjoying the warmth of the sun streaming into this beautiful sunroom on a cold winter day.

- Living Room: This large living room seems even more spacious, thanks to its 14-ft. ceiling.

- Master Bath: This luxurious master bath features a his-and-her arrangement and a wraparound mirrored dressing table.

Copyright by designer/architect.

Plan #271078

Dimensions: 83' W x 52' D

Levels: 1

Square Footage: 1,855

Bedrooms: 1-2

Bathrooms: 1½-2½

Foundation: Daylight basement

Materials List Available: No

Price Category: D

Images provided by designer/architect.

Optional Basement Level Floor Plan

Copyright by designer/architect.

Plan #271060

Dimensions: 72' W x 52' D

Levels: 1

Square Footage: 1,726

Bedrooms: 2-4

Bathrooms: 2½-3½

Foundation: Daylight basement

Materials List Available: No

Price Category: C

Images provided by designer/architect.

Copyright by designer/architect.

Optional Basement Level Floor Plan

Plan #271059

Dimensions: 67' W x 57' D
Levels: 1
Square Footage: 1,790
Bedrooms: 1-3
Bathrooms: 1½-2½
Foundation: Daylight basement
Materials List Available: No
Price Category: C

Images provided by designer/architect.

**Optional
Basement Level
Floor Plan**

Plan #111018

Dimensions: 67' W x 79' D
Levels: 1
Square Footage: 2,745
Bedrooms: 4
Bathrooms: 3½
Foundation: Basement
Materials List Available: No
Price Category: F

Images provided by designer/architect.

Plan #351005

Dimensions: 61' W x 47'4" D

Levels: 1

Square Footage: 1,501

Bedrooms: 3

Bathrooms: 2

Foundation: Basement, crawl space, or slab

Materials List Available: Yes

Price Category: C

Images provided by designer/architect.

Copyright by designer/architect.

Plan #201032

Dimensions: 66'10" W x 50'10" D

Levels: 1

Square Footage: 1,556

Bedrooms: 3

Bathrooms: 2

Foundation: Crawl space, slab, or basement

Materials List Available: Yes

Price Category: C

Images provided by designer/architect.

Copyright by designer/architect.

Images provided by designer/architect.

Plan #211065

Dimensions: 72' W x 70' D

Levels: 1

Square Footage: 3,158

Bedrooms: 4

Bathrooms: 3

Foundation: Crawl space

Materials List Available: Yes

Price Category: G

Copyright by designer/architect.

Plan #211067

Dimensions: 96' W x 90' D

Levels: 1

Square Footage: 4,038

Bedrooms: 4

Bathrooms: 4½

Foundation: Crawl space

Materials List Available: Yes

Price Category: I

Images provided by designer/architect.

Copyright by designer/architect.

Copyright by designer/architect.

Images provided by designer/architect.

Plan #321034

Dimensions: 75'8" W x 52'6" D
Levels: 1
Square Footage: 3,508
Bedrooms: 4
Bathrooms: 3
Foundation: Daylight basement
Materials List Available: Yes
Price Category: H

Optional Basement Level Floor Plan

Rear View

Plan #321029

Dimensions: 50' W x 56' D
Levels: 1
Square Footage: 2,334
Bedrooms: 3
Bathrooms: 2
Foundation: Daylight basement
Materials List Available: Yes
Price Category: E

Images provided by designer/architect.

Optional Basement Level Floor Plan

Copyright by designer/architect.

Plan #391028

Dimensions: 54' W x 50' D

Levels: 1

Square Footage: 1,771

Bedrooms: 2

Bathrooms: 2

Foundation: Crawl space, slab

Materials List Available: Yes

Price Category: C

Images provided by designer/architect.

Copyright by designer/architect.

Plan #201036

Dimensions: 67'10" W x 44'10" D

Levels: 1

Square Footage: 1,671

Bedrooms: 3

Bathrooms: 2

Foundation: Crawl space, slab

Materials List Available: Yes

Price Category: C

Images provided by designer/architect.

SMARTtip

Bathroom Style Without Fallbacks

Retrofit an antique chest for bathroom storage, but make sure that you seal the wood against moisture. Even smarter—buy a new cabinet that's made to look like an antique and won't fall prey to the assaults of humidity and water. Leave chest open to display linens, soaps, and pretty bottled toiletries to create a focal point.

Copyright by designer/architect.

Plan #321008

Dimensions: 57' W x 52'2" D
Levels: 1
Square Footage: 1,761
Bedrooms: 4
Bathrooms: 2
Foundation: Basement
Materials List Available: Yes
Price Category: C

One look at the roof dormers and planter boxes that grace the outside of this ranch, and you'll know that the interior is planned for comfortable family living.

Features:

- Great Room: A vaulted ceiling in this room points up its generous dimensions. Put a grouping of chairs near the fireplace to take advantage of the cozy spot it creates in chilly weather.

- Kitchen: Open to the great room, this kitchen has been planned for convenience. It features a pass-through to the dining area for easy serving when you've got a crowd to feed.

- Master Bedroom: A vaulted ceiling here makes you feel especially pampered, and the walk-in closet and amenity-filled bath add to that feeling.

- Additional Bedrooms: Great closet space characterizes all the rooms in this home, making it easy for children of any age to keep it organized and tidy.

Copyright by designer/architect.

SMARTtip

Hanging Wallpaper

Use liner paper to smooth out a damaged wall and to provide uniform support for expensive paper.

Plan #131020

Dimensions: 67'2" W x 48'10" D
Levels: 1
Square Footage: 1,735
Bedrooms: 3
Bathrooms: 2
Foundation: Basement, crawl space, or slab
Materials List Available: Yes
Price Category: C

This gorgeous ranch is designed for entertaining but is also comfortable for family living.

Features:

- **Living Room:** A 9-ft. stepped ceiling highlights the spaciousness of this room, which gives a view of one of the two covered porches.

- **Dining Room:** Also with a 9-ft. stepped ceiling and a view of the porch, this room features a bay window.

- **Family Room:** An 11-ft. vaulted ceiling and gliding French doors to the porch define this central gathering area.

- **Kitchen:** Enjoy the skylight, a fireplace that's shared with the family room, a central island cooktop, and a snack bar in this room.

- **Master Suite:** The tray ceiling is 9 ft. 9 in. high, and this area includes a sitting area and a bath with a whirlpool tub and dual-sink vanity.

Images provided by designer/architect.

Copyright by designer/architect.

Photos provided by designer/architect.

Kitchen

Foyer/Dining Room

Plan #161009

Dimensions: 60'9" W x 49' D

Levels: 1

Square Footage: 1,651

Bedrooms: 3

Bathrooms: 2

Foundation: Slab

Materials List Available: Yes

Price Category: C

The warm, textured exterior combines with the elegance of double-entry doors to preview both the casual lifestyle and formal entertaining capabilities of this versatile home.

Features:

• Great Room: Experience the openness provided by the sloped ceiling topping both this great room and the formal dining area. Enjoy the warmth and light supplied by the gas fireplace and dual sliding doors.

• Kitchen: This kitchen, convenient to the living space, is designed for easy work patterns and features an open bar that separates the work area from the more richly decorated gathering rooms.

• Master Bedroom: Separated for privacy, this master bedroom includes a tray ceiling and lavishly equipped bath.

• Basement: This full basement allows you to expand your living space to meet your needs.

Images provided by designer/architect.

Copyright by designer/architect.

Right Side Elevation

Rear Elevation

Left Side Elevation

Copyright by
designer/architect.

Images provided by
designer/architect.

Plan #391025

Dimensions: 54' W x 48'4" D
Levels: 1
Square Footage: 1,625
Bedrooms: 3
Bathrooms: 2
Foundation: Crawl space, basement, slab
Materials List Available: Yes
Price Category: C

SMARTtip

Assembling Wall Frames

It's important to square up the pieces to start with.
Then, even a tick mark across the joint will serve as an
accurate registration mark for the plate joiner.

Images provided by
designer/architect.

Plan #391021

Dimensions: 54' W x 48'4" D
Levels: 1
Square Footage: 1,568
Bedrooms: 3
Bathrooms: 2
Foundation: Crawl space, basement, slab
Materials List Available: Yes
Price Category: C

Copyright by
designer/architect.

Images provided by designer/architect.

Plan #121013

Dimensions: 40' W x 55'8" D
Levels: 1
Square Footage: 1,375
Bedrooms: 1
Bathrooms: 2
Foundation: Basement
Materials List Available: Yes
Price Category: B

This convenient open plan is well-suited to retirement or as a starter home.

Features:

- Ceiling Height: 8 ft., unless otherwise noted.

- Den: To the left of the entry, French doors lead to a den that can convert to a second bedroom.

- Kitchen: A center island doubles as a snack bar while the breakfast area includes a pantry and a desk for compiling shopping lists and menus.

- Open Plan: The sense of spaciousness is enhanced by the large open area that includes the family room, kitchen, and breakfast area.

- Family Room: A handsome fireplace invites family and friends to gather in this area.

- Porch: Step through the breakfast area to enjoy the fresh air on this secluded porch.

- Master Bedroom: This distinctive bedroom features a boxed ceiling. It's served by a private bath with a walk-in closet.

Copyright by designer/architect.

SMARTtip
Paint Color Choices for Your Home

Earth tones are easy to decorate with because they are neutral colors. Use neutral or muted tones, such as light grays, browns, or greens with either lighter or darker shades for accenting.

Use bright colors sparingly, to catch the eye. Painting the front door a bright color creates a cheerful entryway.

Investigate home shows, magazines, and houses in your area for color ideas. Paint suppliers can also give you valuable tips on appropriate color schemes.

Colors that look just right on a color card may need to be toned down for painting large areas. If in doubt, buy a quart of paint and test it.

Plan #271080

Dimensions: 71' W x 83' D

Levels: 1

Square Footage: 2,581

Bedrooms: 3

Bathrooms: 3

Foundation: Basement

Materials List Available: Yes

Price Category: E

Images provided by designer/architect.

An open floor plan and beautiful adornments promise comfortable living within this appealing one-story home.

Features:

- **Living Room:** Beyond the sidelighted entry, this spacious living room is bordered on two sides by striking arched openings.

- **Kitchen:** This island kitchen flows into a bayed eating nook, which shares a two-sided fireplace with the living room.

- **Master Suite:** A bright sitting room is a nice feature in this luxurious suite, which is secluded to the rear of the home. The private bath boasts a corner tub, a separate shower, two vanities, and a walk-in closet.

Copyright by designer/architect.

Plan #221012

Dimensions: 71' W x 51' D

Levels: 1

Square Footage: 1,802

Bedrooms: 3

Bathrooms: 2½

Foundation: Basement

Materials List Available: No

Price Category: D

Images provided by designer/architect.

Rear Elevation

The interesting roofline and covered porch on this one-story beauty give it great curb appeal.

Features:

• Ceiling Height: 8 ft.

• Great Room: Highlighted by a fireplace flanked by large windows on both sides, this large room also boasts a tall cathedral ceiling.

• Dining Room: This room opens from the entry for the convenience of your guests. Thanks to the nook by the kitchen, you can save this space for formal family dining and hosting dinner parties.

• Kitchen: This well-planned kitchen with ample counter and cabinet space also has an island and opens to the family room. Use the large, adjacent nook for casual meals, and take advantage of the sliding glass doors that open to the backyard.

• Master Suite: Relax in this suite's bedroom, where you'll find a large walk-in closet. The bath features both a soaking tub and a standing shower for the ultimate in versatility.

Copyright by designer/architect.

Plan #101012

Dimensions: 69'4" W x 62'9" D

Levels: 1

Square Footage: 2,288

Bedrooms: 3

Bathrooms: 2½

Foundation: Slab, crawl space, or basement

Materials List Available: No

Price Category: E

This classic brick ranch boasts traditional styling and an exciting up-to-date floor plan.

Features:

- Ceiling Height: 9 ft. unless otherwise noted.

- Front Porch: Guests will be welcome by this inviting front porch, which features a 12-ft. ceiling.

- Family Room: This warm and inviting room measures 16 ft. x 19 ft. It features a 14-ft. ceiling and a rear wall of windows. French doors lead to an enormous deck.

- Kitchen: This unique angled kitchen is open to the hearth room and eating areas, all of which enjoy vaulted ceilings and are surrounded by windows. The hearth room has a TV niche.

- Master Suite: This 16-ft. x 15-ft. master suite is truly sumptuous, with its 12-ft. ceiling, sitting area, two walk-in closets, and full-featured bath.

Images provided by designer/architect.

Copyright by designer/architect.

- Bonus Room: Here is plenty of storage or room for future expansion. Just beyond the entry are stairs leading to a bonus room measuring approximately 12 ft. x 21 ft.

Hearth Room

Copyright by designer/architect.

Plan #321030

Dimensions: 61' W x 51' D

Levels: 1

Square Footage: 2,029

Bedrooms: 4

Bathrooms: 2

Foundation: Basement, crawl space, slab or daylight basement

Materials List Available: Yes

Price Category: D

Images provided by designer/architect.

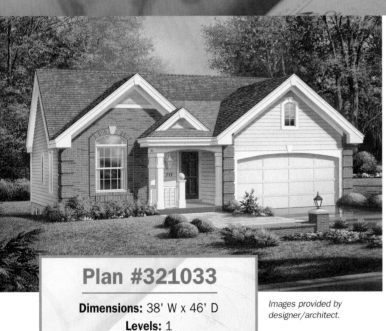

Plan #321033

Dimensions: 38' W x 46' D

Levels: 1

Square Footage: 1,268

Bedrooms: 3

Bathrooms: 2

Foundation: Basement

Materials List Available: Yes

Price Category: B

Images provided by designer/architect.

Copyright by designer/architect.

Images provided by designer/architect.

Plan #391035

Dimensions: 84' W x 56'8" D

Levels: 1

Square Footage: 1,430

Bedrooms: 3

Bathrooms: 2

Foundation: Crawl space, basement, slab

Materials List Available: Yes

Price Category: B

Copyright by designer/architect.

SMARTtip

Two Dishwashers

Sometimes two is better than one. If you have the need (yours is a large household, you do a lot of cooking and baking, or you entertain often), two dishwashers make sense. That way, when one is full, you won't have to pile the sink with dirty dishes, pots, and pans. If you don't have space for a second full-size model, consider a dishwasher drawer.

Images provided by designer/architect.

Plan #391039

Dimensions: 50' W x 45'4" D

Levels: 1

Square Footage: 1,539

Bedrooms: 3

Bathrooms: 2

Foundation: Crawl space, basement, slab

Materials List Available: Yes

Price Category: C

Copyright by designer/architect.

Plan #321031

Dimensions: 79'4" W x 59'6' D
Levels: 1
Square Footage: 3,200
Bedrooms: 3
Bathrooms: 2½
Foundation: Daylight basement
Materials List Available: Yes
Price Category: G

Images provided by designer/architect.

Copyright by designer/architect.

Optional Basement Level Floor Plan

Plan #321032

Dimensions: 109' W x 57'6" D
Levels: 1
Square Footage: 4,826
Bedrooms: 4
Bathrooms: 2½
Foundation: Daylight basement
Materials List Available: Yes
Price Category: I

Images provided by designer/architect.

Copyright by designer/architect.

Optional Basement Level Floor Plan

Plan #341005

Dimensions: 66' W x 30' D
Levels: 1
Square Footage: 1,334
Bedrooms: 3
Bathrooms: 2
Foundation: Crawl space, slab, or basement
Materials List Available: Yes
Price Category: B

Images provided by designer/architect.

Copyright by designer/architect.

Plan #341010

Dimensions: 42'6" W x 35'4" D
Levels: 1
Square Footage: 1,261
Bedrooms: 3
Bathrooms: 2
Foundation: Crawl space, slab, or basement
Materials List Available: Yes
Price Category: B

Images provided by designer/architect.

Copyright by designer/architect.

Plan #221013

Dimensions: 48' W x 58'8" D

Levels: 1

Square Footage: 1,495

Bedrooms: 3

Bathrooms: 2

Foundation: Basement

Materials List Available: No

Price Category: B

Images provided by designer/architect.

If you love rooms with unusual shapes, angled features, and interesting ceilings, this could be the home of your dreams.

Features:

- Ceiling Height: 8 ft.

- Great Room: A cathedral ceiling complements this huge room, and the fireplace and flanking windows make a lovely focal point.

- Dining Room: You'll love the cathedral ceiling that gives elegance to this open dining room, as well as its doors, which lead to both the backyard and the screened-in porch.

- Kitchen: Arched openings let you look into the dining room and the great room, and the angled counter area gives distinction to this room, with its step-saving floor plan.

- Master Suite: Enjoy the tray ceiling, walk-in closet, plant ledge, and luxurious bath.

- Additional Bedrooms: Bedroom #2 has a cathedral ceiling, and shares a bath with bedroom #3.

Rear Elevation

Copyright by designer/architect.

Plan #101013

Dimensions: 72' W x 66' D

Levels: 1

Square Footage: 2,564

Bedrooms: 3

Bathrooms: 2½

Foundation: Slab, crawl space, basement

Materials List Available: No

Price Category: E

This exciting design combines a striking classic exterior with a highly functional floor plan.

Features:

- Ceiling Height: 9 ft. unless otherwise noted.

- Family Room: This warm and inviting room measures 18 ft. x 22 ft. It features a 14-ft. ceiling and a rear wall of windows. French doors lead to an enormous deck.

- Kitchen: This unique angled kitchen is open to the hearth room and eating areas, all of which enjoy vaulted ceilings and are surrounded by windows. The hearth room has a TV niche.

- Master Suite: This 19-ft. x 18-ft. master suite is truly sumptuous, with its 12-ft. ceiling, sitting area, two walk-in closets, and full-featured bath.

- Secondary Bedrooms: Each of the secondary bedrooms measures 11 ft. x 14 ft. and has direct access to a shared bath.

Images provided by designer/architect.

- Bonus Room: Just beyond the entry are stairs leading to this bonus room, which measures approximately 12 ft. x 21 ft.—plenty of room for storage or future expansion.

Copyright by designer/architect.

Plan #111014

Dimensions: 78' W x 47' D
Levels: 1
Square Footage: 1,865
Bedrooms: 4
Bathrooms: 2
Foundation: Crawl space
Materials List Available: No
Price Category: D

Images provided by designer/architect.

Copyright by designer/architect.

Plan #111019

Dimensions: 49' W x 62' D
Levels: 1
Square Footage: 1,936
Bedrooms: 4
Bathrooms: 2
Foundation: Pier
Materials List Available: No
Price Category: D

Images provided by designer/architect.

Optional Gameroom

Copyright by designer/architect.

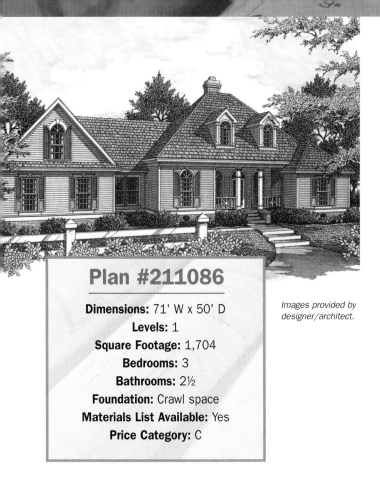

Plan #211086

Dimensions: 71' W x 50' D

Levels: 1

Square Footage: 1,704

Bedrooms: 3

Bathrooms: 2½

Foundation: Crawl space

Materials List Available: Yes

Price Category: C

Images provided by designer/architect.

Copyright by designer/architect.

Bonus Area

attic

bonus rm
20 x 14

attic

Plan #251006

Dimensions: 65'5" W x 59'11" D

Levels: 1

Square Footage: 1,849

Bedrooms: 3

Bathrooms: 2

Foundation: Crawl space

Materials List Available: Yes

Price Category: D

Images provided by designer/architect.

Copyright by designer/architect.

SMARTtip

Tile for a Creative Fireplace

Tile on a fireplace face can offer a low-cost and unique alternative to masonry. Use reproduction tiles for an Arts and Crafts look, add European flair with painted ceramic tiles, drama with a mosaic design, or sleek contemporary styling with granite, terrazzo, or limestone tiles.

Plan #341018

Dimensions: 53'6" W x 35' D

Levels: 1

Square Footage: 1,191

Bedrooms: 3

Bathrooms: 2

Foundation: Crawl space, slab, or basement

Materials List Available: Yes

Price Category: B

Plan #341012

Dimensions: 43'2" W x 33'6" D

Levels: 1

Square Footage: 1,316

Bedrooms: 3

Bathrooms: 2

Foundation: Crawl space, slab, or basement

Materials List Available: Yes

Price Category: B

Plan #201061

Dimensions: 64'10" W x 54'10" D

Levels: 1

Square Footage: 2,387

Bedrooms: 4

Bathrooms: 2½

Foundation: Crawl space, slab

Materials List Available: Yes

Price Category: E

Images provided by designer/architect.

Floor plan:
- mbr 15 x 14
- br 4 12 x 11
- br 3 12 x 12⁴
- br 2 11⁶ x 12⁶
- foy 9 x 12
- den 19 x 20
- porch 19 x 8
- garage 21 x 22
- sto
- util
- kit 15 x 14
- dining 14 x 12⁶
- eating 10 x 15

Copyright by designer/architect.

Plan #201063

Dimensions: 74'10" W x 70'10" D

Levels: 1

Square Footage: 2,697

Bedrooms: 4

Bathrooms: 3

Foundation: Crawl space, slab

Materials List Available: Yes

Price Category: F

Images provided by designer/architect.

Floor plan:
- por 33⁸ x 5
- eating 14 x 10
- den 20⁶ x 18
- br 4 12 x 14
- mbr 19⁸ x 16
- kit 14 x 14
- dining 14' x 16
- foy 8 x 14
- br 2 12 x 12
- br 3 12 x 16
- sto 7 x 8
- util 8x8
- por
- garage 22 x 22

Copyright by designer/architect.

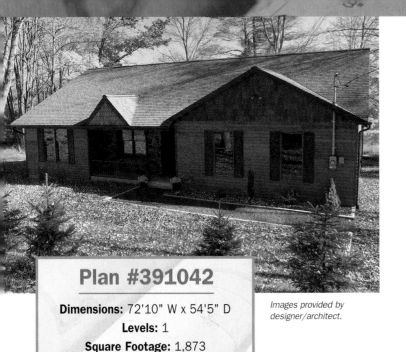

Plan #391042

Dimensions: 72'10" W x 54'5" D

Levels: 1

Square Footage: 1,873

Bedrooms: 4

Bathrooms: 2

Foundation: Crawl space, slab

Materials List Available: Yes

Price Category: D

Images provided by designer/architect.

Bonus Area

Copyright by designer/architect.

Plan #201064

Dimensions: 68'10" W x 67'4" D

Levels: 1

Square Footage: 2,682

Bedrooms: 4

Bathrooms: 3

Foundation: Crawl space, slab

Materials List Available: Yes

Price Category: F

Images provided by designer/architect.

Copyright by designer/architect.

Plan #211090

Dimensions: 66' W x 72' D

Levels: 1

Square Footage: 1,932

Bedrooms: 3

Bathrooms: 2

Foundation: Crawl space

Materials List Available: No

Price Category: D

Images provided by designer/architect.

This home has a magnificent raised-cottage exterior that makes it seem much larger than it actually is.

Features:

- Ceiling Height: 8 ft.

- Living Room: There is plenty of room for entertaining and family activities in this living room. Pairs of French doors lead from here to the rear covered deck and porch.

- Kitchen: The smart, modern design of this kitchen makes cooking a pleasure. The room is angled to provide a commanding view to the outside through the parallel angles of the adjacent eating area. This kitchen includes a built-in pantry and a desk for menu planning and compiling shopping lists.

- Master Suite: This luxurious master suite includes a bath with a large walk-in closet, twin lavatories, a dressing area, linen storage, a soaking tub, and a separate shower.

- Room to Expand: A conveniently located stairwell leads to an abundance of space waiting for future expansion.

Copyright by designer/architect.

Plan #131044

Dimensions: 57'6" W x 42'4" D
Levels: 1
Square Footage: 1,994
Bedrooms: 3
Bathrooms: 2
Foundation: Basement, crawl space, or slab
Materials List Available: Yes
Price Category: E

Under a covered porch, Victorian-detailed bay windows grace each side of the brick-faced facade at the center of this ranch-style home, giving it a formal air.

Features:

- Ceiling Height: 10-ft. ceilings grace the central living area and the master bedroom of this home.

- Entry: Round top windows make this area and the flanking rooms bright and cheery.

- Great Room: A fireplace and built-ins that are visible from anywhere in this large room make it a natural gathering place for friends and family.

- Optional Office: Use the room just off the central hall as a home office, fourth bedroom, or study.

- Master Suite: You'll love the bay window, tray ceiling, two walk-in closets, and private bath.

- Bonus Space: Finish this large area in the attic for extra living space, or use it for storage.

Rear Elevation

Bonus Area

Plan #161010

Dimensions: 50'8" W x 54'2" D
Levels: 1
Square Footage: 1,544
Bedrooms: 3
Bathrooms: 2
Foundation: Basement
Materials List Available: Yes
Price Category: C

Images provided by designer/architect.

This one-story home's many distinctive and elegant features—including arched openings and sloped ceilings—will surprise and excite you at every turn.

Features:

- **Great Room:** Decorative columns frame the entrance from the foyer to this great room and are repeated at the opening to the formal dining area.

- **Kitchen:** Designed for quick meals or to accommodate an oversized crowd, this kitchen features a curved countertop with seating that functions as a delightful bar.

- **Master Bedroom:** This master bedroom is split to afford you more privacy and features a compartmented bath that forms a separate vanity area.

- **Additional Bedrooms:** Take advantage of the double doors off the foyer to allow one bedroom to function as a library.

Right Side Elevation

Left Side Elevation

Rear Elevation

Copyright by designer/architect.

Plan #221014

Dimensions: 72' W x 44'8" D

Levels: 1

Square Footage: 1,906

Bedrooms: 3

Bathrooms: 2½

Foundation: Basement

Materials List Available: No

Price Category: D

Images provided by designer/architect.

If elegance is your cup of tea but you also have a practical streak, you'll love everything about this home.

Features:

- Ceiling Height: 8 ft.

- Living Room: The tall vaulted ceiling gives stature to this spacious room. Decorate to highlight the cozy fireplace, and let your guests flow into the adjacent dining room.

- Dining Room: A bayed area with a central doorway to the backyard highlights this room, which is open to the kitchen.

- Kitchen: The family chefs will love the central island and ample counter and cabinet space in this well-planned kitchen, which opens to a fully equipped laundry room and half-bath.

- Master Suite: A tray ceiling and large bay window are the elegant features in this suite's bedroom. The bath includes a whirlpool tub, standing shower, and two-sink vanity. The adjacent walk-in closet gives a practical touch.

Rear Elevation

Copyright by designer/architect.

Plan #131045

Dimensions: 81'4" W x 68'3" D
Levels: 1
Square Footage: 2,347
Bedrooms: 4
Bathrooms: 2½
Foundation: Basement, crawl space, or slab
Materials List Available: Yes
Price Category: E

You'll love the character and flexibility in siting that the angled design gives to this contemporary ranch-style home.

Features:

- **Porch:** A wraparound rear porch adds distinction to this lovely home.

- **Great Room:** Facing the rear of the house, this great room has a high, stepped ceiling, fireplace, and ample space for built-ins.

- **Kitchen:** This large room sits at an angle to the great room and is adjacent to both a laundry room and extra powder room.

- **Office:** Use the 4th bedroom as a home office, study, or living room, depending on your needs.

- **Master Suite:** This area is separated from the other bedrooms in the house to give it privacy. The beautiful bay window at the rear, two large walk-in closets, and luxurious bath make it an ideal retreat after a hectic day.

Images provided by designer/architect.

Copyright by designer/architect.

Plan #341004

Dimensions: 56'10" W x 28'6" D

Levels: 1

Square Footage: 1,101

Bedrooms: 3

Bathrooms: 2

Foundation: Crawl space, slab, or basement

Materials List Available: Yes

Price Category: B

Images provided by designer/architect.

You'll love the romantic feeling that the gables and front porch give to this well designed home, with its family-oriented layout.

Features:

• **Living Room:** The open design between this spacious room and the kitchen/dining area makes this home as ideal for family activities as it is for entertaining.

• **Outdoor Living Space:** French doors open to the back deck, where you're sure to host alfresco dinners or easy summer brunches.

• **Kitchen:** Designed for the cook's convenience, this kitchen features ample work area as well as excellent storage space in the nearby pantry.

• **Laundry Area:** Located behind closed doors to shut out the noise, this laundry closet is conveniently placed.

• **Master Suite:** With triple windows, a wide closet, and a private bath, this is a luxurious suite.

SMARTtip

Creating Depth with Wall Frames

Wall frames create an illusion of depth and density because 1) they are three-dimensional and 2) they divide the wall area into smaller, denser segments. The three- dimensional quality of wall frames is fundamentally different from that of the alternative treatment: raised panels. Despite the name, raised panels actually produce a concave-like, or receding, effect whereas wall frames are more convex, protruding outward. In terms of sculpture, concave units create negative space while convex units create positive space. Raised panels, therefore, deliver a uniform sense of volume, mass, and density, while wall frames create a higher level of tension and dramatic interest.

DECK

Copyright by designer/architect.

GARAGE
21'-0" X 14'-0"

W. D
PAN
WH

DINING/KITCH.
18'-6" X 9'-0"

BEDROOM 3
11'-4" X 9'-0"

BA. 1

COATS

BA. 2

LIVING ROOM
15'-6" X 12'-0"

LIN

BEDROOM 1
11'-4" X 12'-8"

PORCH

BEDROOM 2
11'-4" X 10'-8"

28'-6"

56'-10"

Plan #121034

Dimensions: 92'8" W x 59'4" D
Levels: 1
Square Footage: 2,223
Bedrooms: 2
Bathrooms: 2
Foundation: Basement
Materials List Available: Yes
Price Category: E

Images provided by designer/architect.

This home features a flowing, open floor plan coupled with an abundance of amenities.

Features:

• Ceiling Height: 8 ft. unless otherwise noted.

• Foyer: This elegant entry features a curved staircase and a view of the formal dining room.

• Formal Dining Room: Magnificent arched openings lead from the foyer into this dining room. The boxed ceiling adds to the architectural interest.

• Great Room: A wall of windows, a see-through fireplace, and built-in entertainment center make this the perfect gathering place.

• Covered Deck: The view of this deck, through the wall of windows in the great room, will lure guests out to this large deck.

• Hearth Room: This room share a panoramic view with the eating area.

• Kitchen: This kitchen features a corner pantry, a built-in desk, and a curved island.

Main Level Floor Plan

Optional Basement Level Floor Plan

Copyright by designer/architect.

Plan #341047

Dimensions: 50' W x 54'9" D

Levels: 1

Square Footage: 1,670

Bedrooms: 3

Bathrooms: 2

Foundation: Crawl space, slab (basement option for fee)

Materials List Available: Yes

Price Category: C

Images provided by designer/architect.

Copyright by designer/architect.

Plan #201068

Dimensions: 74'10" W x 73'10" D

Levels: 1

Square Footage: 2,780

Bedrooms: 4

Bathrooms: 3

Foundation: Crawl space, slab

Materials List Available: Yes

Price Category: F

Images provided by designer/architect.

Copyright by designer/architect.

Plan #341041

Dimensions: 48' W x 56'8" D
Levels: 1
Square Footage: 1,454
Bedrooms: 3
Bathrooms: 2
Foundation: Crawl space, slab (basement option for fee)
Materials List Available: Yes
Price Category: B

Images provided by designer/architect.

Copyright by designer/architect.

Plan #201074

Dimensions: 56' W x 59' D
Levels: 1
Square Footage: 1,692
Bedrooms: 3
Bathrooms: 2
Foundation: Crawl space, slab
Materials List Available: Yes
Price Category: C

Images provided by designer/architect.

Copyright by designer/architect.

Plan #391006

Dimensions: 66' W x 69' D

Levels: 1

Square Footage: 1,788

Bedrooms: 3

Bathrooms: 2

Foundation: Basement

Materials List Available: Yes

Price Category: C

Celebrating the union of beauty and function, this single-level layout makes a large appearance, with its peaked rooflines, elongated windowing, and sloping ceilings in the living room and bedroom #3 (or home office).

Features:

• Foyer: Soft angles define the space in the house, beginning with this foyer entry that curves to all the important rooms.

• Master Suite: Private rooms gather on the opposite side of the plan, with this master suite owning special windowing, an enormous walk-in closet, and a highly specialized bathroom with compartments that maintain privacy as two people use the various facilities at once.

• Bedroom: This other secondary bedroom enjoys a full bath and plenty of closet space.

• Utility Areas: Laundry facilities are easy to access, and a two-car garage has convenient front entry.

Slab/Crawl Space Option

Option

Plan #221015

Dimensions: 69'8" W x 46' D

Levels: 1

Square Footage: 1,926

Bedrooms: 3

Bathrooms: 2½

Foundation: Basement; optional walk-out basement available for extra fee

Materials List Available: No

Price Category: D

Images provided by designer/architect.

You'll love the open plan in this lovely ranch and admire its many features, which are usually reserved for much larger homes.

Features:

- Ceiling Height: 8 ft.

- Great Room: A vaulted ceiling and tall windows surrounding the centrally located fireplace give distinction to this handsome room.

- Dining Room: Positioned just off the entry, this formal room makes a lovely spot for quiet dinner parties.

- Dining Nook: This nook sits between the kitchen and the great room. Central doors in the bayed area open to the backyard.

- Kitchen: An island will invite visitors while you cook in this well-planned kitchen, with its corner pantry and ample counter space.

- Master Suite: A tray ceiling, bay window, walk-in closet, and bath with whirlpool tub, dual-sink vanity, and standing shower pamper you here.

Rear Elevation

Copyright by designer/architect.

Plan #271081

Dimensions: 86' W x 54' D
Levels: 1
Square Footage: 2,539
Bedrooms: 3
Bathrooms: 2
Foundation: Slab
Materials List Available: No
Price Category: E

Images provided by designer/architect.

This traditional home is sure to impress your guests and even your neighbors.

Features:

• Living Room: This quiet space off the foyer is perfect for pleasant conversation.

• Family Room: A perfect gathering spot, this room is nicely enhanced by a fireplace.

• Kitchen: This room easily serves the bayed morning room and the formal dining room.

• Master Suite: The master bedroom overlooks a side patio, and boasts a private bath with a skylight and a whirlpool tub.

• Library: This cozy room is perfect for curling up with a good novel. It would also make a great extra bedroom.

SMARTtip

Determining Curtain Length

Follow length guidelines for foolproof results, but remember that they're not rules. Go ahead and play with curtain and drapery lengths. Instead of shortening long panels at the hem, for instance, take up excess material by blousing them over tiebacks for a pleasing effect.

Images provided by designer/architect.

Plan #121060

Dimensions: 50' W x 46' D

Levels: 1

Square Footage: 1,339

Bedrooms: 3

Full Bathrooms: 2

Foundation: Basement

Materials List Available: Yes

Price Category: B

You'll love this compact design if you're looking for either a starter home or a luxurious place to spend your retirement years.

Features:

- **Foyer:** A covered stoop and arched entry open to this gracious foyer, where you'll love to greet guests.

- **Great Room:** From the foyer, you'll walk into this large area with its 10-ft. ceilings. A fireplace gives you a cozy spot on chilly days and cool evenings.

- **Kitchen:** This kitchen is truly step-saving and convenient. In addition to plenty of counter and storage space, it features a snack bar and an adjoining breakfast area.

- **Master Suite:** A 9-ft. ceiling gives a touch of elegance to the bedroom, and the walk-in closet adds practicality. In the bath, you'll find two vanities and a whirlpool tub.

- **Garage:** There's room for storage, a work bench, and three cars in this huge garage.

Copyright by designer/architect.

Plan #341048

Dimensions: 58' W x 39' D

Levels: 1

Square Footage: 1,471

Bedrooms: 3

Bathrooms: 2

Foundation: Crawl space, slab (basement option for fee)

Materials List Available: Yes

Price Category: B

Images provided by designer/architect.

Copyright by designer/architect.

Bonus Area

Copyright by designer/architect.

Plan #201081

Dimensions: 65'10" W x 55'10" D

Levels: 1

Square Footage: 1,940

Bedrooms: 3

Bathrooms: 2

Foundation: Crawl space, slab

Materials List Available: Yes

Price Category: D

Images provided by designer/architect.

Copyright by designer/architect.

Images provided by designer/architect.

Copyright by designer/architect.

Plan #341042

Dimensions: 52'8" W x 28'6" D

Levels: 1

Square Footage: 1,055

Bedrooms: 3

Bathrooms: 2

Foundation: Crawl space, slab (basement option for fee)

Materials List Available: Yes

Price Category: B

Images provided by designer/architect.

Copyright by designer/architect.

Plan #201085

Dimensions: 58'10" W x 63'4" D

Levels: 1

Square Footage: 2,015

Bedrooms: 3

Bathrooms: 2

Foundation: Crawl space, slab

Materials List Available: Yes

Price Category: D

Plan #161012

Dimensions: 69' W x 50'10" D

Levels: 1

Square Footage: 1,648

Bedrooms: 3

Bathrooms: 2

Foundation: Basement

Materials List Available: Yes

Price Category: C

Images provided by designer/architect.

This delightful brick home, with multiple gables and an inviting front porch, offers an exciting interior with varied ceiling heights and an open floor plan.

Features:

- **Great Room:** This great room showcases an 11-ft. ceiling and a gas fireplace. Enjoy a beverage seated at the convenient bar, and move freely through a generous opening to the relaxed dining area.

- **Kitchen:** This galley kitchen is expanded by easy access to the garage and laundry room.

- **Master Bedroom:** You will appreciate the openness of this large master bedroom, which features an 11-ft. ceiling. You can also retreat to the privacy of an adjoining covered porch.

- **Library:** Thoughtful design allows you to exercise the option of converting the bedroom off the foyer into a library.

Right Side Elevation

Rear Elevation

Left Side Elevation

Copyright by designer/architect.

Plan #221016

Dimensions: 56' W x 42' D

Levels: 1

Square Footage: 1,461

Bedrooms: 3

Bathrooms: 2

Foundation: Basement

Materials List Available: No

Price Category: B

Images provided by designer/architect.

The interesting roofline and classic siding give this traditional ranch home an instant appeal.

Features:

- Ceiling Height: 8 ft.

- Great Room: From the entry, you'll look into this great room, where a handsome fireplace with large flanking windows makes you feel at home.

- Dining Room: Open to the great room, this room features access to the rear deck. An eating island shared with the kitchen allows the whole living area to flow together.

- Kitchen: The step-saving layout and ample counter space will delight the family chef.

- Master Suite: With a large walk-in closet and deluxe bath with a whirlpool tub, separate shower, and two-sink vanity, this private area will become a real retreat at the end of the day.

- Additional Bedrooms: Add the optional door from the entry to transform bedroom #2 into a quiet den, or use it as a bedroom.

Rear Elevation

Copyright by designer/architect.

Plan #221017

Dimensions: 65' W x 56' D

Levels: 1

Square Footage: 2,229

Bedrooms: 3

Bathrooms: 2

Foundation: Basement

Materials List Available: No

Price Category: E

You'll love both the traditional appearance and practical layout of this gracious home.

Features:

- Ceiling Height: 9 ft.

- Great Room: A cathedral ceiling highlights the spaciousness of this room. Large rear windows and a handsome fireplace give it a comfortable atmosphere.

- Dining Room: Featuring a high tray ceiling, this dining room has an arched entryway to the great room and opens to the kitchen for convenience.

- Kitchen: This large room has a center cooktop island with space for an eating area, a corner pantry, and an arched doorway to the dining nook with easy access to the backyard.

- Master Suite: A cathedral ceiling and large windows looking out to the backyard give a graceful feeling to the bedroom. Two walk-in closets, plus a bath with a whirlpool tub, standing shower, and dual-sink vanity, add a practical and luxurious touch.

Rear Elevation

Copyright by designer/architect.

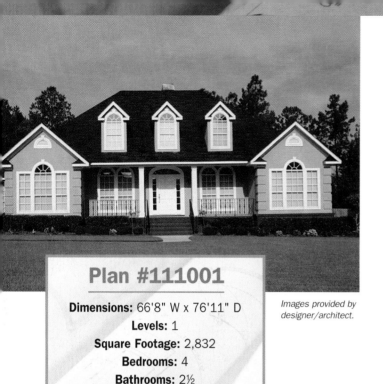

Plan #111001

Dimensions: 66'8" W x 76'11" D

Levels: 1

Square Footage: 2,832

Bedrooms: 4

Bathrooms: 2½

Foundation: Slab

Materials List Available: No

Price Category: F

Images provided by designer/architect.

Copyright by designer/architect.

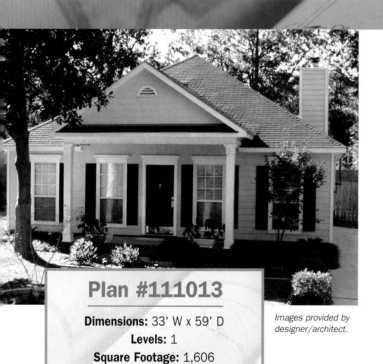

Plan #111013

Dimensions: 33' W x 59' D

Levels: 1

Square Footage: 1,606

Bedrooms: 3

Bathrooms: 2

Foundation: Slab

Materials List Available: No

Price Category: C

Images provided by designer/architect.

Plan #111030

Dimensions: 74'10" W x 85'5" D

Levels: 1

Square Footage: 2,905

Bedrooms: 4

Bathrooms: 3

Foundation: Slab

Materials List Available: No

Price Category: F

Images provided by designer/architect.

Bonus Gameroom

Plan #211007

Dimensions: 72' W x 60' D

Levels: 1

Square Footage: 2,252

Bedrooms: 4

Bathrooms: 2

Foundation: Slab

Materials List Available: Yes

Price Category: E

Images provided by designer/architect.

Plan #201086

Dimensions: 68'6" W x 46' D

Levels: 1

Square Footage: 1,573

Bedrooms: 3

Bathrooms: 2

Foundation: Crawl space, slab

Materials List Available: Yes

Price Category: C

Images provided by designer/architect.

Bonus Room

bonus 10 x 22⁴

porch

br 3 12 x 11

den 16 x 17

eating 9 x 11

util

mbr 13 x 16

kit 11x11

br 2 12 x 12

foy

dining 11 x 12

sto 8⁸x10

garage 22 x 22

Copyright by designer/architect.

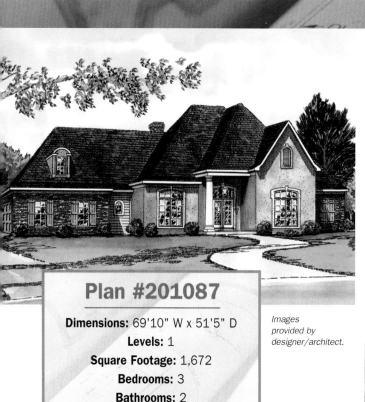

Plan #201087

Dimensions: 69'10" W x 51'5" D

Levels: 1

Square Footage: 1,672

Bedrooms: 3

Bathrooms: 2

Foundation: Crawl space, slab

Materials List Available: Yes

Price Category: C

Images provided by designer/architect.

Bonus Room

bonus rm 15⁸ x 12

mbr 14 x 14

util 6⁴ x 7¹⁰

eating 11⁸ x 9

por 4 x 21

br 3 12 x 11

garage 22 x 23

kit 9 x 9

den 17 x 16

sto 6x7⁸

dining 12 x 11

foy 9 x 9

br 2 12 x 12

por 9 x 5

Copyright by designer/architect.

*Images provided by
designer/architect.*

Plan #201069

Dimensions: 70'10" W x 64'10" D

Levels: 1

Square Footage: 2,735

Bedrooms: 4

Bathrooms: 3½

Foundation: Crawl space, slab

Materials List Available: Yes

Price Category: F

**Optional
Basement Level
Floor Plan**

*Images provided by
designer/architect.*

Plan #321039

Dimensions: 31'8" W x 45' D

Levels: 1

Square Footage: 1,231

Bedrooms: 2

Bathrooms: 2

Foundation: Basement

Materials List Available: Yes

Price Category: B

Plan #221018

Dimensions: 67' W x 53' D

Levels: 1

Square Footage: 2,007

Bedrooms: 3

Bathrooms: 2

Foundation: Basement

Materials List Available: No

Price Category: D

You'll love this ranch design, with its traditional stucco facade and interesting roofline.

Features:

- Ceiling Height: 9 ft.

- Great Room: A cathedral ceiling points up the large dimensions of this room, and the handsome fireplace with tall flanking windows lets you decorate for a formal or a casual feeling.

- Dining Room: A tray ceiling imparts elegance to this room, and a butler's pantry just across from the kitchen area lets you serve in style.

- Kitchen: You'll love the extensive counter space in this well-designed kitchen. The adjoining nook is large enough for a full-size dining set and features a door to the outside deck, where you can set up a third dining area.

- Master Suite: Located away from the other bedrooms for privacy, this suite includes a huge walk-in closet, windows overlooking the backyard, and a large bath with a whirlpool tub, standing shower, and dual-sink vanity.

Images provided by designer/architect.

Rear Elevation

Copyright by designer/architect.

Plan #221019

Dimensions: 64'8" W x 57' D

Levels: 1

Square Footage: 1,591

Bedrooms: 3

Bathrooms: 2

Foundation: Basement

Materials List Available: No

Price Category: C

Images provided by designer/architect.

You'll be delighted with the many luxurious elements included in this compact home.

Features:

• Ceiling Height: 9 ft.

• Great Room: A vaulted ceiling sets the elegant tone you'll find reflected in the rest of this gracious home. The fireplace, flanked by windows, and the open entry to the dining room make everyone feel comfortable.

• Dining Room: A tray ceiling distinguishes this formal room. You'll find a door to the large screened porch from this room, so it's easy to serve meals here when the weather's fine or relax with a beverage at the end of the day.

• Kitchen: The ample counter and cabinet space make this kitchen a delight, and the eating bar encourages lots of little visitors.

• Master Suite: With a tray ceiling and huge walk-in closet, this suite's bedroom makes you feel elegant. The large bathroom, with its whirlpool tub, standing shower, and dual-sink vanity, confirms the feeling.

Rear Elevation

Copyright by designer/architect.

Plan #221020

Dimensions: 69'8" W x 43' D

Levels: 1

Square Footage: 1,859

Bedrooms: 3

Bathrooms: 2½

Foundation: Basement

Materials List Available: No

Price Category: D

Images provided by designer/architect.

You'll love this design if you're looking for a compact home with amenities usually found in much larger designs.

Features:

- Ceiling Height: 8 ft.

- Living Room: A vaulted ceiling gives an elegant feeling, and a bank of windows lets natural light pour in during the daytime.

- Dining Room: Located just off the entry for the convenience of your guests, this room is ideal for intimate family meals or formal dinner parties.

- Kitchen: Just across from the dining room, this kitchen is distinguished by its ample counter space. The adjacent nook is large enough to use as a casual dining area, and it features access to the backyard.

- Master Suite: The large bay window lends interest to this room, and you'll love the walk-in closet and private bath, with its whirlpool tub, standing shower, and dual-sink vanity.

Rear Elevation

Copyright by designer/architect.

Plan #271082

Dimensions: 71' W x 62' D
Levels: 1
Square Footage: 2,074
Bedrooms: 4
Bathrooms: 2
Foundation: Crawl space or slab
Materials List Available: No
Price Category: D

Magnificent pillars and a huge transom window add stature to the impressive entry of this traditional home.

Features:

- Living Room: A corner fireplace warms this spacious room, which shares a 12-ft. ceiling with the dining room and the kitchen.

- Backyard: A French door provides direct access to a covered porch, which in turn flows into a wide deck and a sunny patio.

- Master Suite: A cathedral ceiling enhances the master bedroom, which offers a large walk-in closet. The private bath is certainly luxurious, with its whirlpool tub and two vanities

Copyright by designer/architect.

SMARTtip

Making a Cornice

Any new cornice or cornice shelf includes mounting hardware and directions for its installation. But you'll probably need to purchase mounting brackets to install older or homemade cornices. If you're not comfortable with the idea of working on a ladder, especially while handling the cornice and various tools, call a pro. A professional installer will charge a flat rate for coming to your house plus an additional fee for each treatment. Prices vary, but your location, the size of the treatment (measured by the foot), and the difficulty of the job will determine its price.

Plan #211009

Dimensions: 72' W x 60' D

Levels: 1

Square Footage: 2,396

Bedrooms: 4

Bathrooms: 2

Foundation: Slab

Materials List Available: Yes

Price Category: E

Images provided by designer/architect.

Beautiful arched windows lend a luxurious feeling to the exterior of this one-story home.

Features:

• Ceiling Height: 9 ft. unless otherwise noted.

• Entry: Guests will be greeted by a dramatic 12-ft. ceiling in this elegant foyer.

• Living Room: The 12-ft. ceiling continues through the foyer into this inviting living room. Everyone will feel welcomed by the crackling fire in the handsome fireplace.

• Covered Porch: When the weather is warm, invite guests to step out of the living room directly into this covered porch.

• Kitchen: This bright and cheery kitchen is designed for the way we live today. It includes a pantry and an angled eating bar that will see plenty of impromptu family meals.

• Energy-Efficient Walls: All the outside walls are framed with 2x6 lumber instead of 2x4. The extra thickness makes room for more insulation to lower your heating and cooling bills.

Copyright by designer/architect.

SMARTtip

Ornaments in a Garden

Placement is everything with ornaments in a garden. Some elements are best sitting by themselves. Others are better when they are part of a cohesive whole, perhaps placed in the greenery at a corner or flanking a structure.

Images provided by designer/architect.

Copyright by designer/architect.

Plan #341033

Dimensions: 57' W x 32'3" D

Levels: 1

Square Footage: 1,297

Bedrooms: 3

Bathrooms: 2

Foundation: Crawl space, slab, or basement

Materials List Available: Yes

Price Category: B

Copyright by designer/architect.

Images provided by designer/architect.

Plan #301001

Dimensions: 99'10" W x 46'2" D

Levels: 1

Square Footage: 2,720

Bedrooms: 3

Bathrooms: 2

Foundation: Crawl space, slab

Materials List Available: Yes

Price Category: F

Images provided by designer/architect.

Plan #231001

Dimensions: 67'6" W x 58' D
Levels: 1
Square Footage: 2,177
Bedrooms: 3
Bathrooms: 2½
Foundation: Crawl space
Materials List Available: No
Price Category: D

Copyright by designer/architect.

Images provided by designer/architect.

Plan #231004

Dimensions: 44' W x 37'6" D
Levels: 1
Square Footage: 1,463
Bedrooms: 2
Bathrooms: 2
Foundation: Crawl space
Materials List Available: No
Price Category: A

Copyright by designer/architect.

Plan #211049

Dimensions: 73' W x 66' D
Levels: 1
Square Footage: 2,000
Bedrooms: 3
Bathrooms: 2
Foundation: Slab
Materials List Available: Yes
Price Category: D

Images provided by designer/architect.

This European-style home features an open floor plan that maximizes use and flexibility of space.

Features:

- Ceiling Height: 8 ft. unless otherwise noted.

- Living/Dining Area: This combined living-and-dining area features high ceilings, which make the large area seem even more spacious. Corner windows will fill the room with light. The wet bar and cozy fireplace make this the perfect place for entertaining.

- Backyard Porch: This huge covered backyard porch is accessible from the living/dining area, so the entire party can step outdoors on a warm summer night.

- Kitchen: More than just efficient, this modern kitchen is actually an exciting place to cook. It features a dramatic high ceiling and plenty of work space.

- Utility Area: Located off the kitchen, this area has extra freezer space, a walk-in pantry, and access to the garage.

- Eating Nook: Informal family meals will be a true delight in this nook that adjoins the kitchen and faces a lovely private courtyard.

Copyright by designer/architect.

Plan #321036

Dimensions: 78'4" W x 68'6" D

Levels: 1, optional lower

Square Footage: 2,900

**Optional Basement Level
Sq. Ft.:** 1,018

Bedrooms: 4

Bathrooms: 2½

Foundation: Basement

Materials List Available: Yes

Price Category: F

Images provided by designer/architect.

This classic contemporary is wrapped in brick.

Features:

- **Great Room:** This grand-scale room offers a vaulted ceiling and Palladian windows flanking an 8-ft.-wide brick fireplace.

- **Kitchen:** This built-in-a-bay room features a picture window above the sink, a huge pantry, and a cooktop island. It opens to the large morning room.

- **Breakfast Area:** Open to the kitchen, this area features 12 ft. of cabinetry.

- **Master Bedroom:** This room features a coffered ceiling, and a walk-in closet gives you good storage space in this luxurious bedroom.

- **Garage:** This area can fit three cars with plenty of room to spare.

**Optional Basement Level
Floor Plan**

Images provided by designer/architect.

Plan #121009

Dimensions: 50' W x 58' D
Levels: 1
Square Footage: 1,422
Bedrooms: 3
Bathrooms: 2
Foundation: Basement
Materials List Available: Yes
Price Category: B

This amenity-filled home is perfect for the growing family or as a retirement retreat.

Features:

- Ceiling Height: 8 ft. unless otherwise noted.
- Great Room: This inviting space is the perfect place for gatherings of all sizes. It shares 12-ft. ceilings with the dining room and kitchen.

- Dining Room: In addition to the 12-ft. ceiling, arched openings, and built-in book cases make this an elegant place to dine.

- Private Porch: After dinner, step through a door in the dining room to enjoy a summer breeze in this inviting porch.

- Master Suite: The boxed ceiling lends drama to this suite and a walk-in closet adds convenience. Luxury comes from the whirlpool bath.

- Garage: You won't be short of parking and storage space in this two-bay garage. As a bonus there is space for a workbench.

SMARTtip
Window Cornices

You can transform plain rooms by making jogs in cornice molding that will hold shades, blinds, and other window treatments. You can create individual pockets over each window or continue the molding past narrow wall sections between windows to form a more expansive detail. Housings below the cornice can be painted or papered.

Plan #121011

Dimensions: 50' W x 50' D
Levels: 1
Square Footage: 1,724
Bedrooms: 3
Bathrooms: 2
Foundation: Basement
Materials List Available: Yes
Price Category: C

Images provided by designer/architect.

This one-level home is perfect for retirement or for convenient living for the growing family.

Features:

- Ceiling Height: 8 ft.
- Master Suite: For privacy and quiet, the master suite is segregated from the other bedrooms.
- Family Room: Sit by the fire and read as light streams through the windows flanking the fireplace. Or enjoy the built-in entertainment center.
- Breakfast Area: Located just off the family room, the sunny breakfast area will lure you to linger over impromptu family meals. Here you will find a built-in desk for compiling shopping lists and menus.
- Private Porch: Step out of the breakfast area to enjoy a breeze on this porch.
- Kitchen: Efficient and attractive, this kitchen offers an angled pantry and an island that doubles as a snack bar.

SMARTtip

Measuring for Kitchen Countertops

Custom cabinetmakers will sometimes come to your house to measure for a countertop, but home centers and kitchen stores may require that you come to them with the dimensions already in hand. Be sure to double-check measurements carefully. Being off by only ½ in. can be quite upsetting.

To ensure accuracy, sketch out the countertop on a sheet of graph paper. Include all the essential dimensions. To be on the safe side, have someone else double-check your numbers.

Copyright by designer/architect.

Decks

Many people are reluctant to make design decisions because they don't think of themselves as designers. But if you take the time to think things through carefully, you may be surprised at the ideas you generate. Start with memories of places you have enjoyed. Of course, dreams can rarely be re-created in the real world. But by letting your imagination run loose and tapping into those images, you can develop a font of design concepts that will help you come up with a deck design.

Beginning Your Design

Begin by imagining your ideal deck, and ask family members to do the same. Think about its design, accessories, and any special elements you would like your deck to contain. Keep track of your ideas by drawing a series of rough sketches as you proceed. Expect to fill a wastebasket or two with these. Don't think of them as actual designs so much as focal points for conversations—it's easier to point to a drawing than to walk around the house.

Feel free to steal ideas from other people. (The best architects do not hesitate to do so.) When you see a deck you like, take photos and jot down some notes. Talk to the owners about how their deck works for them. Most people will be flattered that you like their deck and will be more than glad to talk to you about it. You will not only learn about pleasing designs and materials, but you can avoid the mistakes they made.

Screened porches, left, are popular deck amenities.

Eating areas, above, require ample room for tables and chairs.

Multilevel decks, opposite, provide room for separate activity areas.

Uses for Your New Deck

Call a family meeting to discuss your deck plans. Find out everyone's vision of the deck. What would they like it to look like? Where would they like it to be? The backyard is the logical choice, but an enlarged front porch may better suit your needs. Or it may make more sense to design a deck that wraps around two sides of your house. How large a deck do you want? If a large deck would cut into your yard area, making it tough to play croquet, or if it would throw shade on the flower bed, you may want to scale back your plans. But if you rarely use your yard or hate maintaining the lawn, a larger deck will make gardening chores easier. Most importantly at this point, consider the activities that will take place on the deck.

Cooking and Entertaining

Entertainment is high on many people's list. Plan for a cooking area as well as a place for a good-sized table for seating smaller groups or for buffet settings if you have large parties. For nighttime entertaining, think about installing lighting.

Locate the grill area as far as possible from other use areas so that you don't have to worry about kids bumping into a hot barbecue. Leave ample room for cooking "assistants" so that friends can gather around and talk as you turn the steaks.

Make the deck easy to get to. The more entrances, the better. Large doorways and oversized windows tend to entice people outside. If you plan on eating on the deck often, make sure it is close to the kitchen. Ideally, try to plan for a direct connection between the deck and kitchen.

A Place to Relax

Consider what your future deck will be like during all the seasons when you are likely to use it.

Decide how much sun and how much shade you want, and take this into account when siting your deck. If you live in the northern hemisphere, a north-facing space will be in shade most of the day. This can be an advantage if you live in a very hot climate and a disadvantage for most everyone else. An eastern exposure gives the deck morning sun and afternoon shade; this is often the best choice in warm climates. In cold climates, a southwest exposure usually provides full and late afternoon sun.

Shade structures, left, offer protection from late afternoon sun.

Built-in seating, below, makes a deck inviting and contributes to its design.

Separate activity areas, opposite, help define the uses of the new deck.

Lighting. If you tend to eat and entertain after dark, consider your deck's lighting. A motion-sensing floodlight provides security and lights your way as you bring in groceries, but it makes for an unappealing dining ambiance. Subtle, low-voltage fixtures set into steps or posts provide a better solution for dining and entertaining on the deck. Most lighting plans call for a combination of both types of lighting.

In addition to placing low-voltage lights in steps and posts, consider lining a path that leads up to the deck with small lights. When choosing these fixtures, be sure to select fixtures that are attractive during the day as well as at night.

You may also want to consider using lights for decorative effect. For example, you can install low-voltage lights in the garden to highlight plantings that are visible from the deck. In-ground fixtures cast their light upward, creating interesting areas of shadow and light on trees and shrubs. Many fixtures have lenses that let you aim the light beam.

Avoid installing too many lights. With low-voltage layouts, a few well-placed lights is more dramatic than the glare produced by too many lights.

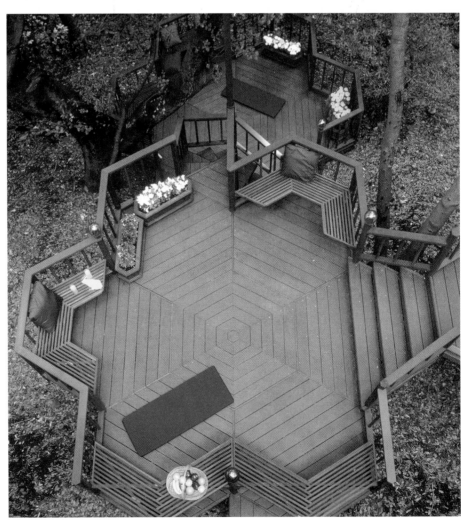

Private Spaces

Decks are often raised off the ground, which might mean you and your family will be on display for all the neighborhood to see. Existing fences may be too low to shield you from view. Sometimes the problem can be solved by stepping the deck down in stages. In most settings, decks work best when built low to the ground. If your entry door occupies a high position, you'll find it best to build a landing and stairs or a series of tiers leading down to a low-built main deck.

Privacy Options. You may have to take direct action to achieve privacy. You don't have to build an unfriendly, solid wall to avoid the feeling you are being watched. If you feel overexposed, a well-placed trellis provides the base for some nice climbing plants to look at and creates a pleasant enclosure. Another solution is to plant border trees and shrubs.

Fences are another option. There are many styles and materials from which to choose. High solid fences provide the most privacy, but an imposing design isn't very friendly, and it can make your yard seem closed in and smaller than it really is. Soften fences by using them as a backdrop for plantings.

Family members need some privacy among themselves as well. By building with different levels, including a conversation pit, or even by just letting the deck ramble a bit, you can create areas that are separate but not walled off. Careful placement of activity areas can also help create private sections. For example, if you are installing a spa or a cooking center—areas that tend to draw a crowd—place private areas on the other side of the deck.

Open or Cozy. Think about whether you want your deck to feel airy and open to the world or cozy and secluded. These effects can be achieved in many ways. A small deck will feel cozier than a large deck. Low benches and railings designed with large open spaces in them give an open feeling. A deck that hugs the house will have a more sequestered feel than one that juts out into the yard.

Plan #271005

Dimensions: 48' W x 50' D
Levels: 1
Square Footage: 1,368
Bedrooms: 3
Bathrooms: 2
Foundation: Basement
Materials List Available: Yes
Price Category: B

This traditional home boasts an open floor plan that is further expanded by soaring vaulted ceilings.

Features:

- **Great Room:** Front and center, this large multipurpose room features a gorgeous corner fireplace, an eye-catching boxed out window, and dedicated space for casual dining—all beneath a vaulted ceiling.

- **Kitchen:** A vaulted ceiling crowns this galley kitchen and its adjoining breakfast nook.

- **Master Suite:** This spacious master bedroom, brightened by a boxed-out window, features a vaulted ceiling in the sleeping chamber and the private bath.

Images provided by designer/architect.

Copyright by designer/architect.

SMARTtip

Design with Computers

Consider using a computer-aided design (CAD) program to plan your deck. Some programs let you see three-dimensional views of your design complete with railings, stairs, planters, hot tubs, and the surrounding landscaping.

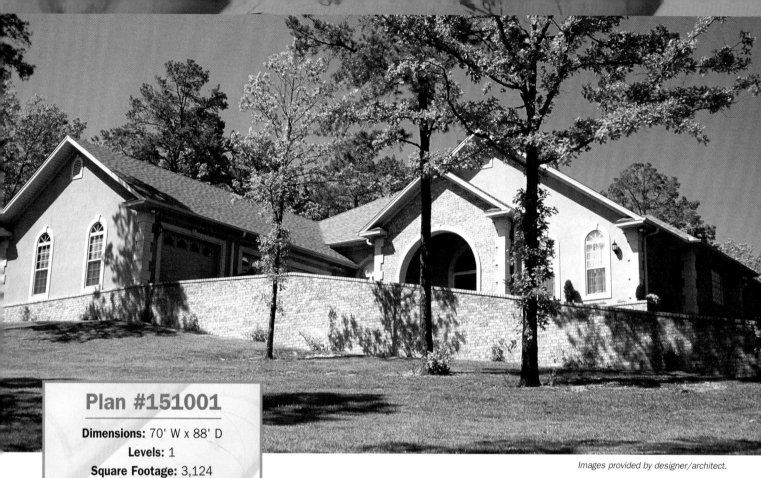

Plan #151001

Dimensions: 70' W x 88' D

Levels: 1

Square Footage: 3,124

Bedrooms: 4

Bathrooms: 3½

Foundation: Crawl space, slab

Materials List Available: No

Price Category: G

Images provided by designer/architect.

From the double front doors to sleek arches, columns, and a gallery with arched openings to the bedrooms, you'll love this elegant home.

Features:

- **Grand Room:** With a 13-ft. pan ceiling and column entry, this room opens to the rear covered porch as well as through French doors to the bay-windowed morning room that, in turn, leads to the gathering room.

- **Gathering Room:** A majestic fireplace, built-in entertainment center, and book shelves give comfort and ease.

- **Kitchen:** A double oven, built-in desk, and a work island add up to a design for efficiency.

- **Master Suite:** Enjoy the practicality of walk-in closets, the comfort of a private sitting area, and the convenience of an adjacent study or nursery. The bath features a step-up whirlpool tub and separate shower.

Copyright by designer/architect.

Images provided by designer/architect.

Plan #371007

Dimensions: 72'10" W x 48'4½" D

Levels: 1

Square Footage: 1,944

Bedrooms: 4

Bathrooms: 2

Foundation: Slab
(crawl space option for fee)

Materials List Available: No

Price Category: D

Copyright by designer/architect.

Images provided by designer/architect.

Plan #341030

Dimensions: 52' W x 40' D

Levels: 1

Square Footage: 1,660

Bedrooms: 3

Bathrooms: 2

Foundation: Crawl space, slab, or basement

Materials List Available: Yes

Price Category: C

Copyright by designer/architect.

Images provided by designer/architect.

Copyright by designer/architect.

Plan #341034

Dimensions: 50' W x 38'2" D

Levels: 1

Square Footage: 1,445

Bedrooms: 3

Bathrooms: 2

Foundation: Crawl space, slab, or basement

Materials List Available: Yes

Price Category: B

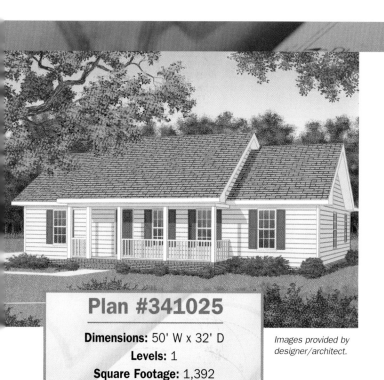

Images provided by designer/architect.

Copyright by designer/architect.

Plan #341025

Dimensions: 50' W x 32' D

Levels: 1

Square Footage: 1,392

Bedrooms: 3

Bathrooms: 2

Foundation: Crawl space, slab, or basement

Materials List Available: Yes

Price Category: B

SMARTtip

Neoclassical Style

Instead of expensive hand-crafted plasterwork, look into the many prefabricated moldings, ceiling medallions, pillars, cornices, and the like that are made of lightweight molded plastic. They can be faux painted to resemble marble or stone and are fairly easy to install yourself.

Plan #131040

Dimensions: 50' W x 37' D
Levels: 1
Square Footage: 1,630
Bedrooms: 3
Bathrooms: 2
Foundation: Basement, crawl space, or slab
Materials List Available: Yes
Price Category: D

Images provided by designer/architect.

The raised main level of this home makes this plan ideal for any site that has an expansive view, and you can finish the lower level as an office, library, or space for the kids to play.

Features:

- **Living Room:** This sunken living room with a prow-shaped front is sure to be a focal point where both guests and family gather in this lovely ranch home. A see-through fireplace separates this room from the dining room.

- **Dining Room:** A dramatic vaulted ceiling covers both this room and the adjacent living room, creating a spacious feeling.

- **Kitchen:** Designed for efficiency, you'll love the features and location of this convenient kitchen.

- **Master Suite:** Luxuriate in the privacy this suite affords and enjoy the two large closets, sumptuous private bath, and sliding glass doors that can open to the optional rear deck.

Rear Elevation

Main Level Floor Plan

Copyright by designer/architect.

Lower Level Floor Plan

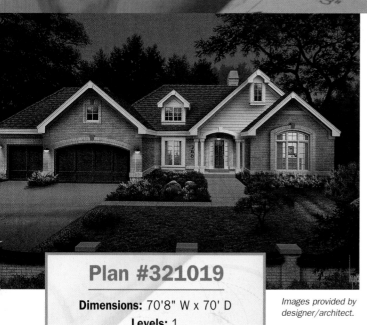

Plan #321019

Dimensions: 70'8" W x 70' D

Levels: 1

Square Footage: 2,452

Bedrooms: 4

Bathrooms: 2½

Foundation: Basement

Materials List Available: Yes

Price Category: E

Images provided by designer/architect.

Copyright by designer/architect.

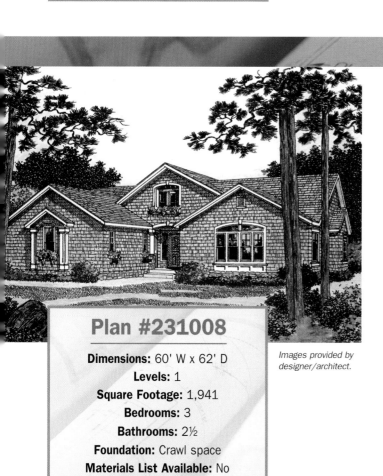

Plan #231008

Dimensions: 60' W x 62' D

Levels: 1

Square Footage: 1,941

Bedrooms: 3

Bathrooms: 2½

Foundation: Crawl space

Materials List Available: No

Price Category: D

Images provided by designer/architect.

Copyright by designer/architect.

Plan #121006

Dimensions: 46' W x 58' D

Levels: 1

Square Footage: 1,762

Bedrooms: 3

Bathrooms: 2

Foundation: Slab, crawl space, or basement

Materials List Available: Yes

Price Category: C

Images provided by designer/architect.

The entry has a trio of arched openings that leads you to other areas of this amenity-packed home.

Features:

- Ceiling Height: 8 ft. except as noted.

- Eating Bar: Conveniently located between the kitchen and family room, this is sure to be a favorite spot for informal entertaining and family gatherings.

- Family room: A wall of windows, a fireplace, and a vaulted ceiling stretching to 11 ft. work together to make this a bright and warm room.

- Kitchen: There's no shortage of counter space in this well-planned kitchen that features a center island in addition to the eating bar.

- Master Suite: Luxuriate at the end of the day in this large bedroom with its decorative tray ceiling and walk-in closet. Enjoy the pampering bath with its sunlit corner whirlpool flanked by vanities.

- Garage: Two bays provide room for cars and plenty of storage as well.

Copyright by designer/architect.

Plan #131001

Dimensions: 72'4" W x 32'4" D
Levels: 1
Square Footage: 1,615
Bedrooms: 3
Bathrooms: 2
Foundation: Basement, crawl space, or slab
Materials List Available: Yes
Price Category: D

Cathedral ceilings and illuminating skylights add drama and beauty to this practical ranch house.

Features:

Ceiling Height: 8 ft.

- **Front Porch:** Watch the rain in comfort from the covered front porch.

- **Foyer:** The stone-tiled foyer flows into the living areas.

- **Living Room:** Oriented towards the front of the house, the living room opens to the dining room and shares a lovely three-sided fireplace with the family room.

- **Family Room:** Conveniently located to share the fireplace with the living room, this room is bright and cheery thanks to its skylights as well as the sliding glass doors that open onto the rear patio.

- **Kitchen:** An island makes this sunny room both efficient and attractive.

- **Breakfast Nook:** Located just off the kitchen, this area can serve double-duty as a spot for kitchen visitors to sit.

- **Dining Room:** The open design between the dining and living rooms adds to the spacious feeling that the cathedral ceiling creates in this area.

- **Laundry Room:** This area opens from the kitchen for convenience.

- **Master Suite:** A walk-in closet makes this room practical, but the master bathroom with a skylight, dual-sink vanity, soaking tub, and separate shower makes it luxurious.

- **Bedrooms:** The two additional bedrooms share a bathroom.

Images provided by
designer/architect.

Plan #171009

Dimensions: 68' W x 50' D
Levels: 1
Square Footage: 1,771
Bedrooms: 3
Bathrooms: 2
Foundation: Slab, crawl space
Materials List Available: Yes
Price Category: C

SMARTtip

Deck Awnings

Awnings come in bright colors. As light filters through, it
will cast a hue to anything under the deck. Warm colors,
such as red or pink, will create a rosy glow; cool colors,
such blues or greens, will enhance the shade.

Plan #151045

Dimensions: 68'6" W x 65' D
Levels: 1
Square Footage: 2,250
Bedrooms: 4
Bathrooms: 2
Foundation: Crawl space, slab
(basement option for fee)
Materials List Available: No
Price Category: E

Images provided by
designer/architect.

Copyright by designer/architect.

Plan #361011

Dimensions: 41' W x 60' D

Levels: 1

Square Footage: 1,632

Bedrooms: 3

Bathrooms: 2

Foundation: Crawl space

Materials List Available: No

Price Category: C

Images provided by designer/architect.

Copyright by designer/architect.

Plan #341046

Dimensions: 50'8" W x 51' D

Levels: 1

Square Footage: 1,495

Bedrooms: 3

Bathrooms: 2

Foundation: Crawl space, slab (basement option for fee)

Materials List Available: Yes

Price Category: B

Images provided by designer/architect.

Copyright by designer/architect.

Planning Your Landscape

Landscapes change over the years. As plants grow, the overall look evolves from sparse to lush. Trees cast cool shade where the sun used to shine. Shrubs and hedges grow tall and dense enough to provide privacy. Perennials and ground covers spread to form colorful patches of foliage and flowers. Meanwhile, paths, arbors, fences, and other structures gain the comfortable patina of age.

Constant change over the years—sometimes rapid and dramatic, sometimes slow and subtle—is one of the joys of landscaping. It is also one of the challenges. Anticipating how fast plants will grow and how big they will eventually get is difficult, even for professional designers, and was a major concern in formulating the designs for this book.

As Your Landscape Grows

To illustrate the kinds of changes to expect in a planting, these pages show one of the designs at three different "ages." Even though a new planting may look sparse at first, it will soon fill in. And because of careful spacing, the planting will look as good in 10 to 15 years as it does after 3 to 5. It will, of course, look different, but that's part of the fun.

At Planting

Dwarf Lilac

Rose

Viburnum

Clematis

Perennials

Switchgrass

Three to Five Years

Rose

Switchgrass

Dwarf Lilac

Juniper

Viburnum

Juniper

Clematis

Perennials

At Planting—Here's how a raised-deck planting might appear in late spring immediately after planting. The rose and clematis haven't begun to climb the new lattice trellis. The viburnum and lilac, usually sold in 2- to 5-gal. cans, start blooming as young plants and may have flowers when you buy them, but there will be enough space that you may want to plant some short annuals around them for the first few growing seasons. You can put short annuals between the new little junipers, too. The switchgrass and perennials, transplanted from quart- or gallon-size containers, are just low tufts of foliage now, but they grow fast enough to produce a few flowers the first summer.

Three to Five Years—As shown here in midsummer, the rose and clematis now reach most of the way up the supports. Although they aren't mature yet, the lilac, viburnum, and junipers look nice and bushy, and they're big enough that you don't need to fill around them with annuals. So far, the vines and shrubs have needed only minimal pruning. Most grasses and perennials reach full size about three to five years after planting; after that, they need to be divided and replanted in freshly amended soil to keep them healthy and vigorous.

Ten to Fifteen Years—Shown again in summer, the rose and clematis now cover their supports, and the lilac and viburnum are as tall as they'll get. To maintain all of these plants, you'll need to start pruning out some of the older stems every year in early spring. The junipers have spread sideways to form a solid mass; prune them as needed along the edge of the lawn and pathways. When the junipers crowd them out, move the daylilies to another part of your property, or move them to the front of the bed to replace the other perennials, as shown here.

Ten to Fifteen Years

A Step Up

Plant a Foundation Garden

Homes on raised foundations usually have foundation plantings. These simple skirtings of greenery hide unattractive concrete-block underpinnings and help overcome the impression that the house is hovering a few feet above the ground. Useful as these plantings are, they are too often just monochromatic expanses of clipped junipers, dull as dishwater. But, as this design shows, a durable, low-maintenance foundation planting can be more varied, more colorful, and more fun.

Because a foundation planting should look good year-round, the design is anchored by a row of cherry laurels, broad-leaved evergreens covered each spring by heavily scented flowers. A small garden of shrubs, perennials, and a graceful arching grass will catch the eye of visitors approaching the front door. Colorful perennials bloom from spring to fall along the edge of the bed. At the far end is a tidy viburnum, whose spicy-scented flowers will encourage springtime strolls around that corner of the house.

'Morning Light' D
Japanese silver grass

'Autumn Joy' sedum E

'Crimson Pygmy' C
Japanese barberry

Lamb's ears I

Plants & Projects

From spring to fall, something is always blooming here, but foliage texture and color play an even greater role than flowers in this design. From the slender, shimmering leaves of Japanese silver grass rising behind mounded barberries, to furry lamb's ears, feathery coreopsis, and fleshy sedum, textures abound, colored in a variety of reds, greens, and silvers. Winter offers glossy green cherry laurels, the tawny leaves and striking seed heads of silver grass, and the rich russets of the sedum. Other than an annual cutback in spring and a little pruning to shape the viburnum, the planting requires little maintenance.

A **Korean spice viburnum** (use 1 plant)
At the corner of the house, this deciduous shrub produces spicy-scented flowers in spring (preceded by pretty pink buds) and dense green foliage in summer and fall. Shape by annual pruning.

B **'Otto Luyken' cherry laurel** (use 4)
The glossy dark leaves and spreading habit of these evergreen shrubs will clothe the foundation year-round. As a bonus, spring produces a profusion of fragrant white flowers in spikes.

C **'Crimson Pygmy' Japanese barberry** (use 3)
A compact deciduous shrub with small, teardrop-shaped maroon leaves that turn crimson in fall, when they are joined by bright red berries.

D **'Morning Light' Japanese silver grass** (use 1)
A rustling sentinel by the door, this grass is silvery all summer, then turns tawny after frost. Its fluffy seed heads last through the winter.

E **'Autumn Joy' sedum** (use 3)
Flat-topped flower clusters emerge in late summer above clumps of fleshy gray-green leaves, turning from white through shades of ever deeper pink to rust-colored seed heads that can stand through the winter.

F **'East Friesland' salvia** (use 4)
Shown against the green backdrop, reddish purple flower spikes cover these perennials from May through fall.

G **'Longwood Blue' bluebeard** (use 1)
A small deciduous shrub with silvery gray foliage and fringed blue flowers from late summer to frost.

H **'Moonbeam' coreopsis** (use 4)
A perennial with fine foliage and tiny pale yellow flowers from July into September.

I **Lamb's ears** (use 3)
A perennial with fuzzy silver-white leaves. Use the large-leaved, wide-spreading cultivar 'Helene von Stein' (sometimes called 'Big Ears').

J **'Big Blue' lilyturf** (use 4)
This grasslike evergreen perennial under the viburnum has dark blue flowers in summer.

G 'Longwood Blue' bluebeard

H 'Moonbeam' coreopsis

B 'Otto Luyken' cherry laurel

F 'East Friesland' salvia

A Korean spice viburnum

J 'Big Blue' lilyturf

Site: Sunny

Season: Early fall

Concept: Mixture of perennials and shrubs provides colorful setting for a home's public face.

Stoop

Steps

Window   House

Lawn

Cherry laurels will not grow tall enough to block windows that are more than 4 ft. above grade.

1 square = 1 ft.

Note: All plants are appropriate for USDA Hardiness Zones 5, 6, and 7.

Plan #211048

Dimensions: 66' W x 60'8" D

Levels: 1

Square Footage: 2,002

Bedrooms: 3

Bathrooms: 2

Foundation: Crawl space, slab

Materials List Available: Yes

Price Category: D

This southern-style home is filled with inviting spaces and will fit into any neighborhood.

Features:

- Ceiling Height: 8 ft.

- Front Porch: Enjoy summer breezes on this porch, which features accented shutters that are both functional and stylish.

- Living Room: From the porch, French doors lead into the side-lit entry and this gracious living room.

- Sundeck: You can bask in the summer sun on this private rear deck, or if you prefer, enjoy a cool breeze under the shade of the rear porch. Each is accessible through its own set of French doors.

- Master Suite: This suite is secluded from the rest of the house for privacy, making it the perfect retreat at the end of a busy day. From the bedroom, open double doors to gain access to the luxurious bath, with a dual-sink vanity and his and her walk-in closets.

Images provided by designer/architect.

Copyright by designer/architect.

SMARTtip

Eye Appeal

Not everything in a landscaping plan needs to be in the ground. You might want to consider hanging flowering plants on a front porch or placing hardy potted plants on outdoor steps and decks or strategically along a paved walkway. Even a window box, viewed from outside, becomes a part of the landscaping.

Plan #201084

Dimensions: 66'10" W x 54'5" D

Levels: 1

Square Footage: 2,056

Bedrooms: 3

Bathrooms: 2

Foundation: Crawl space, slab

Materials List Available: Yes

Price Category: D

This classic family home features beautiful country styling with lots of curb appeal.

Features:

- Ceiling Height: 8 ft.

- Open Plan: When guests arrive, they'll enter a foyer that is open to the dining room and den. This open area makes the home seem especially spacious and offers the flexibility for all kinds of entertaining and family activities.

- Kitchen: You'll love preparing meals in this large, well-designed kitchen. There's plenty of counter space, and the breakfast bar is perfect impromptu family meals.

- Master Suite: This spacious and elegant master suite is separated from the other bedroom for maximum privacy.

- Bonus Room: This unfinished bonus room awaits the time to add another bedroom or a home office.

- Garage: This attached garage offers parking for two cars, plus plenty of storage space.

Copyright by designer/architect.

Bonus Room

Images provided by designer/architect.

Plan #211024

Dimensions: 61' W x 44' D

Levels: 1

Square Footage: 1,418

Bedrooms: 3

Bathrooms: 2

Foundation: Slab

Materials List Available: Yes

Price Category: B

Copyright by designer/architect.

SMARTtip

Brackets in Window Treatments

Although it is rarely noticed, a bracket plays an important role in supporting rods and poles. If a treatment rubs against a window frame, an extension bracket solves the problem. It projects from the wall at an adjustable length, providing enough clearance. A hold-down bracket anchors a cellular shade or a blind to the bottom of a door, preventing the treatment from moving when the door is opened or closed.

Plan #211030

Dimensions: 75' W x 37' D

Levels: 1

Square Footage: 1,600

Bedrooms: 3

Bathrooms: 2

Foundation: Slab

Materials List Available: Yes

Price Category: C

Images provided by designer/architect.

Copyright by designer/architect.

Plan #241007

Dimensions: 58'10" W x 59'1" D

Levels: 1

Square Footage: 2,036

Bedrooms: 3

Bathrooms: 2

Foundation: Slab, crawlspace

Materials List Available: No

Price Category: D

Images provided by designer/architect.

Enjoy summer breezes while relaxing on the large front porch of this charming country cottage.

Features:

- Great Room: Whether you enter from the front door or from the kitchen, you will feel welcome in this comfortable great room, which features a corner fireplace.

- Kitchen: This well-designed kitchen with extensive counter space offers a delightful eating bar, perfect for quick or informal meals.

- Master Suite: This luxurious master suite, located on the first floor for privacy, features his and her walk-in closets, separate vanities, a deluxe corner tub, a linen closet, and a walk-in shower.

- Additional Bedrooms: Two secondary bedrooms and an optional, large game room —well suited for a growing family—are located on the second floor.

Copyright by designer/architect.

Plan #181021

Dimensions: 37' W x 44' D

Levels: 1

Square Footage: 1,124

Bedrooms: 2

Bathrooms: 1

Foundation: Basement

Materials List Available: Yes

Price Category: B

Images provided by designer/architect.

This cozy country cottage is enhanced by lattice trim details over the porch and garage.

Features:

- Ceiling Height: 8 ft.

- Living Room: This living room gets extra architectural interest from a sunken floor. The room, located directly to the left of the entry hall, has plenty of space for entertaining.

- Dining Room: This dining room is located in center of the home. It's adjacent to the kitchen to make it easy to serve meals.

- Kitchen: This bright and efficient kitchen is a real pleasure in which to work. It includes a pantry and double sinks. There's a breakfast bar that will see plenty of informal meals for families on the go.

- Covered Porch: This is the perfect place to which to retire after dinner on a warm summer evening.

- Bedrooms: Each of the two bedrooms has its own closet. They share a full bathroom.

Copyright by designer/architect.

Plan #251001

Dimensions: 61'3" W x 40'6" D

Levels: 1

Square Footage: 1,253

Bedrooms: 3

Bathrooms: 2

Foundation: Crawl space, slab

Materials List Available: Yes

Price Category: B

This charming country home has a classic full front porch for enjoying summertime breezes.

Features:

• Ceiling Height: 8 ft.

• Foyer: Guests will walk through the front porch into this foyer, which opens to the family room.

• Screened Porch: A second porch is screened and is located at the rear of the home off the dining room, so your guests can step out for a bit of fresh air after dinner.

• Family Room: Family and friends will be drawn to this large open space, with its handsome fireplace and sloped ceiling.

• Kitchen: This open and airy kitchen is a pleasure in which to work. It has ample counter space and a pantry.

Images provided by designer/architect.

• Master Bedroom: This master bedroom features a large walk-in closet. It has its own master bath with a single vanity, a tub, and a walk-in shower.

• Garage: This attached garage provides plenty of extra storage space, as well as parking for two cars.

Plan #171002

Dimensions: 44' W x 41' D
Levels: 1
Square Footage: 1,458
Bedrooms: 3
Bathrooms: 2
Foundation: Slab, crawl space
Materials List Available: Yes
Price Category: B

Images provided by designer/architect.

Plan #171015

Dimensions: 79' W x 52' D
Levels: 1
Square Footage: 2,089
Bedrooms: 3
Bathrooms: 2½
Foundation: Slab, crawl space
Materials List Available: Yes
Price Category: D

Images provided by designer/architect.

Bonus Area

Plan #341013

Dimensions: 44' W x 34' D

Levels: 1

Square Footage: 1,363

Bedrooms: 3

Bathrooms: 2

Foundation: Crawl space, slab, or basement

Materials List Available: Yes

Price Category: B

Images provided by designer/architect.

Copyright by designer/architect.

Plan #371001

Dimensions: 52' W x 45' D

Levels: 1

Square Footage: 1,418

Bedrooms: 3

Bathrooms: 2

Foundation: Slab
(crawl space option for fee)

Materials List Available: No

Price Category: B

Images provided by designer/architect.

Copyright by designer/architect.

Plan #251002

Dimensions: 55'6" W x 64'3" D
Levels: 1
Square Footage: 1,333
Bedrooms: 3
Bathrooms: 2
Foundation: Crawl space, slab
Materials List Available: Yes
Price Category: B

Although compact, this farmhouse has all the amenities for comfortable modern living.

Features:

- Ceiling Height: 8 ft. unless otherwise noted.

- Foyer: This gracious and welcoming foyer opens to the family room.

- Family Room: This inviting family room is designed to accommodate all kinds of family activities. It features a 9-ft. ceiling and a handsome, warming fireplace.

- Kitchen: Cooking in this kitchen is a real pleasure. It includes a center island, so you'll never run out of counter space for food preparation.

- Master Bedroom: This master bedroom features a large walk-in closet and an elegant 9-ft. recessed ceiling.

- Master Bath: This master bath offers a double vanity, a tub, and a walk-in shower.

- Garage: This attached garage provides plenty of extra storage space, as well as parking for two cars.

Images provided by designer/architect.

SMARTtip

Arts and Crafts Style

The heart of this style rests in its earthy connection. The more you can bring nature into it, the more authentic it will be. An easy way to do this is with plants. A bonus is that plants naturally thrive in the bathroom, where they enjoy the humid environment.

Copyright by designer/architect.

Plan #131013

Dimensions: 50' W x 41'8" D
Levels: 1
Square Footage: 1,489
Bedrooms: 3
Bathrooms: 2
Foundation: Basement, crawl space, or slab
Materials List Available: Yes
Price Category: C

Images provided by designer/architect.

You'll love the Victorian details on the exterior of this charming ranch-style home.

Features:

- **Front Porch:** This porch is large enough so that you can sit out on warm summer nights to catch a breeze or create a garden of potted ornamentals.

- **Great Room:** Running from the front of the house to the rear, this great room is bathed in natural light from both directions. The volume ceiling adds a luxurious feeling to it, and the fireplace creates a cozy place on chilly afternoons.

- **Kitchen:** Cooking will be a pleasure in this kitchen, thanks to the thoughtful layout and well-designed work areas.

- **Master Suite:** Enjoy the quiet in this room, where it will be easy to relax and unwind, no matter what the time of day. The walk-in closet gives you plenty of storage space, and you're sure to appreciate both the privacy and large size of the master bath.

Copyright by designer/architect.

Rear Elevation

Plan #141001

Dimensions: 37' W x 61' D

Levels: 1

Square Footage: 1,208

Bedrooms: 3

Bathrooms: 2

Foundation: Basement

Materials List Available: Yes

Price Category: B

Images provided by designer/architect.

The spacious feel of this raised ranch belies its compact floor plan.

Features:

• Ceiling Height: 8 ft. unless otherwise noted.

• Porch: This country-style porch lends character and lots of curb appeal.

• Drive-Under Garage: The garage is tucked below for a more attractive facade but can also be built with a front entry if lot restrictions dictate.

• Living Room: The cathedral ceiling in the living room creates a dramatic fireplace wall.

• Kitchen: You'll love cooking in this super-efficient U-shaped kitchen, with its generous counter space and storage.

• Laundry: The laundry closet is conveniently located in the hall bath.

• Master Suite: A cathedral ceiling makes this bedroom seem spacious. The oversize tub has a showerhead so that you can enjoy an oversize shower as well.

Copyright by designer/architect.

SMARTtip

Hydro-seeding

An alternative to traditional seeding is hydro-seeding. In this process, a slurry of grass seed, wood fibers, and fertilizer is spray-applied in one step. Hydro-seeding is relatively inexpensive. Compared with seeding by hand, hydro-seeding is also very fast.

Plan #251004

Dimensions: 50'9" W x 42'1" D
Levels: 1
Square Footage: 1,500
Bedrooms: 3
Bathrooms: 2
Foundation: Crawl space, slab
Materials List Available: Yes
Price Category: C

Images provided by designer/architect.

Combine the old-fashioned appeal of a country farmhouse with all the comforts of modern living.

Features:

- Ceiling Height: 9 ft.
- Foyer: When guests enter this inviting foyer, they will be greeted by a view of the lovely family room.
- Family Room: Usher family and friends into this welcoming family room, where they can warm up in front of the fireplace. The room's 12-ft. ceiling enhances its sense of spaciousness.

- Kitchen: Gather around and keep the cook company at the snack bar in this roomy kitchen. There's still plenty of counter space for food preparation, thanks to the kitchen island.
- Master Bedroom: This elegant master bedroom features a large walk-in closet and a 9-ft. recessed ceiling.
- Master Bath. This master bath includes a double vanity, a tub, and a walk-in shower.
- Garage: This attached garage provides plenty of extra storage space, as well as parking for two cars.

Copyright by designer/architect.

Garage
22 x 22
8' Clg.

Storage
16 x 4

Master
16 x 13/7
Recessed Clg.
9' Clg.

Rear Porch
24 x 6

Dining
11/8 x 13
8' Clg.

Kitchen
12 x 13

Snack Bar

Br. #3
11 x 10/5
8' Clg.

Br. #2
10 x 12
8' Clg.

Family Room
21/8 x 15/7
12' Clg.

Sloped Ceiling

W D

Front Porch
49 x 6   8' Clg.

SMARTtip

Shaker Style in Your Bathroom

This warm, likable style fits in perfectly with a country home because of its old-fashioned values. But it blends in well with contemporary interiors, too, because of its clean lines and plain geometric shapes. In fact, adding a few Shaker elements can warm up the sometimes cold look of a thoroughly modern room.

Copyright by designer/architect.

Plan #201004

Dimensions: 60'10" W x 34'10" D

Levels: 1

Square Footage: 1,121

Bedrooms: 3

Bathrooms: 2

Foundation: Crawl space, slab, or basement

Materials List Available: Yes

Price Category: B

Images provided by designer/architect.

SMARTtip

Color Basics

Use color effectively to enhance the perception of the space itself. Make a large room feel cozy with warm colors, which tend to advance. Conversely, open up a small room with cool colors or neutrals, which tend to recede.

Plan #151168

Dimensions: 66' W x 65'2" D

Levels: 1

Square Footage: 2,261

Bedrooms: 4

Bathrooms: 2½

Foundation: Basement, daylight basement, crawl space, or slab

Materials List Available: Yes

Price Category: E

Images provided by designer/architect.

Copyright by designer/architect.

Bonus Room

Plan #361019

Dimensions: 66' W x 47' D

Levels: 1

Square Footage: 1,619

Bedrooms: 3

Bathrooms: 2

Foundation: Basement, crawl space

Materials List Available: No

Price Category: C

Images provided by designer/architect.

Alternate Basement Stairs Location

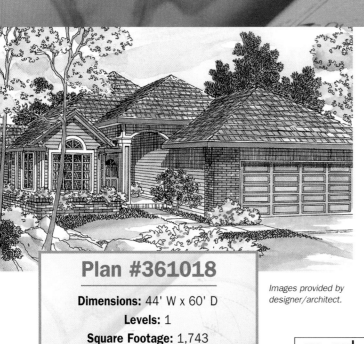

SMARTtip

Bathroom Fans

Especially in large bathrooms, more than one fan is recommended for efficient venting. Of course, first check with your local building department about codes that may stipulate where to install bathrooms fans. If possible, include a fan in the toilet area, one near the shower, and one over the bathtub.

Plan #361018

Dimensions: 44' W x 60' D

Levels: 1

Square Footage: 1,743

Bedrooms: 3

Bathrooms: 2

Foundation: Crawl space

Materials List Available: No

Price Category: C

Images provided by designer/architect.

Optional Basement Stair Location

Plan #131016

Dimensions: 75' W x 45' D
Levels: 1
Square Footage: 1,902
Bedrooms: 3
Bathrooms: 2
Foundation: Basement, crawl space, or slab
Materials List Available: Yes
Price Category: E

If traditional country looks appeal to you, you'll be delighted by the wraparound covered porch that forms the entryway to this comfortable home.

Features:

- Great Room: Sit by the fireplace in this room with feature walls so large that they'll suit a home theater or large media center.

- Kitchen: Overlooking the great room, this well-designed kitchen has great cabinets and ample counter space to make all your cooking and cleaning a pleasure.

- Master Suite: A large bay window makes the bedroom in this private suite sophisticated, and two walk-in closets make it practical. You'll love to relax in the master bath, whether in the whirlpool tub or the separate shower. A dual-sink vanity completes the amenities in this room.

- Garage: Find extra storage space in this two-bayed, attached garage.

Great Room

Plan #171006

Dimensions: 68' W x 50' D
Levels: 1
Square Footage: 2,296
Bedrooms: 3
Bathrooms: 2½
Foundation: Slab, crawl space
Materials List Available: Yes
Price Category: E

Images provided by designer/architect.

This classic country farmhouse features a large, open rocking-chair front porch.

Features:

• Ceiling Height: 9 ft. unless otherwise noted.

• Great Room: This spacious great room is perfect for all types of entertaining.

• Dining Room: This dining room is designed to accommodate formal dinner parties as well as less-formal family occasions. After dinner, step from the dining room onto the covered rear porch.

• Family Room: On cool evenings, enjoy the handsome fireplace in this family room. There's plenty of room for all kinds of family activities.

• Kitchen: This is truly a cook's kitchen with its cooktop range and U-shaped open traffic pattern. The snack bar will see lots of use for quick family meals.

• Master Suite: This master suite is separated from the other bedrooms for additional privacy. The large bedroom has a paddle fan and a roomy walk-in closet. The bathroom features his and her vanities, a deluxe bath, and a walk-in shower.

Copyright by designer/architect.

Plan #271074

Dimensions: 68' W x 86' D
Levels: 1
Square Footage: 2,400
Bedrooms: 4
Bathrooms: 3
Foundation: Crawl space or slab
Materials List Available: No
Price Category: E

Perfect for families with aging relatives or boomerang children, this home includes a completely separate suite at the rear.

Features:

- **Living Room:** A corner fireplace casts a friendly glow over this gathering space.

- **Kitchen:** This efficient space offers a serving bar that extends toward the eating nook

and the formal dining room.

- **Master Suite:** A cathedral ceiling presides over this deluxe suite, which boasts a whirlpool tub, dual-sink vanity, and walk-in closet.

- **In-law Suite:** This separate wing has its own vaulted living room, plus a kitchen, a dining room, and a bedroom suite.

Copyright by designer/architect.

SMARTtip

Adding Professional Flair to Window Treatments

You can give your window treatment designs a professional look by using decorator tricks to customize readymades or dress your own home-sewn designs. These could include contrast linings, tassels, cording, ribbons, or couture trimmings such as buttons, coins, or bows applied to edges. Another trick is to sew a fine wire into the hem of curtains or valances to create a pliable edge that you can shape yourself. Small weights that you can sew into the hem of drapery panels or jabots will make them hang better. For more inspiration look at fashion magazines and visit showrooms.

Plan #131004

Dimensions: 59'4" W x 35'8" D
Levels: 1
Square Footage: 1,097
Bedrooms: 3
Bathrooms: 2
Foundation: Basement, crawl space, or slab
Materials List Available: Yes
Price Category: B

Images provided by designer/architect.

You'll love the extra features you'll find in this charming but easy-to-build ranch home.

Features:

• Porch: This full-width porch is graced with impressive round columns, decorative railings, and ornamental moldings.

• Living Room: Just beyond the front door, the living room entrance has a railing that creates the illusion of a hallway. The 10-ft. tray ceiling makes this room feel spacious.

• Dining Room: Flowing from the living room, this room has a 9-ft.-high stepped ceiling and leads to sliding glass doors that open to the large rear patio.

• Kitchen: This kitchen is adjacent to the dining room for convenience and has a large island for efficient work patterns.

• Master Suite: Enjoy the privacy in this bedroom with its private bathroom.

Alternate Basement Floor Plan

Copyright by designer/architect.

Plan #241016

Dimensions: 58'10" W x 59'1" D

Levels: 1

Square Footage: 2,011

Bedrooms: 3

Bathrooms: 2

Foundation: Slab

Materials List Available: No

Price Category: D

Images provided by designer/architect.

Copyright by designer/architect.

MASTER SUITE 14'-0" X 15'-0"

MORNING ROOM 12'-6" X 12'-4"

PORCH

BEDR'M 2 11'-0" X 12'-8"

GREAT ROOM 15'-0" X 20'-7"

BATH-2

KIT

MASTER BATH

UTIL

DOUBLE GARAGE 21'-3" X 20'-0"

DINING 12'-0" X 12'-0"

FOYER

BEDR'M 3 11'-0" X 12'-0"

PORCH

58'-10"

59'-1"

FUTURE BATH

FUTURE GAMEROOM 15'-0" X 20'-0"

DN

Plan #241015

Dimensions: 67'2" W x 46'10" D

Levels: 1

Square Footage: 1,609

Bedrooms: 3

Bathrooms: 2

Foundation: Slab

Materials List Available: No

Price Category: C

Images provided by designer/architect.

Copyright by designer/architect.

MASTER BATH

MASTER SUITE 13'-3" X 16'-0"

BATH-2

GREAT ROOM 16'-6" X 16'-0"

PATIO AREA

STOR

STOR

DOUBLE GARAGE 20'-0" X 21'-3"

KIT

BEDR'M 2 12'-6" X 11'-3"

BEDR'M 3 12'-8" X 11'-3"

HALL

FOYER

DINING 12'-0" X 11'-4"

PORCH

67'-2"

46'-10"

Images provided by designer/architect.

Copyright by designer/architect.

Plan #351010

Dimensions: 61'8" W x 45'8" D

Levels: 1

Square Footage: 1,502

Bedrooms: 3

Bathrooms: 2

Foundation: Basement, crawl space, or slab

Materials List Available: Yes

Price Category: C

Images provided by designer/architect.

Copyright by designer/architect.

Plan #201025

Dimensions: 62' W x 46' D

Levels: 1

Square Footage: 1,379

Bedrooms: 3

Bathrooms: 2

Foundation: Crawl space, slab

Materials List Available: Yes

Price Category: B

SMARTtip

Arrangement of Mantle Objects

On a fireplace mantle, group objects of different heights for visual interest—a straight line can be boring. Raise one or two pieces with a small pedestal or stand, and stagger the pieces from back to front. If you have three or more objects, make a triangle or overlapping triangles.

Plan #291001

Dimensions: 63' W x 37' D

Levels: 1

Square Footage: 1,550

Bedrooms: 3

Bathrooms: 2

Foundation: Basement

Materials List Available: No

Price Category: C

Images provided by designer/architect.

A handsome porch with Greek Revival details greets visitors to this Early-American style home.

Features:

- Ceiling Height: 8 ft. unless otherwise noted.

- Foyer: Upon entering this foyer you'll be struck by the space provided by the vaulted ceiling in the dining room, living room, and kitchen.

- Dining Room: This dining room is perfectly suited for formal dinner parties as well as less formal family meals.

- Decks: Two rear decks are conveniently accessible from the master bedroom, kitchen, and living room.

- Kitchen: You'll enjoy cooking in this well-designed kitchen, which features an eating area that is perfect for informal family meals.

- Master Bedroom: This master retreat is separated from the other bedrooms for additional privacy. It features an elegant vaulted ceiling and is graced with a dressing area, private bath, and walk-in closet.

Rear View

Copyright by designer/architect.

Plan #171011

Dimensions: 70' W x 58' D
Levels: 1
Square Footage: 2,069
Bedrooms: 3
Bathrooms: 2½
Foundation: Slab, crawl space
Materials List Available: Yes
Price Category: D

Images provided by designer/architect.

This home combines the charm of a country cottage with all the modern amenities.

Features:

- Ceiling Height: 9 ft. unless otherwise noted.
- Front Porch: Watch the sun set, read a book, or just relax on this spacious front porch.

- Foyer: This gracious foyer has two closets and opens to the formal dining room and the study.
- Dining Room: This big dining room works just as well for family Sunday dinner as it does for entertaining guests on Saturday night.
- Family Room: This inviting family room features an 11-ft. ceiling, a paddle fan, and a corner fireplace.
- Kitchen: This smart kitchen includes lots of counter space, a built-in desk, and a breakfast bar.
- Master Bedroom: This master bedroom is separate from the other bedrooms for added privacy. It includes a paddle fan.
- Master Bath: This master bath has two vanities, walk-in closets, a deluxe tub, and a walk-in shower.

Copyright by designer/architect.

Plan #281022

Dimensions: 48' W x 58' D

Levels: 1

Square Footage: 1,506

Bedrooms: 3

Bathrooms: 2

Foundation: Basement

Materials List Available: Yes

Price Category: C

Images provided by designer/architect.

Rear Elevation

Copyright by designer/architect.

Plan #351011

Dimensions: 73'8" W x 53'2" D

Levels: 1

Square Footage: 2,251

Bedrooms: 3

Bathrooms: 2½

Foundation: Basement, crawl space, or slab

Materials List Available: Yes

Price Category: E

Images provided by designer/architect.

Bonus Room

Copyright by designer/architect.

Plan #201034

Dimensions: 66'10" W x 46'10" D

Levels: 1

Square Footage: 1,660

Bedrooms: 3

Bathrooms: 2

Foundation: Crawl space, slab

Materials List Available: Yes

Price Category: C

Images provided by designer/architect.

Wall Frame Widths

Trim Tip: Depending on the room, widths of wall frames usually vary from wall to wall. This is okay as long as you keep variations as small as possible while trying to maintain dimensions close to the ideal 1:0.635 ratio of the Golden Rectangle. Doors and windows will dictate exceptions to the rule.

Plan #341022

Dimensions: 58'4" W x 31'10" D

Levels: 1

Square Footage: 1,281

Bedrooms: 3

Bathrooms: 2

Foundation: Crawl space, slab, or basement

Materials List Available: Yes

Price Category: B

Images provided by designer/architect.

Plan #141002

Dimensions: 48' W x 29' D
Levels: 1
Square Footage: 1,365
Bedrooms: 3
Bathrooms: 2
Foundation: Slab, basement
Materials List Available: No
Price Category: B

Images provided by designer/architect.

This warm country cottage-style house is perfect for the growing family.

Features:

- Ceiling Height: 8 ft. unless otherwise noted.

- Foyer: Guests will be greeted by a full vaulted ceiling that soars to a height of 11 ft. 8 in.

- Dining Area: This dining area flows from the foyer but is defined by a plant shelf over a column.

- Kitchen: This kitchen is open and spacious, with large windows facing the front of the house so that the cook can keep an eye on the kids playing in the front yard. It includes a pass-through over the sink.

- Master Bedroom: This bedroom is separated from the others to create more privacy. Its distinctive look comes from a ceiling that slopes to flat at 9 ft. 6 in.

- Laundry: For maximum efficiency, the washer and dryer are closeted in the hall of the secondary bedrooms.

Copyright by designer/architect.

Plan #131017

Dimensions: 69'8" W x 39'4" D
Levels: 1
Square Footage: 1,480
Bedrooms: 3
Bathrooms: 2
Foundation: Basement, crawl space, or slab
Materials List Available: Yes
Price Category: C

Images provided by designer/architect.

This fully accessible home is designed for wheelchair access to every area, giving everyone true enjoyment and freedom of movement.

Features:

- **Great Room:** Facing towards the rear, this great room features a volume ceiling that adds to the spacious feeling of the room.

- **Kitchen:** Designed for total convenience and easy work patterns, this kitchen also offers a view out to the covered front porch.

- **Master Bedroom:** Enjoy the quiet in this room which is sure to become your favorite place to relax at the end of the day.

- **Additional Bedrooms:** Both rooms have easy access to a full bath and feature nicely sized closet spaces.

- **Garage:** Use the extra space in this attached garage for storage..

Copyright by designer/architect.

Rear Elevation

Plan #131002

Dimensions: 70'1" W x 60'7" D
Levels: 1
Square Footage: 1,709
Bedrooms: 3
Bathrooms: 2½
Foundation: Basement, crawl space, or slab
Materials List Available: Yes
Price Category: D

Images provided by designer/architect.

COV. PORCH
30'-5" x 8'-0"

FRENCH DR

BUILT IN

DINING RM
14'-0" x 10'-0"

SNACK BAR

TRAY CEIL

MSTR BEDRM
12'-0" x 18'-4"

KITCHEN
14'-8" x 9'-4"

10' HIGH
STEPPED CLG

GREAT RM
14'-0" x 22'-8"

CL

BEDRM #2
10'-0" x 12'-8"

T.V.

BUILT IN

FOYER

BATH

VAULTED CEIL

MSTR BATH

DRSG AREA

STOR

UTIL

CL PANT

CL

LAV

COV. PORCH

BEDRM #3
12'-4" x 12'-0"

LOCATION OF BSMT STAIR

LAUN RM

TWO CAR GARAGE
20'-0" x 21'-0"

Copyright by designer/architect.

Rear View

You'll love the way this angled ranch brings out the best in a corner lot or on a slope.

Features:

- Ceiling Height: 8 ft.

- Front Porch: Hang baskets of plants from the roof of this porch, which is just the right size for a couple of rockers and a side table.

- Dining Room: Well-placed windows flood this room with sunlight during the day and a built-in cabinet gives ample storage space for all your china, linens, and collectables.

- Foyer: Open to the great room, the foyer gives a lovely area to greet your visitors.

- Great Room: A built-in media center surrounds the fireplace where friends and family are sure to gather.

- Master Suite: You'll love the privacy of this somewhat isolated but easily accessed room. Decorate to show off the large bay window and tray ceiling, and enjoy the luxury of a compartmented bathroom.

Living Room

Plan #121012

Dimensions: 40' W x 48'8" D
Levels: 1
Square Footage: 1,195
Bedrooms: 3
Bathrooms: 2
Foundation: Basement
Materials List Available: Yes
Price Category: B

Note: The photographed home has been modified to suit homeowner preferences

Images provided by designer/architect.

This compact one-level home uses an open plan to make the most of its square footage.

Features:

- Ceiling Height: 8 ft.

- Covered Porch: This delightful area, located off the kitchen, provides a private spot to enjoy some fresh air.

- Open Plan: The family room, dining area and kitchen share a big open space to provide a sense of spaciousness. Moving so easily between these interrelated areas provides the convenience demanded by a busy lifestyle.

- Master Suite: An open plan is convenient, but it is still important for everyone to have their private space. The master suite enjoys its own bath and walk-in closet. The secondary bedrooms share a nearby bath.

- Garage: Here you will find parking for two cars and plenty of extra storage space as well.

Copyright by designer/architect.

Rendering reflects floor plan

Images provided by designer/architect.

Copyright by designer/architect.

Plan #211036

Dimensions: 80' W x 40' D

Levels: 1

Square Footage: 1,800

Bedrooms: 3

Bathrooms: 2

Foundation: Slab

Materials List Available: Yes

Price Category: D

SMARTtip

Dimmer Switches

You can dim lights just slightly to extend lamp life and save energy, and there will be very little perceptible change in light level. For instance, dimming the light to 50 percent will be perceived as though the light were only dimmed to 70 percent. Therefore, there is no dramatic dilation or constriction of the eye due to light level change.

Images provided by designer/architect.

Plan #251003

Dimensions: 42' W x 42' D

Levels: 1

Square Footage: 1,393

Bedrooms: 3

Bathrooms: 2

Foundation: Crawl space, slab

Materials List Available: Yes

Price Category: B

Copyright by designer/architect.

Images provided by
designer/architect.

Copyright by designer/architect.

Plan #351008

Dimensions: 64'6" W x 61'4" D

Levels: 1

Square Footage: 2,002

Bedrooms: 3

Bathrooms: 2

Foundation: Basement, crawl space

Materials List Available: Yes

Price Category: D

Images provided by
designer/architect.

Plan #351009

Dimensions: 54' W x 47' D

Levels: 1

Square Footage: 1,400

Bedrooms: 3

Bathrooms: 2

Foundation: Crawl space, slab
(basement option for fee)

Materials List Available: Yes

Price Category: B

**Optional Basement
Floor Plan**

Copyright by designer/architect.

Plan #131035

Dimensions: 65'4" W x 45'10" D
Levels: 1
Square Footage: 1,892
Bedrooms: 3
Bathrooms: 2½
Foundation: Basement, crawl space, or slab
Materials List Available: Yes
Price Category: D

Images provided by designer/architect.

Families who love a mixture of traditional — a big front porch, simple roofline, and bay windows—and contemporary—an open floor plan—will love this charming home.

Features:

- **Great Room:** Central to this home, the open living and entertaining areas allow the family to gather effortlessly and create the perfect spot for entertaining.

- **Dining Room:** Volume ceilings both here and in the great room further enhance the spaciousness the open floor plan creates.

- **Master Suite:** Positioned on the opposite end of the other two bedrooms in the split-bedroom plan, this master suite gives an unusual amount of privacy and quiet in a home of this size.

- **Bonus Room:** Located over the attached garage, this bonus room gives you a place to finish for a study or a separate game room.

Rear Elevation

Bonus Area

Copyright by designer/architect.

Plan #131047

Dimensions: 69'10" W x 51'8" D
Levels: 1
Square Footage: 1,793
Bedrooms: 3
Bathrooms: 2
Foundation: Basement, crawl space, or slab
Materials List Available: Yes
Price Category: C

Images provided by designer/architect.

The country charm of this well-designed home is mixed with the convenience and luxury normally reserved for more contemporary plans.

Features:

• Great Room: The spaciousness of this great room is enhanced by the 11-ft. stepped ceiling. A fireplace makes it cozy on cool evenings or on chilly winter days, and two sets of French sliding glass doors open to the back porch.

• Kitchen: In addition to the convenient layout of this design, you'll also love its bright, airy position. It includes an old-fashioned pantry,

a sink under a window, and a sunny breakfast area that opens to the wraparound porch.

• Master Suite: You'll find 11-ft. ceilings in both the master bedroom and the bayed sitting area that the suite includes. In the bath, the circular spa tub is surrounded by a glass-block wall.

• Bonus Space: A permanent staircase leads to an unfinished bonus space on the upper level.

Copyright by designer/architect.

Rear View

Bonus Area

Plan #131048

Dimensions: 67'6" W x 53'2" D
Levels: 1
Square Footage: 1,579
Bedrooms: 3
Bathrooms: 2
Foundation: Basement, crawl space, or slab
Materials List Available: Yes
Price Category: D

Images provided by designer/architect.

You'll love the country appearance of this expandable ranch, with its covered porch and shuttered windows.

Features:

- **Foyer:** This foyer flows into the great room but gives you a gracious space to welcome guests.

- **Great Room:** Enjoy the 9-ft. ceiling, fireplace, and tall windows in this room, which gives you a view of the front porch.

- **Dining Room:** Adjoining the great room, this dining room opens through French doors to the backyard terrace, making this area ideal

for hosting a party or grilling a family meal.

- **Kitchen:** The dinette in this kitchen area opens to the terrace, and an angled pass-through to the dining room makes entertaining a pleasure.

- **Mudroom:** With access to the garage and terrace, this mudroom also includes laundry facilities.

Copyright by designer/architect.

Plan #301005

Dimensions: 71' W x 42' D
Levels: 1
Square Footage: 1,930
Bedrooms: 3
Bathrooms: 2
Foundation: Crawl space, slab
Materials List Available: Yes
Price Category: D

This home features an old-fashioned rocking-chair porch that enhances the streetscape.

Features:

• Ceiling Height: 8 ft.

• Dining Room: When the weather is warm, guests can step through French doors from this elegant dining room and enjoy a breeze on the rear screened porch.

• Family Room: This family room is a warm and inviting place to gather, with its handsome fireplace and built-in bookcases.

• Kitchen: This kitchen offers plenty of counter space for preparing your favorite recipes. Its U-shape creates a convenient open traffic pattern.

• Master Suite: You'll look forward to retiring at the end of the day in this truly luxurious master suite. The bedroom has a fireplace and opens through French doors to a private rear deck. The bath features a corner spa tub, a walk-in shower, double vanities, and a linen closet.

Images provided by designer/architect.

Copyright by designer/architect.

SMARTtip

Light With Shutters

For the maximum the amount of light coming through shutters, use the largest panel possible on the window. Make sure the shutters have the same number of louvers per panel so that all of the windows in the room look unified. However, don't choose a panel that is over 48 inches high, because the shutter becomes unwieldy. Also, any window that is wider than 96 inches requires extra framing to support the shutters.

Plan #121010

Dimensions: 50' W x 62' D
Levels: 1
Square Footage: 1,902
Bedrooms: 2
Bathrooms: 2
Foundation: Basement
Materials List Available: Yes
Price Category: D

This home is replete with architectural details that provide a convenient and gracious lifestyle.

Features:

• Ceiling Height: 8 ft.

• Great Room: The entry enjoys a long view into this room. Family and friends will be drawn to the warmth of its handsome fireplace flanked by windows.

• Breakfast Area: You'll pass through cased openings from the great room into the cozy breakfast area that will lure the whole family to linger over informal meals.

• Kitchen: Another cased opening leads from the breakfast area into the well-designed kitchen with its convenient island.

• Master Bedroom: To the right of the great room special ceiling details highlight the master bedroom where a cased opening and columns lead to a private sitting area.

• Den/Library: Whether you are listening to music or relaxing with a book, this special room will always enhance your lifestyle.

SMARTtip

Accentuating Your Fireplace with Faux Effects

Experiment with faux effects to add an aged look or a specific style to a fireplace mantel and surround. Craft stores sell inexpensive kits with directions for adding the appearance of antiqued or paneled wood or plaster, rusticated stone, marble, terra cotta, and other effects that make any style achievable.

Plan #241017

Dimensions: 74'4" W x 55'4" D

Levels: 1

Square Footage: 2,431

Bedrooms: 4

Bathrooms: 2½

Foundation: Slab

Materials List Available: No

Price Category: E

The turret, arched window details, and wraparound porch hint at the interesting interior design of this lovely home.

Features:

- **Great Room:** This room features a 12-ft. ceiling, angled walls, a corner fireplace, and sliding doors leading to the rear porch.

- **Dining Room:** Located in the turret, the highlights of this room are the deep bay and 10-ft. ceiling.

- **Morning Room:** The angled walls and windows over the rear porch echo those in the great room.

- **Kitchen:** With an angled snack bar accessible from the great room and morning room, this well-designed kitchen is ideal for the family cooks.

- **Master Suite:** Situated for privacy, the master suite has an angled wall in the bedroom and a door onto the rear porch. The bath has two walk-in closets, two vanities, a garden tub, and a separate shower stall.

Plan #151010

Dimensions: 38'4" W x 68'6" D

Levels: 1

Square Footage: 1,379

Bedrooms: 3

Bathrooms: 2

Foundation: Crawl, slab

Materials List Available: No

Price Category: B

Images provided by designer/architect.

This French Country home has a spacious great room for friends and family to gather, but you can sneak away to the covered rear porch or patio off the master suite for cozy tête-à-têtes.

Features:

- **Entry:** Take advantage of the marvelous 10-ft. ceilings to hang groups of potted flowering plants.

- **Great Room:** This spacious room, with an optional 10-ft. boxed ceiling, is the place to curl up by the gas fireplace on a cold winter night.

- **Kitchen:** The kitchen includes a bar for casual meals, and is open to the breakfast room.

- **Rear Porch:** Enjoy leisurely meals on the covered rear porch that you can access from both the master suite and the breakfast room.

- **Master Suite:** The 10-ft. boxed ceiling in the bedroom and the master bath with a whirlpool tub and separate shower make this suite a luxurious place to end a long day.

Copyright by designer/architect.

Plan #111007

Dimensions: 72' W x 91' D
Levels: 1
Square Footage: 3,668
Bedrooms: 4
Bathrooms: 2½
Foundation: Crawl space
Materials List Available: No
Price Category: H

This Mediterranean-inspired, traditional manor home offers an enormous amount of space and every amenity you can imagine, but to do it justice, site it on a large lot with wonderful views.

Features:

- **Living Room:** With a fireplace and built-in media center, this room has the potential to become a gathering place for guests as well as family members.

- **Kitchen:** Enjoy this well-designed kitchen which will surely have you whistling as you work.

- **Breakfast Area:** Unusually large for a breakfast room, this space invites a crowd at any time of day. French doors at the back of the room open to the gracious rear porch.

- **Master Suite:** Privacy is guaranteed by the location of this spacious suite. The separate walk-in closets give plenty of storage space, and the master bath features separate vanities as well as a large corner whirlpool tub.

Copyright by designer/architect.

Copyright by designer/architect.

Plan #341027

Dimensions: 54' W x 55'10" D

Levels: 1

Square Footage: 1,657

Bedrooms: 3

Bathrooms: 2

Foundation: Crawl space, slab, or basement

Materials List Available: Yes

Price Category: C

Images provided by designer/architect.

SMARTtip

Using a Miter Trimmer

Most pros who use this type of tool hold the molding by hand close to the fence. But watch those fingertips; the blade is extremely sharp.

Plan #341032

Dimensions: 76' W x 38' D

Levels: 1

Square Footage: 1,528

Bedrooms: 3

Bathrooms: 2

Foundation: Crawl space, slab, or basement

Materials List Available: Yes

Price Category: C

Images provided by designer/architect.

Copyright by designer/architect.

Images provided by designer/architect.

Copyright by designer/architect.

Plan #151065

Dimensions: 51' W x 71'4" D

Levels: 1

Square Footage: 1,881

Bedrooms: 3

Bathrooms: 2

Foundation: Crawl space, slab

Materials List Available: No

Price Category: D

Copyright by designer/architect.

Images provided by designer/architect.

Plan #341023

Dimensions: 72'7" W x 34' D

Levels: 1

Square Footage: 1,469

Bedrooms: 3

Bathrooms: 2

Foundation: Crawl space, slab, or basement

Materials List Available: Yes

Price Category: B

Plan #361015

Dimensions: 81' W x 44'2" D

Levels: 1

Square Footage: 1,778

Bedrooms: 3

Bathrooms: 2½

Foundation: Slab

Materials List Available: No

Price Category: C

Images provided by designer/architect.

Optional Basement Stair Location

Copyright by designer/architect.

Plan #361016

Dimensions: 92'4" W x 55' D

Levels: 1

Square Footage: 2,383

Bedrooms: 3

Bathrooms: 2½

Foundation: Crawl space

Materials List Available: No

Price Category: E

Images provided by designer/architect.

Copyright by designer/architect.

Plan #151054

Dimensions: 71'2" W x 54'10" D

Levels: 1

Square Footage: 1,746

Bedrooms: 3

Bathrooms: 2

Foundation: Crawl space, slab, with basement option for fee

Materials List Available: Yes

Price Category: C

Images provided by designer/architect.

Copyright by designer/architect.

SMARTtip

Mixing and Matching Windows

Windows, both fixed and operable, are made in various styles and shapes. While mixing styles should be carefully avoided, a variety of interesting window sizes and shapes may nevertheless be combined to achieve symmetry, harmony, and rhythm on the exterior of a home.

Plan #151057

Dimensions: 73'6" W x 80'6" D

Levels: 1

Square Footage: 2,951

Bedrooms: 4

Bathrooms: 3

Foundation: Crawl space, slab, or basement

Materials List Available: No

Price Category: F

Images provided by designer/architect.

Plan #151170

Dimensions: 57' W x 64'4" D

Levels: 1

Square Footage: 1,965

Bedrooms: 4

Bathrooms: 2

Foundation: Crawl space, slab (basement or walkout basement option for fee)

Materials List Available: No

Price Category: D

Images provided by designer/architect.

The clean lines of the open floor plan and high ceilings match the classic good looks of this home's exterior.

Features:

- Foyer: The 10-ft. ceiling here sets the stage for the open, airy feeling of this lovely home.

- Dining Room: Set off by columns from the foyer and great room, this area is ideal for entertaining.

- Great Room: Open to the breakfast room beyond, this great room features a masonry fireplace and a door to the rear grilling porch.

- Breakfast Room: A deep bay overlooking the porch is the focal point here.

- Kitchen: Planned for efficiency, the kitchen has an angled island with storage and snack bar.

- Master Suite: A boxed ceiling adds elegance to the bedroom, and the bath features a whirlpool tub, double vanity, and separate shower.

Copyright by designer/architect.

Bonus Area

Plan #121050

Dimensions: 64' W x 50' D
Levels: 1
Square Footage: 1,996
Bedrooms: 2
Bathrooms: 2
Foundation: Basement
Materials List Available: Yes
Price Category: D

This compact design includes features usually reserved for larger homes and has styling that is typical of more-exclusive home designs.

Features:

- **Entry:** As you enter this home, you'll see the formal living and dining rooms—both with special ceiling detailing—on either side.

- **Great Room:** Located in the rear of the home for convenience, this great room is likely to be your favorite spot. The fireplace is framed by transom-topped windows, so you'll love curling up here, no matter what the weather or time of day.

- **Kitchen:** Ample counter and cabinet space make this kitchen a dream in which to work.

- **Master Suite:** A tray ceiling and lovely corner windows create an elegant feeling in the bedroom, and two walk-in closets make it easy to keep this space tidy and organized. The private bath has a skylight, corner whirlpool tub, and two separate vanities.

Plan #151070

Dimensions: 54'2" W x 57'4" D

Levels: 1

Square Footage: 1,786

Bedrooms: 3

Bathrooms: 2

Foundation: Crawl space, slab (basement option for fee)

Materials List Available: No

Price Category: C

Images provided by designer/architect.

Copyright by designer/architect.

SMARTtip

Using Wall Anchors

Where a pilaster doesn't fall over a stud, use a combination of construction adhesive and an anchor-type fastener.

Plan #341043

Dimensions: 44'7" W x 50' D

Levels: 1

Square Footage: 1,213

Bedrooms: 3

Bathrooms: 2

Foundation: Crawl space, slab (basement option for fee)

Materials List Available: Yes

Price Category: B

Images provided by designer/architect.

Copyright by designer/architect.

Plan #341021

Dimensions: 40' W x 35' D

Levels: 1

Square Footage: 1,208

Bedrooms: 3

Bathrooms: 2

Foundation: Crawl space, slab, or basement

Materials List Available: Yes

Price Category: B

Images provided by designer/architect.

DECK

BEDROOM 3
11'-8"X10'-0"

KITCHEN
15'-6"X11'-4"

DW

DINING

LN

BA. 2

COAT

VAULTED
CEILING

D

W

GREAT ROOM
14'-8"X12'-4"

BEDROOM 1
12'-7"X15'-0"

BEDROOM 2
11'-8"X11'-0"

PORCH

35'-0"

40'-0"

Copyright by designer/architect.

Plan #341019

Dimensions: 44' W x 32' D

Levels: 1

Square Footage: 1,258

Bedrooms: 3

Bathrooms: 2

Foundation: Crawl space, slab, or basement

Materials List Available: Yes

Price Category: B

Images provided by designer/architect.

SMARTtip

Resin Outdoor Furniture

Resin furniture is made of molded plastic. Most resin pieces are quite affordable, but lacquered resin with brass fittings is a high-end item. Resin doesn't corrode and cleans easily, but a scratched finish cannot be repaired. Lacquered resin can be touched up, however.

DECK
10'-0" X 10'-0"

BEDROOM 3
10'-0" X 10'-2"

CLOSET

COATS

RANGE

SINK

DW

KITCHEN/DINING
15'-9" X 10'-2"

REF

WASH

DRY

SHWR

WH

BATH 1

GARDEN TUB

BATH 2

CLOSET

LINENS

BEDROOM 2
11'-0" X 10'-2"

CLOSET

FAMILY ROOM
15'-9" X 15'-7"

VAULTED CEILING

MASTER SUITE
13'-3" X 16'-5"

PORCH

32'-0"

44'-0"

Copyright by designer/architect.

Plan #171003

Dimensions: 69' W x 64' D

Levels: 1

Square Footage: 2,098

Bedrooms: 4

Bathrooms: 3

Foundation: Slab, crawl space

Materials List Available: Yes

Price Category: D

Images provided by designer/architect.

Copyright by designer/architect.

Plan #171010

Dimensions: 76' W x 61' D

Levels: 1

Square Footage: 1,972

Bedrooms: 3

Bathrooms: 2

Foundation: Slab, crawl space

Materials List Available: Yes

Price Category: D

Images provided by designer/architect.

Copyright by designer/architect.

SMARTtip

Testing Grill Hoses for Leaks

Hoses on gas grills can develop leaks. To check the hose on your gas grill, brush soapy water over it. If you see any bubbles, turn off the gas valve and disconnect the tank. Then replace the hose.

Images provided by designer/architect.

Plan #341029

Dimensions: 49' W x 57' D

Levels: 1

Square Footage: 1,737

Bedrooms: 3

Bathrooms: 2

Foundation: Crawl space, slab, or basement

Materials List Available: Yes

Price Category: C

Copyright by designer/architect.

Images provided by designer/architect.

Plan #341028

Dimensions: 40' W x 32' D

Levels: 1

Square Footage: 1,248

Bedrooms: 3

Bathrooms: 2

Foundation: Crawl space, slab, or basement

Materials List Available: Yes

Price Category: B

Copyright by designer/architect.

Images provided by designer/architect.

Copyright by designer/architect.

Plan #111016

Dimensions: 72' W x 76' D

Levels: 1

Square Footage: 2,240

Bedrooms: 3

Bathrooms: 2½

Foundation: Basement

Materials List Available: No

Price Category: E

Rear View

Images provided by designer/architect.

Copyright by designer/architect.

Plan #111017

Dimensions: 61' W x 70' D

Levels: 1

Square Footage: 2,323

Bedrooms: 3

Bathrooms: 2½

Foundation: Monolithic slab

Materials List Available: No

Price Category: E

Plan #111015

Dimensions: 64' W x 58' D

Levels: 1

Square Footage: 2,208

Bedrooms: 4

Bathrooms: 2½

Foundation: Crawl space

Materials List Available: No

Price Category: E

Images provided by designer/architect.

Copyright by designer/architect.

Copyright by designer/architect.

Plan #121055

Dimensions: 51' W x 52' D

Levels: 1

Square Footage: 1,622

Bedrooms: 3

Bathrooms: 2

Foundation: Basement

Materials List Available: Yes

Price Category: C

Images provided by designer/architect.

Optional Third Bedroom Floor Plan

Color

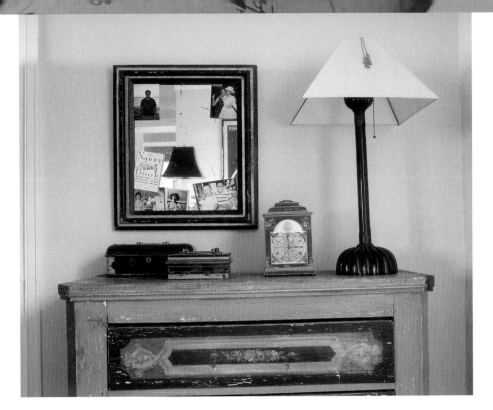

No other decorating component has more power and greater effect at such little cost than color. It can fill a space and make furnishings look fresh and new. Color can also show off fine architectural details or downplay a room's structural flaws. A particular color can make a cold room cozy, while another hue can cool down a sunny cooker. And color comes cheap, giving a tremendous impact for your decorating dollar: elbow grease, supplies, prep work, and paint will all cost pretty much the same if you choose a gorgeous hue over plain white.

But finding the color—the right color—isn't easy. Where do you begin to look? Like the economy, color has leading indicators. You have a market basket full of choices, and there are lots of signposts to direct you where to go.

The Lay of the Land

For the past 200 years, white has been the most popular choice for American home exteriors. And it still is, followed by tan, brown, and beige. You can play it safe and follow the leader. But you should also think about the architecture of your house and where you live when you're considering exterior color. For example, traditional Colonials have a color-combination range of about two that look appropriate: white with black or green shutters and gray with white trim. Mediterranean-style houses typically pick up the colors of terra-cotta and the tile that are indigenous to the regions that developed the architecture—France, Italy, and Spain. A ranch-style house shouldn't be overdone—it is, after all, usually a modest structure. On the other hand, a cottage can be fanciful. Whimsical colors also look charming on Victorian houses in San Francisco, but they would be out of place in conservative Scarsdale, New York, where you must

check with the local building board even when you want to change the exterior color of your house.

How's the Weather?

Like exteriors, interiors often take their color cues from their environs and local traditions. In the rainy and often chilly Pacific Northwest, cozy blanket plaids in strong reds and black abound. In the hot-and-arid climate of the West, indigo or brown ticking-stripes and faded denim look appropriately casual and cool. Subtle grays and neutrals, reflecting steel, limestone, and concrete, look apropos for sophisticated city life. In extremely warm southern climates, the brilliant sun tends to overpower lighter colors. That explains the popularity of strong hues in tropical, sun-drenched locales.

Natural Light. That's the one you don't pay for. Its direction and intensity greatly affects color. A room with a window that faces trees will look markedly different in summer, when warm white sunlight is filtered through the leaves, than in winter, when the trees are bare and the color of natural light takes on a cool blue cast. Time of day affects color, too. Yellow walls that are pleasant and cheerful in the early morning can be stifling and blinding in the afternoon. That's because afternoon

The yellow-colored wall, above, complements the antique painted dresser.

Warm neutral-color walls, opposite, and touches of red make this bedroom cozy.

sun is stronger than morning sun.

When you're choosing a color for an interior, always view it at different times of day, but especially during the hours in which you will inhabit the room.

Artificial Light. Because artificial light affects color rendition as much as natural light, don't judge a color in the typically chilly fluorescence of a hardware store. The very same color chip will look completely different when you bring it home, which is why it's so important to test out a paint color in your own home. Most fluorescent light is bluish and distorts colors. It depresses red and exaggerates green, for example. A romantic faded rose on your dining room walls will just wash out in the kitchen if your use a fluorescent light there. Incandescent light, the type produced by the standard bulbs you probably use in your chandelier and in most of your home's light fixtures, is warm but slightly yellow. Halogen light, which comes from another newer type of incandescent bulb, is white and the closest to natural sunlight. Of all three types of bulbs, halogen is truest in rendering color.

red

RED is powerful, dramatic, motivating. Red is also hospitable, and it stimulates the appetite, which makes it a favorite choice for dining rooms. Some studies have indicated that a red room actually makes people feel warmer.

yellow

YELLOW illuminates the colors it surrounds. It warms rooms that receive northern light but can be too bright in a sunny room. It's best for daytime rooms, not bedrooms. It has a short range, which means as white is added to yellow, it disappears. Yellow highlights and calls attention to features—think of bright taxicabs.

green

GREEN is tranquil, nurturing, rejuvenating. It is a psychological primary, and because it is mixed from yellow and blue, it can appear both warm and cool. Time seems to pass more quickly in green rooms. Perhaps that's why waiting rooms off-stage are called "green rooms."

neutrals

GRAY goes with all colors—it is a good neighbor. Various tones of gray range from dark charcoal to pale oyster.

BLACK (technically the absence of color) enhances and brightens other colors, making for livelier decorating schemes when used as an accent.

pink

PINK is perceived as outgoing and active. It's also a color that flatters skin tones. Hot shades are invigorating, while soft, toned-down versions can be relaxed and charming.

order direct: 1-800-523-6789

blue

BLUE, with its associations of sea and sky, offers serenity, which is why it is a favorite in bedrooms. Studies have shown that people think better in blue rooms. Perhaps that explains the popularity of the navy blue suit. Cooler blues show this color's melancholy side, however.

Plan #211002

Dimensions: 68' W x 62' D
Levels: 1
Square Footage: 1,792
Bedrooms: 3
Bathrooms: 2
Foundation: Crawl space
Materials List Available: Yes
Price Category: C

Arched windows on the front of this home give it a European style that you're sure to love.

SMARTtip

Water Features

Water features create the ambiance of a soothing oasis on a deck. A water-filled urn becomes a mirror that reflects the sky—making a small deck look larger. Fish flashing in an ornamental pool add color and act as a focal point for a deck with no view.

A water fountain introduces a pleasant rhythmical sound that helps drown out the background noises of traffic and nearby neighbors.

Features:

• Living Room: The 12-ft. ceiling in this large, open room enhances its spacious feeling. A fireplace adds warmth on chilly days and cool evenings.

• Dining Room: Decorate to accentuate the 12-ft. ceiling and formal feeling of this room.

• Kitchen: Designed for comfort and efficiency, this room also has a 12-ft. ceiling. The cozy breakfast bar is a natural gathering spot for friends and family.

• Master Suite: A split design guarantees privacy here. A sloped cathedral ceiling adds elegance, and a walk-in closet makes it practical. The bath has two vanities, a tub, and a walk-in shower.

• Garage: Park two cars here, and use the balance of this 520 sq. ft. area as a handy storage area.

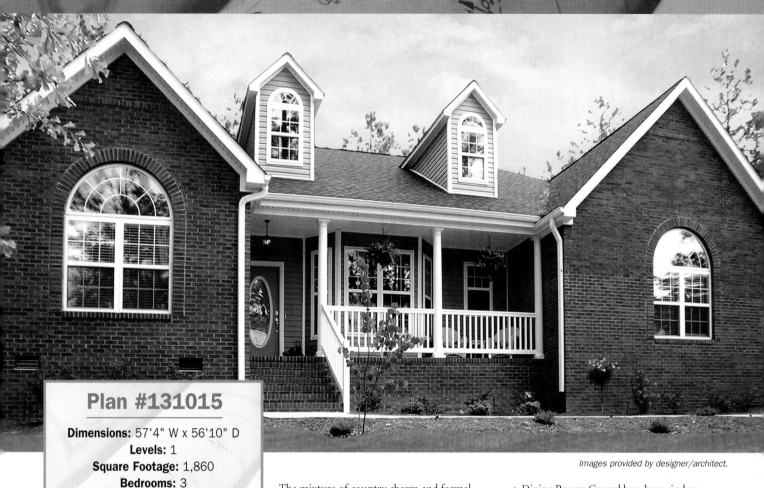

Plan #131015

Dimensions: 57'4" W x 56'10" D
Levels: 1
Square Footage: 1,860
Bedrooms: 3
Bathrooms: 2
Foundation: Basement, crawl space, or slab
Materials List Available: Yes
Price Category: D

Images provided by designer/architect.

The mixture of country charm and formal elegance is sure to thrill any family looking for a distinctive and comfortable home.

Features:

- Great Room: Separated from the dining room by a columned arch, this spacious room has a stepped ceiling, a built-in media center, and a fireplace. French doors within a rear bay lead to the large backyard patio at the rear of the house.

- Dining Room: Graced by a bay window, this formal room has an impressive 11-ft. 6-in.-high stepped ceiling.

- Breakfast Room: With a 12-ft. sloped ceiling, this room shares an eating bar with the kitchen.

- Master Bedroom: The 10-ft. tray ceiling and bay window contribute elegance, and the walk-in closet and bath with a bayed nook, whirlpool tub, and separate shower make it practical.

Copyright by designer/architect.

Rear Elevation

Great Room

Plan #151108

Dimensions: 84'6" W x 58'6" D
Levels: 1
Square Footage: 2,742
Bedrooms: 4
Bathrooms: 2½
Foundation: Crawl space, slab, or basement
Materials List Available: No
Price Category: F

Images provided by designer/architect.

Optional Bonus Space Floor Plan

Plan #151109

Dimensions: 59'9" W x 64'7" D
Levels: 1
Square Footage: 2,132
Bedrooms: 3
Bathrooms: 2
Foundation: Crawl space, slab (basement option for fee)
Materials List Available: Yes
Price Category: D

Images provided by designer/architect.

Optional Bonus Space Floor Plan

Plan #221005

Dimensions: 72' W x 42' D

Levels: 1

Square Footage: 1,868

Bedrooms: 3

Bathrooms: 2

Foundation: Basement

Materials List Available: No

Price Category: D

Images provided by designer/architect.

Rear Elevation

Copyright by designer/architect.

Plan #221006

Dimensions: 59' W x 58' D

Levels: 1

Square Footage: 1,756

Bedrooms: 3

Bathrooms: 2

Foundation: Basement

Materials List Available: No

Price Category: C

Images provided by designer/architect.

Rear Elevation

Copyright by designer/architect.

Plan #151058

Dimensions: 58'8" W x 58'6" D

Levels: 1

Square Footage: 1,854

Bedrooms: 4

Bathrooms: 2

Foundation: Crawl space, slab (basement option for fee)

Materials List Available: No

Price Category: D

Plan #341024

Dimensions: 49'6" W x 39'8" D

Levels: 1

Square Footage: 1,310

Bedrooms: 3

Bathrooms: 2

Foundation: Crawl space, slab, or basement

Materials List Available: Yes

Price Category: B

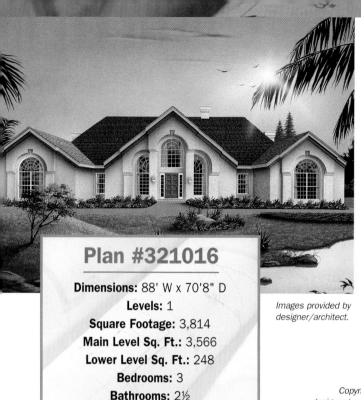

Plan #321016

Dimensions: 88' W x 70'8" D

Levels: 1

Square Footage: 3,814

Main Level Sq. Ft.: 3,566

Lower Level Sq. Ft.: 248

Bedrooms: 3

Bathrooms: 2½

Foundation: Daylight basement

Materials List Available: Yes

Price Category: H

Images provided by designer/architect.

Rear View

Copyright by designer/architect.

Images provided by designer/architect.

Plan #321026

Dimensions: 67' W x 42'4" D

Levels: 1

Square Footage: 1,712

Bedrooms: 3

Bathrooms: 2½

Foundation: Crawl space

Materials List Available: Yes

Price Category: C

Copyright by designer/architect.

SMARTtip

Deck Design with Computers

Consider using a computer-aided design (CAD) program to plan your deck. Some programs let you see three-dimensional views of your design complete with railings, stairs, planters, hot tubs, and the surrounding landscaping.

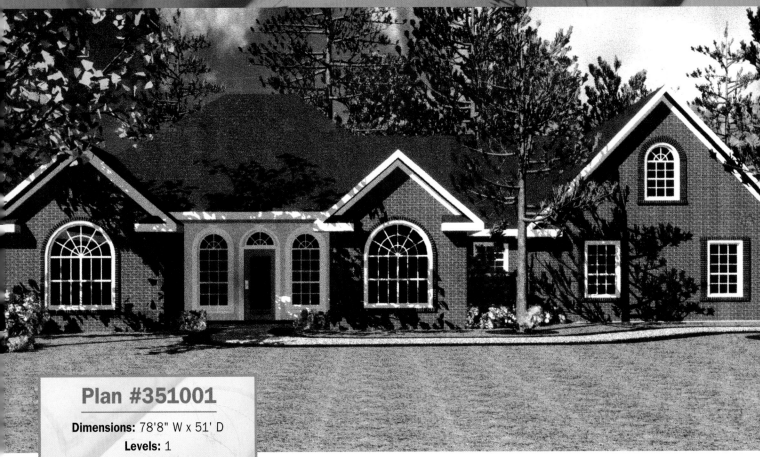

Plan #351001

Dimensions: 78'8" W x 51' D
Levels: 1
Square Footage: 1,855
Bedrooms: 3
Bathrooms: 2½
Foundation: Basement, crawl space, or slab
Materials List Available: Yes
Price Category: D

Images provided by designer/architect.

From the lovely arched windows on the front to the front and back covered porches, this home is as comfortable as it is beautiful.

Features:

• **Great Room:** Come into this room with 12-ft. ceilings, and you're sure to admire the corner gas stove and three windows overlooking the porch.

• **Dining Room:** Set off from the open design, this room is designed to be used formally or not.

• **Kitchen:** You'll love the practical walk-in pantry, broom closet, and angled snack bar here.

• **Breakfast Room:** Brightly lit and leading to the covered porch, this room will be a favorite spot.

• **Bonus Room:** Develop a playroom or study in this area.

• **Master Suite:** The large bedroom is complemented by the private bath with garden tub, separate shower, double vanity, and spacious walk-in closet.

Copyright by designer/architect.

Kitchen/Great Room

Plan #211040

Dimensions: 66' W x 60' D
Levels: 1
Square Footage: 1,800
Bedrooms: 3
Bathrooms: 2
Foundation: Slab
Materials List Available: Yes
Price Category: D

Images provided by designer/architect.

Copyright by designer/architect.

This Louisiana-style raised cottage features shuttered windows and a tin roof.

Features:

• **Front Porch:** You'll enjoy cool summer breezes on this generous and relaxing front porch, which adds to the nostalgic appeal of this Creole classic.

• **French Doors:** These elegant doors lead from the front porch to the formal living areas and the front bedroom.

• **Master Bedroom Suite:** You'll enjoy the open space, walk-in closet, and master bath amenities.

SMARTtip

Folding and Draping Swags

Plaids and stripes are a traditional choice for swags and jabots. But how they are folded and draped has a significant effect on the resulting overall pattern. For example, the lines can be positioned to be vertical and horizontal, or they can be draped as a diagonal. In addition, installing the darker-value stripes as the outer part of the pleat will create a totally different look from the one produced by setting the lighter value there. Try folding the fabric in different ways and pleat depths before you finally decide on the look that you prefer.

Plan #161001

Dimensions: 67'2" W x 47' D

Levels: 1

Square Footage: 1,782

Bedrooms: 3

Bathrooms: 2

Foundation: Basement

Materials List Available: Yes

Price Category: C

Images provided by designer/architect.

An all-brick exterior displays the solid strength that characterizes this gracious home.

Features:

• Gathering Area: A feeling of spaciousness permeates this gathering area, created by the foyer, great room, and dining room. Multiple windows provide natural light that dances along a sloped ceiling, spilling onto decorative columns and a fireplace.

• Breakfast Area: A continuation of the sloped ceiling leads to this breakfast area, where French doors open to a screened porch.

• Kitchen: An abundance of cabinets and counter space are the hallmarks of this large kitchen, with its easy access to a spacious laundry room and storage area.

• Master Suite: A tray ceiling and spacious walk-in closet in the master bedroom, along with a whirlpool tub and double-bowl vanity in the bathroom, enable you to pamper yourself.

Copyright by designer/architect.

Rear Elevation

Left Side Elevation

Right Side Elevation

Front View

Great Room / Foyer

Plan #151004

Dimensions: 64'8" W x 62'1" D

Levels: 1

Square Footage: 2,158

Bedrooms: 4

Bathrooms: 2½

Foundation: Basement, slab, crawl space

Materials List Available: No

Price Category: D

Images provided by designer/architect.

You'll love the spacious feeling in this comfortable home designed for a family.

Features:

• Foyer: A 10-ft. ceiling greets you in this home.

• Great Room: A 10-ft. ceiling complements this large room, with its fireplace, built-in cabinets, and easy access to the rear covered porch.

• Dining Room: The 9-ft. boxed ceiling in this large room helps to create a beautiful formal feeling.

• Kitchen: The island in this kitchen is open to the breakfast room for true convenience.

• Breakfast Room: Morning light will stream through the bay window here.

• Master Suite: A 9-ft. pan ceiling adds a distinctive note to this room with access to the rear porch. In the bath, you'll find a whirlpool tub, separate shower, double vanities, and two walk-in closets.

MAIN FLOOR

Copyright by designer/architect.

Plan #121004

Dimensions: 55'4" W x 48' D

Levels: 1

Square Footage: 1,666

Bedrooms: 3

Bathrooms: 2

Foundation: Basement

Materials List Available: Yes

Price Category: C

An efficient floor plan and plenty of amenities create a luxurious lifestyle.

Features:

• Ceiling Height: 8 ft. except as noted.

• Entry: Enjoy summer breezes on the porch; then step inside the entry where sidelights and an arched transom create a bright, cheery welcome.

• Great Room: The 10-ft. ceiling and the transom-topped windows flooding the room with light provide a sense of spaciousness. The fireplace adds warmth and style.

• Dining Room: You'll usher your guests into this room located just off the great room.

• Breakfast Area: Also located off the great room, the breakfast area offers another dining option.

• Master Suite: The master bedroom is highlighted by a tray ceiling and a large walk-in closet. Luxuriate in the private bath with its sunlit whirlpool, separate shower, and double vanity.

Images provided by designer/architect.

Copyright by designer/architect.

SMARTtip

Carpeting

Install the best underlayment padding available, as well as the highest grade of carpeting you can afford. This will guarantee a feeling of softness beneath your feet and protect your investment for years to come by reducing wear and tear on the carpet.

Plan #211004

Dimensions: 64' W x 62' D
Levels: 1
Square Footage: 1,828
Bedrooms: 4
Bathrooms: 2
Foundation: Slab, crawl space, basement
Materials List Available: Yes
Price Category: D

This super-energy-efficient home has the curb appeal of a much larger house.

Features:

- Ceiling Height: 9 ft.

- Kitchen: You will love cooking in this bright, airy, and efficient kitchen. It features an angled layout that allows a great view to the outside through a window wall in the breakfast area.

- Breakfast Area: With morning sunlight streaming through the wall of windows in

this area, you won't be able to resist lingering over a cup of coffee.

- Rear Porch: This breezy rear porch is designed to accommodate the pleasure of old-fashioned rockers or swings.

- Master Bedroom: Retreat at the end of a long day to this bedroom, which is isolated for privacy yet conveniently located a few steps from the kitchen and utility area.

- Attic Storage: No need to fuss with creaky pull-down stairs. This attic has a permanent stairwell to provide easy access to its abundant storage.

SMARTtip

Resin Furniture

Resin furniture is made of molded plastic. Most resin pieces are quite affordable, but lacquered resin with brass fittings is a high-end item. Resin doesn't corrode and cleans easily, but a scratched finish cannot be repaired. However, lacquered resin can be touched up.

Copyright by designer/architect.

Plan #271063

Dimensions: 62' W x 70' D

Levels: 1

Square Footage: 2,572

Bedrooms: 3

Bathrooms: 2

Foundation: Daylight basement

Materials List Available: No

Price Category: E

Images provided by designer/architect.

European detailing gives this home a unique flair and elegant curb appeal.

Features:

• Entry Rotunda: This welcoming area opens to a quiet den with a cozy fireplace.

• Living Room: This open space leads back to a wall of windows overlooking a backyard deck.

• Country Kitchen: A central island and dramatic overhead glass make for a great spot for meal preparation and eating. A four-season porch is nearby.

• Master Suite: Double doors and a coffered ceiling enhance this secluded suite. The private bath has everything you can imagine, including a whirlpool tub.

Copyright by designer/architect.

**Basement Level
Floor Plan**

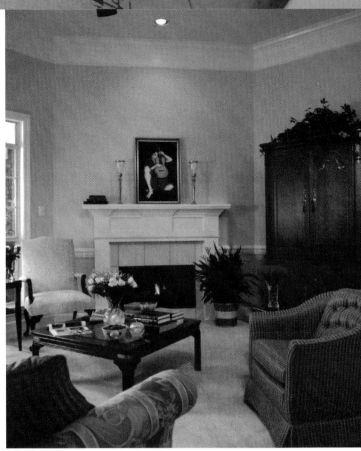

Plan #111051

Dimensions: 72' W x 91' D

Levels: 1

Square Footage: 3,668

Bedrooms: 4

Bathrooms: 2½

Foundation: Crawl space

Materials List Available: No

Price Category: H

You'll find everything you want in this traditional cottage-style home, and it's all on one floor!

Features:

- Living Room: Both this room and the dining room are just off the foyer for convenience. A corner fireplace and windows overlooking the backyard give character to the room.

- Kitchen: The kitchen island contains a sink and dishwasher as well as a bar. A nearby hall way leads to a half-bath, the utility room, and the two-car garage.

- Breakfast Area: Adjacent to the kitchen, the large breakfast area leads to the back porch.

- Master Suite: Featuring a walk-in closet and bath with a garden tub, standing shower, and private toilet area, this room opens to the back porch.

- Additional Bedrooms: Walk-in closets in two bedrooms and a wide closet with a double door in the third provide good storage space.

Kitchen/Breakfast Area

Plan #211006

Dimensions: 61' W x 77' D
Levels: 1
Square Footage: 2,177
Bedrooms: 3
Bathrooms: 2
Foundation: Slab, optional basement
Materials List Available: Yes
Price Category: D

SMARTtip

DECK Furniture Style

Mix-and-match tabletops, frames, and legs are stylish. Combine materials such as glass, metal, wood, and mosaic tiles.

This traditional home with a stucco exterior is distinguished by its 9-ft. ceilings throughout and its sleek, contemporary interior.

Features:

- **Living Room:** A series of arched openings that surround this room adds strong visual interest. Settle down by the fireplace on cold winter nights.

- **Dining Room:** Step up to enter this room with a raised floor that sets it apart from other areas.

- **Kitchen:** Ideal for cooking as well as casual socializing, this kitchen has a stovetop island and a breakfast bar.

- **Master Suite:** The sitting area in this suite is so big that you might want to watch TV here or make it a study. In the bath, you'll find a skylight above the angled tub with a mirror surround and well-placed plant ledge.

- **Rear Porch:** This 200-sq.-ft. covered porch gives you plenty of space for entertaining.

Copyright by designer/architect.

GARAGE
23 x 31

PORCH

w
d
H
P

wh

BEDROOM
10 x 15

BEDROOM
10 x 15

BEDROOM
16 x 16

loft over

pass-thru

KIT.
16 x 13

LIV./ DINING
19 x 25

PORCH

Images provided by designer/architect.

Plan #381010

Dimensions: 62' W x 87'6" D
Levels: 1
Square Footage: 1,905
Main Level Sq. Ft.: 1,905
Opt. Bonus Level Sq. Ft.: 320
Bedrooms: 3
Bathrooms: 2
Foundation: Crawl space
Materials List Available: Yes
Price Category: D

GRILLING PORCH
19'-8" X 8'-0"

BEDROOM 4
11'-8" X 11'-0"

HEARTH ROOM
19'-4" X 12'-10"

BEDROOM 3
11'-0" X 11'-6"

MASTER SUITE
14'-10" X 15'-4"

GREAT RM.
17'-0" X 21'-8"

KITCHEN
12'-4" X 11'-8"

BATH

M. BATH
14'-2" X 18'-8"

FOYER

DINING RM.
11'-0" X 13'-2"

LAU. / HOBBY
10'-4" X 6'-4"

BEDROOM 2
11'-8" X 12'-0"

ENTRY PORCH
10'-8" X 7'-0"

GARAGE
22'-4" X 23'-2"

Images provided by designer/architect.

Plan #151048

Dimensions: 60'6" W x 69'2" D
Levels: 1
Square Footage: 2,238
Bedrooms: 4
Bathrooms: 2
Foundation: Crawl space, slab (basement option for fee)
Materials List Available: Yes
Price Category: E

Plan #151046

Dimensions: 63'4" W x 59'10" D

Levels: 1

Square Footage: 2,525

Bedrooms: 3

Bathrooms: 2½

Foundation: Crawl space, slab, or basement

Materials List Available: No

Price Category: E

Images provided by designer/architect.

Copyright by designer/architect.

Plan #151047

Dimensions: 69'2" W x 63'9" D

Levels: 1

Square Footage: 2,422

Bedrooms: 3

Bathrooms: 2½

Foundation: Crawl space, slab (walkout or basement option for fee)

Materials List Available: Yes

Price Category: E

Images provided by designer/architect.

Copyright by designer/architect.

Images provided by designer/architect.

Plan #121003

Dimensions: 76' W x 55'4" D
Levels: 1
Square Footage: 2,498
Bedrooms: 4
Bathrooms: 2½
Foundation: Basement,
(crawlspace or slab option for fee)
Materials List Available: Yes
Price Category: E

Repeated arches bring style and distinction to the interior and exterior of this spacious home.

Features:

- Ceiling Height: 8 ft. except as noted.

- Den: A decorative volume ceiling helps make this spacious retreat the perfect place to relax after a long day.

- Formal Living Room: The decorative volume ceiling carries through to the living room that invites large formal gatherings.

- Formal Dining Room: There's plenty of room for all the guests to move into this gracious formal space that also features a decorative volume ceiling.

- Master Suite: Retire to this suite with its glamorous bayed whirlpool, his and her vanities, and a walk-in closet.

- Optional Sitting Room: With the addition of French doors, one of the bedrooms can be converted into a sitting room for the master suite.

Copyright by designer/architect.

Plan #211005

Dimensions: 68' W x 64' D

Levels: 1

Square Footage: 2,000

Bedrooms: 3

Bathrooms: 2

Foundation: Slab

Materials List Available: Yes

Price Category: D

A brick veneer exterior complements the columned porch to make this a striking home.

SMARTtip

Do-It-Yourself Ponds

To avoid disturbing utility lines, contact your utility companies before doing any digging. Locate a freestanding container pond on your deck near an existing (GFCI) outlet. For an in-ground pond, have an electrician run a buried line and install a GFCI outlet near the pond so you can plug in a pump or fountain.

Features:

- Ceiling Height: 9 ft. unless otherwise noted.

- Living Room: From the front porch, the foyer unfolds into this expansive living room. Family and friends will be drawn to the warmth of the living room's cozy fireplace.

- Formal Dining Room: This elegant room is designed for dinner parties of any size.

- Kitchen: Located between the formal dining room and the dinette, the kitchen can serve formal meals as easily as quick family repasts.

- Master Suite: There's plenty of room to unwind at the end of a long day in the huge master bedroom. Luxuriate in the private bath, with its spa tub, separate shower, dual sinks, and two walk-in closets.

- Home Office: The home office, accessible from the master bedroom, is the perfect quiet spot to work, study, or pay the bills.

Copyright by designer/architect.

Plan #211041

Dimensions: 49' W x 64' D
Levels: 1
Square Footage: 1,891
Bedrooms: 3
Bathrooms: 2
Foundation: Slab
Materials List Available: Yes
Price Category: D

Images provided by designer/architect.

Privacy is possible in an urban setting, thanks to an entry courtyard and covered rear porch.

Features:

- Ceiling Height: 9 ft. unless otherwise noted.

- Kitchen: The innovative interior design of this home centers on this unique kitchen, which directs traffic away from the working areas while still serving the entire home.

- Family Room: Family and friends will be drawn to this casual sunken family room with its soaring 14-ft. vaulted ceiling and its handsome, warming fireplace.

- Formal Living Room: This room is designed and placed in such a way that it can easily become a third bedroom, den, office or study room, depending on your family's needs and lifestyle.

- Master Suite: This is the perfect retreat at the end of the busy day. The bedroom offers a large walk-in closet. The sumptuous master bath features an oversize shower and a whirlpool tub.

Copyright by designer/architect.

SMARTtip

Window Treatment Trims

If conventional trims and braids don't excite you, look for untraditional or unusual elements for decorating your window treatments. Attach single beads, small shells, or crystal drops at regular intervals along the edge. Either glue them in place or, if they have holes, sew them on. A series of stars, leaves, or some other appropriate shape made of stiffened fabric and then glued or stitched on is another idea. Consider old or new buttons, jewelry, or metal chains. If your embroidery skills are good, use them to embellish the window treatment.

Plan #121051

Dimensions: 64' W x 44' D

Levels: 1

Square Footage: 1,808

Bedrooms: 3

Bathrooms: 2½

Foundation: Basement

Materials List Available: Yes

Price Category: D

Images provided by designer/architect.

You'll love the way that natural light pours into this home from the gorgeous windows you'll find in room after room.

Features:

• Great Room: You'll notice the bayed, transom-topped window in the great room as soon as you step into this lovely home. A wet-bar makes this great room a natural place for entertaining, and the see-through fireplace makes it cozy on chilly days and winter evenings.

• Kitchen: This well-designed kitchen will be a delight for everyone who cooks here, not only because of the ample counter and cabinet space but also because of its location in the home.

• Master Suite: Angled ceilings in both the bedroom and the bathroom of this suite make it feel luxurious, and the picturesque window in the bedroom gives it character. The bath includes a corner whirlpool tub where you'll love to relax at the end of the day.

Copyright by designer/architect.

Plan #211052

Dimensions: 49' W x 74' D
Levels: 1
Square Footage: 2,111
Bedrooms: 3
Bathrooms: 2
Foundation: Slab, crawl space
Materials List Available: No
Price Category: D

This Florida-style home offers convenient gracious living on one level.

Features:

• Ceiling Height: 9 ft. unless otherwise noted.

• Kitchen: You'll love cooking in this kitchen, thanks to its efficient, innovative layout. Its unusual shape makes the kitchen the heart of this design.

• Family Room: This comfortable, informal room features a 6-in. sunken floor complemented by a sloped ceiling with exposed beams. The massive fireplace is flanked by built-in bookshelves, so you can curl up by the fire with a good book.

• Master Suite: This large bedroom provides plenty of room to relax at the end of a hectic day, and the luxurious bathroom features his and her walk-in closets.

SMARTtip

General and Task Lighting Outdoors

General lighting also known as ambient lighting, provides overall diffused illumination. Ceiling lights and wall sconces are good examples of the types of fixtures that can typically provide general lighting. Post-and-rail lighting on a deck may also satisfy this function, but space the fixtures evenly around the deck for the best advantage.

Task lighting illuminates a specific area or activity. In an "outdoor room" like a screened deck, for example, you'll want to use the space during summer evenings as well as on sunny days. That means you'll need good task lighting for an outdoor food-preparation and cooking area. Keep task lights on a switch that you can control separately from other types of outdoor light sources. Flood mounts or cylinder lights, which are typically used for general lighting, can accommodate task-lighting needs because they help to focus and direct light beams.

Plan #121052

Dimensions: 56' W x 70' D
Levels: 1
Square Footage: 2,093
Bedrooms: 4
Bathrooms: 2
Foundation: Basement
Materials List Available: Yes
Price Category: D

You'll love this one story home with all the amenities that usually go with a larger home with more levels.

Features:

- Entry: As you enter this home, you'll have a long view into the great room, letting you feel welcome right away.

- Great Room: Enjoy the fireplace in this large room during cool evenings, and during the day, bask in the sunlight streaming through the arched windows that flank the fireplace.

- Den: French doors from the great room open into this room that features a spider-beamed ceiling.

- Kitchen: An island, pantry, and built-in desk make this kitchen a versatile work space. It includes a lovely breakfast area, too, that opens into the backyard.

- Master Suite: This secluded suite features an angled ceiling in the private bathroom.

Images provided by designer/architect.

Plan #101010

Dimensions: 70' W x 47' D

Levels: 1

Square Footage: 2,187

Bedrooms: 4

Bathrooms: 2½

Foundation: Slab, crawl space, or basement

Materials List Available: Yes

Price Category: D

This stately ranch features a brick-and-stucco exterior, layered trim, and copper roofing returns.

Features:

• Ceiling Height: 11 ft. unless otherwise noted.

• Special Ceilings: Vaulted and raised ceilings adorn the living room, family room, dining room, foyer, kitchen, breakfast room, and master suite.

• Kitchen: This roomy kitchen is brightened by an abundance of windows.

• Breakfast Room: Located off the kitchen, this breakfast room is the perfect spot for informal family meals.

• Master Suite: This truly exceptional master suite features a bath, and a spacious walk in closet.

• Morning Porch: Step out of the master bedroom, and greet the day on this lovely porch.

• Additional Bedrooms: The three additional bedrooms each measure approximately 11 ft. x 12 ft. Two of them have walk-in closets.

Copyright by designer/architect.

SMARTtip

Using Slipcovers in Your Dining Area

Change the look of your dining room by slipcovering chairs. Short-skirted slipcovers give a more informal appearance; fabrics in graphic patterns, such as checks or floral prints, complement this style of slipcover best. Long-skirted covers are elegant additions to a formal dining room, particularly in solid color or tone-on-tone fabrics. Ties, buttons, or trim can add personality.

Rear Elevation

Images provided by designer/architect.

Plan #281008

Dimensions: 74' W x 45' D

Levels: 1

Square Footage: 1,731

Bedrooms: 3

Bathrooms: 2½

Foundation: Basement, crawl space

Materials List Available: Yes

Price Category: C

Here is a cheery ranch home characterized by lots of windows and an open, airy plan.

Features:

• Ceiling Height: 8 ft.

• Foyer: This home was originally designed to sit on the edge of a golf course with panoramic vistas in every direction, hence the open design. As you step into the spacious foyer, your eye travels across the great room out the view at the rear.

• Great Room: This room seems even larger than it is, thanks to the open plan and the great views that seem to bring the outdoors in.

• Kitchen: This open, airy kitchen is a pleasure in which to work. It features an unusual octagonal breakfast nook that's the perfect place to enjoy informal meals with the family or pause with a morning cup of coffee.

• Laundry: This laundry facility is located on the main floor, so you won't have to carry clothing up and down stairs to the basement.

Copyright by designer/architect.

SMARTtip

The Provençal Style in Your Kitchen

No French country kitchen would be complete without a massive harvest table. If you can't find an affordable antique, create your own. Buy a long, unfinished pine table, and stain it a rich walnut color. Because pine is a softwood, you won't have to add "authentic" distress marks because normal wear and tear will do that for you. Pair the table with an assortment of unmatched chairs to add casual ambiance.

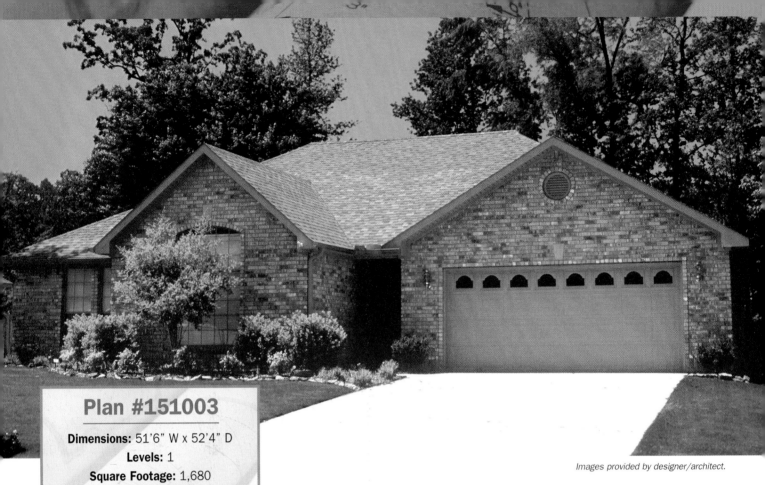

Plan #151003

Dimensions: 51'6" W x 52'4" D

Levels: 1

Square Footage: 1,680

Bedrooms: 3

Bathrooms: 2

Foundation: Basement, crawlspace, slab, or daylight basement.

Materials List Available: No

Price Category: C

A lovely front porch, bay windows, and dormers add sparkle to this country-style home.

Features:

• Great Room: Perfect for entertaining, this room features a tray ceiling, wet bar, and a quiet screened porch nearby.

• Dining Room: This bayed dining room facing the front porch is cozy yet roomy enough for family parties during the holidays.

• Kitchen: This eat-in kitchen also faces the front and is ideal for preparing meals for any occasion.

• Master Suite: The tray ceiling here gives an added feeling of space, while the distance from the other bedrooms allows for all the privacy you'll need.

Plan #211010

Dimensions: 81' W x 84' D
Levels: 1
Square Footage: 2,503
Bedrooms: 3
Bathrooms: 2½
Foundation: Slab
Materials List Available: Yes
Price Category: E

A well-designed floor plan makes maximum use of space and creates convenience and comfort.

Features:

• Ceiling Height: 10 ft. unless otherwise noted.

• Living Room: A stepped ceiling gives this living room special architectural interest. There's a full-service wet bar designed to handle parties of any size. When the weather gets warm, step out of the living room into a lovely screened rear porch.

• Master Bedroom: You'll love unwinding at the end of a busy day in this master suite. It's located away from the other bedrooms for more privacy.

• Study: This charming study adjoins the master bedroom. It's the perfect quiet spot to get some work done, surf the internet, or pay the bills.

Images provided by designer/architect.

SMARTtip

Deck Railings

Install caps and post finials to your railings. A rail cap protects the cut ends of the posts from the weather. Finials add another decorative layer to your design, and the styles are endless—ball, chamfered, grooved, and top hat are a few.

Copyright by designer/architect.

Plan #151008

Dimensions: 42' W x 66'10" D
Square Footage: 1,892
Bedrooms: 3
Bathrooms: 2
Foundation: Crawl space, slab, basement, or daylight basement
Materials List Available: No
Price Category: D

Images provided by designer/architect.

This cozy home features a foyer with 8-in. columns and a wide-open welcoming great room and kitchen.

Features:

- Great Room/Kitchen: Enjoy the fireplace in the great room while seated at the kitchen island or in the breakfast room. Access to the rear patio and covered porch makes this room a natural spot for family as well as for entertaining.

- Dining Room: For a formal evening, entertain in this dining room, with its grand entrance through elegant 8-in. columns.

- Master Suite: Luxuriate in the privacy of this master suite, with its 10-ft. ceiling and private access to the covered porch. The master bath pampers you with a whirlpool tub, separate vanities, a shower, and a walk-in closet.

- Bedrooms: A bedroom with walk-in closet and private access to full bath is a cozy retreat, while the other bedroom makes room for one more!

Copyright by designer/architect.

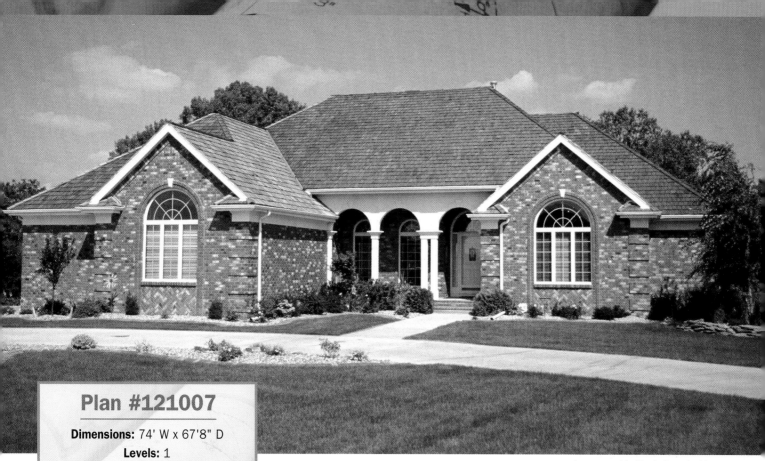

Plan #121007

Dimensions: 74' W x 67'8" D

Levels: 1

Square Footage: 2,512

Bedrooms: 3

Bathrooms: 2½

Foundation: Basement

Materials List Available: Yes

Price Category: E

Images provided by designer/architect.

A series of arches brings grace to this home's interior and exterior.

Features:

- Ceiling Height: 8 ft.

- Formal Dining Room: Tapered columns give this dining room a classical look that lends elegance to any dinner party.

- Great Room: Just beyond the dining room is this light-filled room, with its wall of arched windows and see-through fireplace.

- Hearth Room: On the other side of the fire place you will find this cozy area, with its corner entertainment center.

- Dinette: A gazebo-shaped dinette is the architectural surprise of the house layout.

- Kitchen: This well-conceived working kitchen features a generous center island.

- Garage: With three garage bays you'll never be short of parking space or storage.

Copyright by designer/architect.

Optional Bedroom

Plan #131052

Dimensions: 67' W x 63'10" D

Levels: 1

Square Footage: 2,171

Bedrooms: 2

Bathrooms: 2

Foundation: Basement, crawl space, or slab (walk-out option for fee)

Materials List Available: Yes

Price Category: D

The front and back turrets, in combination with the vaulted ceilings and unusually shaped rooms, make this house a treasure.

Features:

- **Covered Porch:** The circular covered front porch is an endlessly versatile area.
- **Dining Room:** The shape of this room echoes that of the front porch. Windows let in plenty of light; the ceiling is vaulted; and columns separate the room from the Great Room.

- **Great Room:** A fireplace, door to the patio, and vaulted ceiling highlight this spacious room.

- **Library:** Use this room, with its deep bay, as a third bedroom, or turn it into a den or media room.

- **Kitchen:** The center island and U-shaped counter make this a convenient work space.

- **Master Suite:** You'll love the turreted sitting room, tray ceiling, two walk-in closets, whirlpool tub, separate shower, and two vanities here.

Rear Elevation

Plan #121053

Dimensions: 66' W x 68' D
Levels: 1
Square Footage: 2,456
Bedrooms: 3
Bathrooms: 2½
Foundation: Basement
Materials List Available: Yes
Price Category: E

Images provided by designer/architect.

If you're looking for a home that gives comfort at every turn, this could be the one.

Features:

- **Entry:** Airy and open, this entry imparts a welcoming feeling.

- **Great Room:** You'll love the style built into this centrally located room. A row of transom-topped windows adds natural light, and a fireplace gives it character.

- **Dining Room:** Just off the entry for convenience, this formal room has a boxed ceiling that accentuates its interesting angled shape.

- **Gathering Room:** This lovely room features an angled ceiling, snack bar, built-in entertainment center, built-in desk, and abundance of windows. A door leads to the large, covered rear porch with skylights.

- **Master Suite:** Relax in comfort after a long day, or sit on the adjoining, covered rear porch to enjoy the evening breezes.

Copyright by designer/architect.

Plan #211050

Dimensions: 68' W x 64' D
Levels: 1
Square Footage: 2,000
Bedrooms: 3
Bathrooms: 2
Foundation: Slab, crawl space, or basement
Materials List Available: Yes
Price Category: D

SMARTtip

Lighting

For lighting in hard-to-reach areas, use a lamp (bulb) with a long life so that you don't have to replace it often.

Stucco siding creates a distinctive counterpoint to the columned front porch.

Features:

• Ceiling Height: 9 ft. unless otherwise noted.

• Living Room: This truly massive living room will accommodate parties of any size, from large formal affairs to more intimate family gatherings.

• Kitchen: This U-shaped kitchen offers generous counter space to make food preparation a pleasure.

• Dinette: Open to the living room, this dinette is the perfect spot for informal family dining.

• Sunroom: There's nothing more pleasant than basking indoors in the warmth of the sun on a cold winter day. When the winter sun is bright, just throw open the double doors between the living room and this delightful sunroom.

• Master Bedroom: This lush retreat boasts a large bedroom and an adjoining study or home office. The master bath has a spa tub, separate shower, dual sinks, and two walk-in closets.

Copyright by designer/architect.

Plan #211056

Dimensions: 63' W x 74' D
Levels: 1
Square Footage: 2,349
Bedrooms: 3
Bathrooms: 2
Foundation: Crawl space
Materials List Available: No
Price Category: E

This distinctive Florida-style home offers convenient modern living on one level.

Features:

- Ceiling Height: 9 ft. unless otherwise noted.
- Family Room: This inviting and spacious sunken room is the perfect place for casual entertainment or just to relax with the family. It features a handsome fireplace flanked by bookshelves.

- Screened Porch. Located near the family room, this screened porch is the perfect place to catch a breeze on a warm summer evening.
- Kitchen: This well-planned kitchen features a built-in menu desk and an eating nook. Put a round table in this octagonal nook, and you'll have the ideal spot for informal family meals.
- Master Suite: Unwind at the end of a busy day in this luxurious master suite.
- Private Study: Conveniently located next to the master suite, this study is the spot to work at the computer or pay the bills.

Copyright by designer/architect.

SMARTtip

Porch Maintenance

Because most porches are made of wood, they do require upkeep. From time to time and particularly if your porch is old, check it for dry rot and insect damage. Unfortunately, termites love porches almost as much as people do and, very often, older ones need extensive repairs. Once your porch is stable, finish it with paint or stain. This is one of the best ways you can preserve it. Your choice of colors will add to the ambiance, and most paint companies now provide "period palettes" to help you make the best selection for your home.

Plan #381009

Dimensions: 26' W x 46' D

Levels: 1

Square Footage: 950

Opt. Bonus Level Sq. Ft.: 210

Bedrooms: 2

Bathrooms: 1

Foundation: Crawl space

Materials List Available: Yes

Price Category: A

Images provided by designer/architect.

Copyright by designer/architect.

Plan #151067

Dimensions: 46'10" W x 54'10" D

Levels: 1

Square Footage: 1,485

Bedrooms: 3

Bathrooms: 2

Foundation: Crawl space, slab (basement option for fee)

Materials List Available: Yes

Price Category: B

Images provided by designer/architect.

Copyright by designer/architect.

Images provided by designer/architect.

Copyright by designer/architect.

Plan #151043

Dimensions: 53' W x 64' D

Levels: 1

Square Footage: 1,636

Bedrooms: 3

Bathrooms: 2

Foundation: Crawl space, slab (basement option for fee)

Materials List Available: No

Price Category: C

Images provided by designer/architect.

Copyright by designer/architect.

Plan #341037

Dimensions: 48' W x 62'4" D

Levels: 1

Square Footage: 1,784

Bedrooms: 3

Bathrooms: 2

Foundation: Crawl space, slab (basement option for fee)

Materials List Available: Yes

Price Category: C

Plan #211058

Dimensions: 74'6" W x 68' D

Levels: 1

Square Footage: 2,564

Bedrooms: 4

Bathrooms: 4

Foundation: Slab

Materials List Available: No

Price Category: E

The style of this spacious home is traditional but the amenities are attuned to modern life.

SMARTtip

Outdoor Furniture

Too much of the same is too much! Avoid matched sets of outdoor furniture. Instead, pair a cast-iron table with wooden chairs, for example. Another trick is to choose all the same chairs from one collection, but buy them in several different finishes. Finally, when it comes time for chair cushions, select fabrics that feel and look good together but don't necessarily match each other or that of the umbrella.

Features:

- Ceiling Height: 8 ft.

- Family Room: This is a great room for family gatherings and relaxation. Everyone will want to gather around the handsome fireplace. A built-in television niche makes maximum use of floor space.

- Home Office: Whether you work full-time at home or just need a spot for the home computer and bill-paying, you'll appreciate this generous office. It even has its own full bath, so all you need is a sofa bed for double-duty as a guest room.

- Porch: Step through sliding glass doors in the family room onto this generous porch, which is also accessible to the bedroom hallway and the garage.

- Courtyard: This private courtyard off the porch adds offers another spot for relaxation.

- Garage: The garage offers parking for three cars, along with plenty of extra storage.

Plan #171004

Dimensions: 72' W x 52' D
Levels: 1
Square Footage: 2,256
Bedrooms: 3
Bathrooms: 2
Foundation: Slab, crawl space
Materials List Available: Yes
Price Category: E

This home greets you with a front porch featuring a high roofline and stucco columns.

Features:

- Ceiling Height: 9 ft. unless otherwise noted.

- Foyer: Step through the front porch into this impressive foyer, which opens to the formal dining room and the study.

- Dining Room: This dining room's 12-ft. ceiling enhances its sense of spaciousness, with plenty of room for large dinner parties.

- Family Room: With plenty of room for all kinds of family activities, this room also has a 12-ft. ceiling, a fireplace, and two paddle fans.

- Kitchen: This kitchen has all the counter space you'll need to prepare your favorite recipes. There's a pantry, desk, and angled snack bar.

- Master Bedroom: This master retreat is separate from the other bedrooms for added privacy. It has an elegant, high step-up ceiling and a paddle fan.

- Master Bath: This master bath features a large walk-in closet, deluxe corner bath, walk-in shower, and his and her vanities.

SMARTtip

Windows – Privacy

You can easily stencil a work of art onto a windowpane, perhaps only as a border around the edge. Choose or create a design that gives you as little or as much privacy and light control as you need. Use a ready-made stencil or a piece of openwork fabric such as lace, or mask a design onto the glass using tape and a razor knife. Then apply glass paint or frosted glass spray, referring to the instructions and guidelines that come with the product.

Plan #151173

Dimensions: 58' W x 53'6" D
Levels: 1
Square Footage: 1,722
Bedrooms: 3
Bathrooms: 2
Foundation: Basement, crawl space, slab, or daylight basement
Materials List Available: No
Price Category: C

Images provided by designer/architect.

Copyright by designer/architect.

Plan #301003

Dimensions: 84' W x 55'8" D
Levels: 1
Square Footage: 2,485
Bedrooms: 3
Bathrooms: 2½
Foundation: Crawl space, basement
Materials List Available: Yes
Price Category: E

Images provided by designer/architect.

Copyright by designer/architect.

SMARTtip

Making Mitered Returns

Cut the small return piece from a substantial board that you can hold safely and securely against the saw fence.

Plan #211011

Dimensions: 84' W x 54' D

Levels: 1

Square Footage: 2,791

Bedrooms: 3 or 4

Bathrooms: 2

Foundation: Slab or crawl space

Materials List Available: Yes

Price Category: F

Images provided by designer/architect.

Plenty of room plus an open, flexible floor plan make this a home that will adapt to your needs.

Features:

- Ceiling Height: 8 ft. unless otherwise noted.

- Living Room: This distinctive room features a 12-ft. ceiling and is designed so that it can also serve as a master suite with a sitting room.

- Family Room: The whole family will want to gather in this large, inviting family room.

- Morning Room: The family room blends into this sunny spot, which is perfect for informal family meals.

- Kitchen: This spacious kitchen offers a smart layout. It is also contiguous to the family room.

- Master Suite: You'll look forward to the end of the day when you can enjoy this master suite. It includes a huge, luxurious master bath with two large walk-in closets and two vanity sinks.

- Optional Bedroom: This optional fourth bedroom is located so that it can easily serve as a library, den, office, or music room.

Copyright by designer/architect.

Plan #151007

Dimensions: 54'2" W x 56'2" D

Levels: 1

Square Footage: 1,787

Bedrooms: 3

Bathrooms: 2

Foundation: Basement, crawl space, or slab

Materials List Available: No

Price Category: C

Images provided by designer/architect.

This compact, well-designed home is graced with amenities usually reserved for larger houses.

Features:

- Foyer: A 10-ft. ceiling creates unity between the foyer and the dining room just beyond it.

- Dining Room: 8-in. boxed columns welcome you to this dining room, with its 10-ft. ceilings.

- Great Room: The 9-ft. boxed ceiling suits the spacious design. Enjoy the fireplace in the winter and the rear-grilling porch in the summer.

- Breakfast Room: This bright room is a lovely spot for any time of day.

- Master Suite: Double vanities and a large walk-in closet add practicality to this quiet room with a 9-ft. pan ceiling. The master bath includes whirlpool tub with glass block and a separate shower.

- Bedrooms: Bedroom 2 features a bay window, and both rooms are convenient to the bathroom.

Copyright by designer/architect.

Plan #121008

Dimensions: 62' W x 56' D
Levels: 1
Square Footage: 1,651
Bedrooms: 2
Bathrooms: 2
Foundation: Basement
Materials List Available: Yes
Price Category: C

Images provided by designer/architect.

This elegant home is packed with amenities that belie its compact size.

Features:

• Ceiling Height: 8 ft.

• Dining Room: The foyer opens into a view of the dining room, with its distinctive boxed ceiling.

• Great Room: The whole family will want to gather around the fireplace and enjoy the views and sunlight streaming through the transom-topped window.

• Breakfast Area: Next to the great room and sharing the transom-topped windows, this cozy area invites you to linger over morning coffee.

• Covered Porch: When the weather is nice, take your coffee through the door in the breakfast area and enjoy this large covered porch.

• Master Suite: French doors lead to this comfortable suite featuring a walk-in. Enjoy long, luxurious soaks in the corner whirlpool accented with boxed windows.

Optional Bedroom

Br. 3
10² x 10⁰

WHIRLPOOL
LIN.

Mbr.
14⁰ x 13⁰
9'-0" CEILING

Grt. rm.
17⁰ x 17⁰
10'-0" CEILING

TRANSOMS   TRANSOMS

Bfst.
11⁰ x 11⁰
10'-0" CEILING

COVERED PORCH

SNACK BAR

Den
10² x 10⁰
OPTIONAL BEDROOM

SERVERY

Kit.
13⁰ x 11⁸

WET BAR

Din.
12⁰ x 11⁰
9'-0" CEILING

Gar.
30⁰ x 20⁸

Br. 2
11⁰ x 10⁰
10'-0" CLG.

COVERED PORCH

56'-0"

62'-0"

Copyright by designer/architect.

SMARTtip

Finishing Your Fireplace with Tile

An excellent finishing material for a fireplace is tile. Luckily, there are reproductions of art tiles today. Most showrooms carry examples of Arts and Crafts, Art Nouveau, California, Delft, and other European tiles. Granite, limestone, and marble tiles are affordable alternatives to custom stone slabs.

Plan #211059

Dimensions: 68' W x 84' D

Levels: 1

Square Footage: 2,299

Bedrooms: 3

Bathrooms: 2

Foundation: Slab, basement

Materials List Available: No

Price Category: E

Images provided by designer/architect.

This well designed home features plenty of space and all the amenities you seek.

Features:

- Ceiling Height: 9 ft.

- Living Room: This living room is the center of the home's activity. It boasts an attractive, unique angled fireplace and a built-in entertainment room.

- Sunroom: This glass room fills the living room with light. In fact, if you open its interior door on a sunny winter day, it can bring solar heat into the home. The sunroom also has direct access to the porch.

- Master Suite: This suite is located opposite the other bedrooms for maximum privacy. This is truly a master retreat. The private bath features two convenient entries, his and her walk-in closets, dual-sink vanity, luxurious tub, and separate shower.

- Bonus Room: Located over the garage, this room offers 352 ft. of additional space.

Copyright by designer/architect.

SMARTtip

Outdoor Decorating

Arrange outdoor spaces as you would an interior room. Choose a dominant element around which everything else flows. It can be a pool, a fire pit, or the garden. One major furniture piece, such as a dining table, can anchor an area.

Images provided by designer/architect.

Plan #211028

Dimensions: 68' W x 41' D
Levels: 1
Square Footage: 1,507
Bedrooms: 3
Bathrooms: 2
Foundation: Slab
Materials List Available: Yes
Price Category: C

Surprise yourself with this ranch-style home, which features every amenity you'll ever need.

Features:

• Living Room: A 12-ft. ceiling here adds dimension to the room, and the angled wall blends perfectly with the bay window in the adjoining eating nook. Both rooms overlook the rear covered porch.

• Dining Room: The formality of this room complements the stately entry it adjoins.

• Kitchen: Shaped and positioned as a hub of the home, this kitchen is also designed for efficient work patterns while you cook.

• Master Suite: With a skylight over the dressing room, a walk-in closet, and a private bath, this suite affords privacy and luxury.

• Additional Bedrooms: Each has a walk-in closet, and the larger one has an 11-ft.-high ceiling to accommodate its transom windows.

Copyright by designer/architect.

SMARTtip

Nailing Asphalt Roof Shingles

Shingles are typically fastened with four nails—one at each end of the shingle, and one above each tab slot. In windy areas use six nails to affix the shingles, placing one on each side of the tab slots. Position the nails just beneath the adhesive patch but above the tab slots. Roofing nails should be long enough to penetrate sheathing by ¾ inch, whether shingling over or replacing existing roofing.

Plan #151002

Dimensions: 67' W x 66' D

Levels: 1

Square Footage: 2,444

Bedrooms: 3

Bathrooms: 2½

Foundation: Basement, crawl space, or slab

Materials List Available: No

Price Category: E

Images provided by designer/architect.

This gracious, traditional home is designed for practicality and convenience.

Features:

- Ceiling Height: 9 ft. except as noted below.

- Great Room: This room is ideal for entertaining, thanks to its lovely fireplace and French doors that open to the covered rear porch. Built-in cabinets give convenient storage space.

- Family Room: With access to the kitchen as well as the rear porch, this room will become your family's "headquarters."

- Study: Enjoy the quiet in this room with its 12-ft. ceiling and doorway to a private patio on the side of the house.

- Dining Room: Take advantage of the 8-in. wood columns and 12-ft. ceilings to create a formal dining area.

- Kitchen: An eat-in bar is a great place to snack, and the handy computer nook allows the kids to do their homework while you cook.

Copyright by designer/architect.

- Breakfast Room: Opening from the kitchen, this area gives added space for the family to gather any time.

- Master Suite: Featuring a 10-ft. boxed ceiling, the master bedroom also has a door way that opens onto the covered rear porch. The master bathroom has a step-up whirlpool tub, separate shower, and twin vanities with a makeup area.

Plan #211039

Dimensions: 62' W x 64' D

Levels: 1

Square Footage: 1,868

Bedrooms: 3

Bathrooms: 2

Foundation: Slab

Materials List Available: Yes

Price Category: D

This home exudes traditional charm, but its layout and amenities are thoroughly modern.

Features:

• Formal Dining Room: This elegant room is perfect for dinner parties of any size.

• Kitchen: If you love to cook, you will love this kitchen. It's U-shaped for maximum efficiency, and it boasts a built-in desk for making menus and shopping lists, as well as a handy pantry closet. The kitchen has access to the carport, so groceries make a short trip to the counter.

• Eating Area: Just off the kitchen you'll find this informal eating area designed for quick meals on the go.

• Master Suite: Here is the perfect place to unwind after a long day. This generous bedroom hosts a lavish master bath with a spa tub, separate shower, and his and hers dressing areas.

• Secondary Bedrooms: Located across the home from the master suite, the two secondary bedrooms share another full bath.

SMARTtip

Kitchen Wallpapering

For wrapping outside corners, measure from the last piece to the corner, and add ½ inch to the measurement. Cut the paper to size, and place it in position, but before wrapping it around the corner, make small slits in the waste portions of the paper near the ceiling and the baseboard. The cuts will allow you to turn the corner without wrinkling or tearing the paper. Hang the other part of the cut sheet so that it overlaps the first portion.

Plan #291004

Dimensions: 77'4" W x 54'4" D

Levels: 1

Square Footage: 2,529

Bedrooms: 3

Bathrooms: 2½

Foundation: Basement

Materials List Available: No

Price Category: E

Illustration provided by designer/architect.

Rear View

Copyright by designer/architect.

Plan #171016

Dimensions: 68' W x 70' D

Levels: 1

Square Footage: 2,482

Bedrooms: 4

Bathrooms: 3

Foundation: Slab, crawl space

Materials List Available: Yes

Price Category: E

Illustration provided by designer/architect.

Copyright by designer/architect.

Bonus Area

Plan #151059

Dimensions: 41'10" W x 53' D

Levels: 1

Square Footage: 1,382

Bedrooms: 3

Bathrooms: 2

Foundation: Crawl space, slab, with basement option for fee

Materials List Available: No

Price Category: B

Images provided by designer/architect.

Copyright by designer/architect.

Plan #151068

Dimensions: 57' W x 61'8" D

Levels: 1

Square Footage: 1,880

Bedrooms: 4

Bathrooms: 2

Foundation: Crawl space, slab, or basement

Materials List Available: No

Price Category: D

Images provided by designer/architect.

Copyright by designer/architect.

Illustration provided by designer/architect.

Plan #151039

Dimensions: 48'2" W x 50'4" D
Levels: 1
Square Footage: 1,353
Bedrooms: 3
Bathrooms: 2
Foundation: Crawl space, slab
Materials List Available: No
Price Category: B

Copyright by designer/architect.

Copyright by designer/architect.

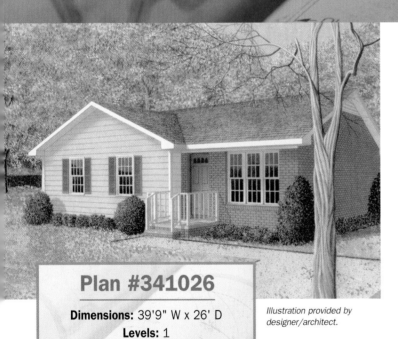

Plan #341026

Dimensions: 39'9" W x 26' D
Levels: 1
Square Footage: 1,009
Bedrooms: 3
Bathrooms: 2
Foundation: Crawl space, slab, or basement
Materials List Available: Yes
Price Category: B

Illustration provided by designer/architect.

Plan #231003

Dimensions: 74' W x 69' D

Levels: 1

Square Footage: 2,254

Bedrooms: 2

Bathrooms: 3

Foundation: Crawl space

Materials List Available: No

Price Category: A

Illustration provided by designer/architect.

Copyright by designer/architect.

Plan #221021

Dimensions: 57' W x 66' D

Levels: 1

Square Footage: 1,642

Bedrooms: 3

Bathrooms: 2½

Foundation: Basement

Materials List Available: No

Price Category: C

Illustration provided by designer/architect.

Rear Elevation

Copyright by designer/architect.

Plan #321037

Dimensions: 78'8" W x 50'6" D
Levels: 1
Square Footage: 2,397
Bedrooms: 3
Bathrooms: 2
Foundation: Basement
Materials List Available: Yes
Price Category: E

Images provided by designer/architect.

Optional Basement Level Floor Plan

Plan #271079

Dimensions: 104' W x 55' D
Levels: 1
Square Footage: 2,228
Bedrooms: 1-3
Bathrooms: 1½
Foundation: Daylight basement
Materials List Available: No
Price Category: E

Images provided by designer/architect.

Optional Basement Level Floor Plan

Copyright by designer/architect.

Plan #241004

Dimensions: 74'9" W x 70'8" D

Levels: 1

Square Footage: 2,771

Bedrooms: 3

Bathrooms: 2½

Foundation: Slab

Materials List Available: No

Price Category: F

Images provided by designer/architect.

Copyright by designer/architect.

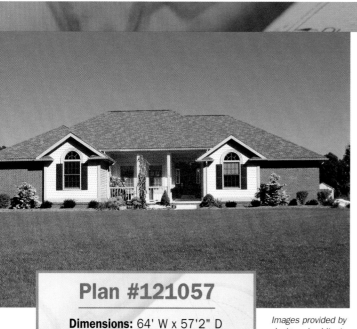

Plan #121057

Dimensions: 64' W x 57'2" D

Levels: 1

Square Footage: 2,311

Bedrooms: 3

Bathrooms: 2½

Foundation: Basement

Materials List Available: Yes

Price Category: E

Images provided by designer/architect.

Copyright by designer/architect.

SMARTtip

Installing Crown Molding

Test for the direction and location of ceiling joists with a stud sensor, by tapping with a hammer to hear the sound of hollow or solid areas or by tapping in test finishing nails.

Plan #211062

Dimensions: 74'6" W x 75' D

Levels: 1

Square Footage: 2,682

Bedrooms: 4

Bathrooms: 3½

Foundation: Slab, optional crawl space

Materials List Available: Yes

Price Category: F

Images provided by designer/architect.

If you're looking for a beautiful home that combines luxurious amenities with a separate, professional office space, this could be the one.

Features:

- **Living Room:** Enjoy an 11-ft. ceiling, brick fireplace, and built-in shelving in this room.

- **Dining Room:** A 2-story ceiling gives presence to this room.

- **Kitchen:** A breakfast bar here is open to the breakfast room beyond for ease of serving.

- **Breakfast Room:** A built-in corner china closet adds to the practicality you'll find here.

- **Office:** A separate entrance makes it possible to run a professional business from this home.

- **Master Suite:** Separated for privacy, this suite includes two vanities and a walk-in closet.

- **Porch:** The rear screened porch opens to a courtyard where you'll love to entertain.

Copyright by designer/architect.

Plan #181001

Dimensions: 38' W x 28' D
Levels: 1
Square Footage: 920
Bedrooms: 2
Bathrooms: 1
Foundation: Basement
Materials List Available: Yes
Price Category: A

Images provided by designer/architect.

This cozy and charming one-story cottage offers many amenities in its well-designed layout.

Features:

- Ceiling Height: 8 ft.

- Porch: Enjoy summer evenings relaxing on the front porch.

- Kitchen: This kitchen has ample work and storage space as well as a breakfast bar and enough room for the family to dine together.

- Family Room: Natural light streaming through the windows makes this an appealing place for family activities.

- Bedrooms: There's a generous master bedroom and one secondary bedroom. Each has its own closet.

- Laundry Room: A fully equipped laundry room is conveniently located adjacent to the kitchen.

- Full Basement: Here is plenty of storage room as well as the opportunity for expanded living space.

28'-0"
8,4 m

19'-0" X 11'-8"
5,70 X 3,50

12'-2" X 11'-8"
3,65 X 3,50

9'-0" X 10'-0"
2,70 X 3,00

15'-4" X 12'-0"
4,60 X 3,60

38'-0"
11,4 m

Copyright by designer/architect.

Images provided by designer/architect.

Plan #371006

Dimensions: 49'9" W x 48'6" D

Levels: 1

Square Footage: 1,374

Bedrooms: 3

Bathrooms: 2

Foundation: Slab
(crawl space option for fee)

Materials List Available: No

Price Category: B

Copyright by designer/architect.

Images provided by designer/architect.

Plan #361013

Dimensions: 54' W x 46' D

Levels: 1

Square Footage: 1,321

Bedrooms: 3

Bathrooms: 2

Foundation: Crawl space

Materials List Available: No

Price Category: B

Copyright by designer/architect.

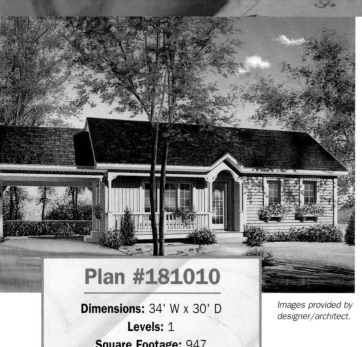

Plan #181010

Dimensions: 34' W x 30' D

Levels: 1

Square Footage: 947

Bedrooms: 2

Bathrooms: 1

Foundation: Full basement

Materials List Available: Yes

Price Category: A

Images provided by designer/architect.

30'-0"
9,0 m

20'-8" X 12'-4"
6,20 X 3,70

14'-8" X 12'-0"
4,40 X 3,60

12'-0" X 9'-8"
3,60 X 2,90

12'-0" X 11'-0"
3,60 X 3,30

34'-0"
10,2 m

Copyright by designer/architect.

Plan #371002

Dimensions: 67'2" W x 48'6" D

Levels: 1

Square Footage: 1,590

Bedrooms: 3

Bathrooms: 2

Foundation: Crawlspace, slab

Materials List Available: No

Price Category: C

Images provided by designer/architect.

PORCH

STORAGE

UT.

KITCH.
9'-0" X 11'-6"

GARAGE
20'-0" X 20'-0"

BREAKFAST BAR

10'-0" HIGH CEILING
FAMILY RM.
17'-0" X 16'-0"

MEDIA CENTER

STEP UP CEILING
MASTER SUITE
12'-0" X 15'-0"

WALK IN CLOSET

GLASS SHOWER

DINING
11'-0" X 15'-0"

B.2

BATH 1

MARBLE TUB

ENTRY

PORCH

SLOPE CLG. UP TO 10'-0"
BED RM.3
11'-0" x 11'-0"

WALK IN CLOSET

BED RM.2
11'-0" x 11'-0"

Copyright by designer/architect.

Plan #181012

Dimensions: 34' W x 34' D

Levels: 1

Square Footage: 1,079

Bedrooms: 2

Bathrooms: 1

Foundation: Full basement

Materials List Available: Yes

Price Category: B

34'-0"
10,2 m

34'-0"
10,2 m

13'-4"x 12'-0"
4,00 x 3,60

19'-0"x 12'-0"
5,70 x 3,60

12'-0"x 16'-0"
3,60 x 4,80

11'-0"x 10'-0"
3,30 x 3,00

Plan #361014

Dimensions: 122'4" W x 77'6" D

Levels: 1

Square Footage: 3,384

Bedrooms: 3

Bathrooms: 4

Foundation: Crawl space

Materials List Available: No

Price Category: G

Vaulted Great Room
25' x 27'8"

Patio

Kitchen

Bedroom
15' x 12'4"

Pantry

Vaulted Dining
16' x 17'

Covered Patio

Bedroom
14'2" x 12'4"

Utility

Library /Den
14'6" x 13'

Entry

Master Suite
16' x 17'

Garage
41'4" x 23'4"

Covered Porch

Vaulted Parlor
16' x 13'8"

PATIO

LIVING
16 x 13

BEDROOM
11 x 11

KIT./DIN.
12 x 13

FLOOR PLAN
910 sq. ft.

BEDROOM
11 x 14

DECK

Images provided by designer/architect.

Copyright by designer/architect.

Plan #381016

Dimensions: 32' W x 39'8" D

Levels: 1

Square Footage: 910

Bedrooms: 2

Bathrooms: 1

Foundation: Basement

Materials List Available: Yes

Price Category: A

15'-0" X 12'-0"
4.50 X 3.60

16'-4" X 15'-0"
4.90 X 4.50

11'-0" X 11'-0"
3.30 X 3.30

19'-4" X 20'-8"
5.80 X 6.20

13'-0" X 14'-0"
3.90 X 4.20

11'-0" X 11'-0"
3.30 X 3.30

12'-0" X 11'-0"
3.60 X 3.30

43'-0"
12.9 m

62'-0"
18.6 m

Copyright by designer/architect.

Plan #181017

Dimensions: 62' W x 43' D

Levels: 1

Square Footage: 1,736

Bedrooms: 3

Bathrooms: 2

Foundation: Full basement

Materials List Available: Yes

Price Category: C

Images provided by designer/architect.

SMARTtip

Simplify Your Deck Design

If your railing is an elaborate Chinese-Chippendale style, you may want to keep the design of benches, planters, and decking basic to prevent visual competition between the elements.

Plan #391004

Dimensions: 66' W x 50' D
Levels: 1
Square Footage: 1,750
Bedrooms: 2
Bathrooms: 2
Foundation: Basement, crawl space, slab
Materials List Available: Yes
Price Category: C

Images provided by designer/architect.

This creatively compact ranch is made especially for effortless everyday living

Features:

• Kitchen: This centralized U-shaped kitchen and look-alike breakfast nook with professional pantry have a wonderful view of the porch.

• Laundry Room: Laundry facilities are cleverly placed within reach while neatly out of the way.

• Great Room: Step into this lavish-looking sunken great room for fire-side gatherings, and move easily into the nearby formal dining area where a screened porch allows you to entertain guests after dinner.

• Master Suite: Flanking one side of the house, this master suit is serenely private and amenity-filled. Its features include full bath, a wall of walk-in closets and a dressing area.

• Bedroom: This second spacious bedroom enjoys great closeting, (with double-doors), a full bath and a close-at-hand den (or bedroom #3).

• Garage: This three-car garage goes beyond vehicle protection, providing plenty of storage and work space.

Copyright by designer/architect.

Plan #181009

Dimensions: 32' W x 36'8" D

Levels: 1

Square Footage: 1,006

Bedrooms: 2

Bathrooms: 1

Foundation: Full basement

Materials List Available: Yes

Price Category: B

Images provided by designer/architect.

36'-8"
11,0 m

32'-0"
9,6 m

11'-0" X 10'-0"
3,30 X 3,00

9'-0" X 10'-0"
2,70 X 3,00

10'-0" X 10'-0"
3,00 X 3,00

15'-6" X 13'-0"
4,65 X 3,90

11'-0" X 13'-0"
3,30 X 3,90

Copyright by designer/architect.

Plan #181011

Dimensions: 41'4" W x 42' D

Levels: 1

Square Footage: 1,347

Bedrooms: 3

Bathrooms: 1

Foundation: Full basement

Materials List Available: Yes

Price Category: B

Images provided by designer/architect.

42'-0"
12,6 m

41'-4"
12,4 m

8'-8" X 12'-0"
2,60 X 3,60

10'-8" X 14'-0"
3,20 X 4,20

10'-0" X 9'-0"
3,00 X 2,70

10'-8" X 9'-0"
3,20 X 2,70

17'-4" X 12'-0"
5,20 X 3,60

14'-0" X 11'-0"
4,20 X 3,30

Copyright by designer/architect.

28'-0"

| Br 2 | R | Kit | Deck |
| 11-0x9-7 | P | 11-0x8-0 | |

28'-0"

Dining

Dn

MBr
11-0x12-0

Living
12-7x19-4

Copyright by designer/architect.

Porch depth 5-0

Illustration provided by designer/architect.

Plan #321025

Dimensions: 28' W x 28' D
Levels: 1
Square Footage: 914
Bedrooms: 2
Bathrooms: 1
Foundation: Daylight basement
Materials List Available: Yes
Price Category: A

Garage

Garage

Up

W D F

Laundry

Optional Basement Level Floor Plan

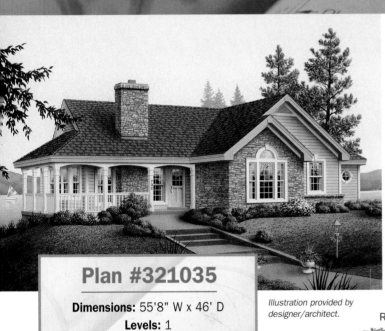

Plan #321035

Dimensions: 55'8" W x 46' D
Levels: 1
Square Footage: 1,384
Bedrooms: 2
Bathrooms: 2
Foundation: Basement
Materials List Available: Yes
Price Category: B

Illustration provided by designer/architect.

Rear View

55'-8"

Atrium below

Dn

Dining Area

Kit
10-2x11-9

Garage
22-0x11-9

Great Rm
18-0x21-8
vaulted

Laundry

D W

MBr
12-8x15-0

46'-0"

Cover porch depth 6-0

Br 2
11-4x12-6

Copyright by designer/architect.

Up

Patio

Family Rm
25-0x21-4

Unexcavated

Unfinished Basement

Optional Basement Level Floor Plan

Images provided by designer/architect.

Plan #321038

Dimensions: 30' W x 51' D

Levels: 1

Square Footage: 1,452

Bedrooms: 4

Bathrooms: 2

Foundation: Basement

Materials List Available: Yes

Price Category: B

Copyright by designer/architect.

Images provided by designer/architect.

Plan #321040

Dimensions: 35' W x 40'8" D

Levels: 1

Square Footage: 1,084

Bedrooms: 2

Bathrooms: 2

Foundation: Basement

Materials List Available: Yes

Price Category: B

Copyright by designer/architect.

Plan #321009

Dimensions: 55'8" W x 46'4" D

Levels: 1

Square Footage: 2,295

Bedrooms: 3

Bathrooms: 2

Foundation: Basement

Materials List Available: Yes

Price Category: E

If you've got a site with great views, you'll love this home, which is designed to make the most of them.

Features:

- Porch: This wraparound porch is an ideal spot to watch the sun come up or go down. Add potted plants to create a lush atmosphere or grow some culinary herbs.
- Great Room: You couldn't ask for more luxury than this room provides, with its vaulted ceiling, large bay window, fireplace, dining balcony, and atrium window wall.
- Kitchen: No matter whether you're an avid cook or not, you'll relish the thoughtful design of this room.
- Master Suite: This suite is truly a retreat you'll treasure. It has two large walk-in closets for good storage space, and sliding doors that open to an exterior balcony where you can sit out to enjoy the stars. The amenity-filled bath adds to your enjoyment of this suite.

Rear View

Optional Basement Level Floor Plan

55'-8"

46'-4"

Balcony

MBr
18-4x13-0

Kit
10-2x
11-9

Dining   Dn

Great Rm
16-0x21-4
vaulted

W D

Entry

Porch depth 6-0

Br 2
12-8x14-0

Br 3
11-4x12-6

Copyright by designer/architect.

Up

Garage
22-4x26-8

Family
15-6x20-8

Unfinished

Plan #131008

Dimensions: 45'4" W x 36'4" D

Levels: 1

Square Footage: 1,299

Bedrooms: 3

Bathrooms: 2

Foundation: Crawl space, basement

Materials List Available: Yes

Price Category: C

Build this home in a vacation spot or any other location where you'll treasure the convenience of having three different outdoor entrances.

Features:

- Ceiling Height: 8 ft.

- Living Room: Sliding glass doors open onto the large deck area and serve to let bright, natural light stream into the home during the day. Add drapes to keep the house cozy at night and on cloudy winter days.

- Kitchen: Shaped like a galley, this kitchen is so well designed that you'll love working in it. Counter space and cabinets add to its practicality, and a windowed nook makes it charming.

- Master Suite: Enjoy the private bath attached to the bedroom in this quiet area.

- Additional Bedrooms: These nicely sized rooms share another full bathroom.

Images provided by designer/architect.

Copyright by designer/architect.

Rear View

Plan #281010

Dimensions: 34' W x 31' D

Levels: 1

Square Footage: 884

Bedrooms: 2

Bathrooms: 1

Foundation: Crawl space

Materials List Available: Yes

Price Category: A

This cute vacation or retirement home is modest in size yet contains all the necessary amenities.

Features:

- Ceiling Height: 8 ft.

- Open Plan: The living room, dining room, and kitchen are all contained in one open space. This makes the space versatile and allows plenty of room for entertaining despite the home's small size.

- Covered Deck: Step outdoors and enjoy warm breezes on this covered deck, which is accessible from the open main living area.

- Master Bedroom: This master bedroom is separated from the other bedroom to allow maximum privacy.

- Second Bedroom: This bedroom is perfect for when friends and family come to spend the night.

- Cedar Siding: This vertical cedar siding weathers to a beautiful silver gray when left unstained.

Illustration provided by designer/architect.

Let Us Help You
Plan Your
Dream Home

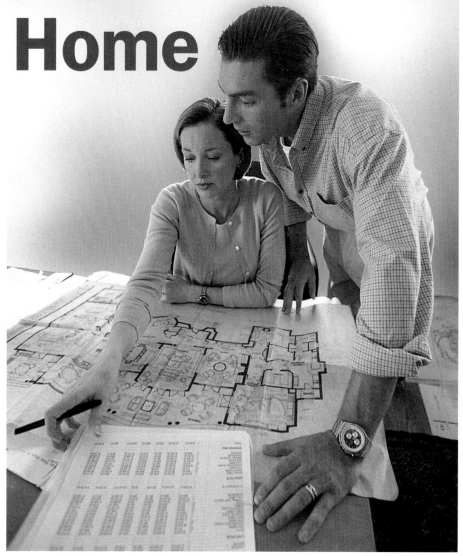

Whether you've always dreamed of building your own home or you can't find the right house from among the dozens you've toured, our collection of one-story plans can help you achieve the home of your dreams.

You could have an architect create a one-of-a-kind home for you, but the design services alone could end up costing up to 15 percent of the cost of construction—a hefty premium for any building project. Isn't it a better idea to select from among the hundreds of unique designs shown in our collection for a fraction of the cost?

What does Creative Homeowner Offer?

In this book, Creative Homeowner provides hundreds of home plans from the country's best architects and designers. Our designs are among the most popular available. Whether your taste runs from traditional to contemporary, Victorian to early American, you are sure to find the best house design for you and your family. Our plans packages include detailed drawings to help you or your builder construct your dream house. **(See page 344.)**

Can I Make Changes to the Plans?

Creative Homeowner offers three ways to help you achieve a truly unique home design. Our customizing service allows for extensive changes to our designs. **(See page 345.)** We also provide reverse images of our plans, or we can give you and your builder the tools for making minor changes on your own. **(See page 346.)**

Can You Help Me Stay on Budget?

Building a house is a large financial investment. To help you stay within your budget, Creative Homeowner can provide you with general construction costs based on your zip code. **(See page 346.)** Also, many of our plans come with the option of buying detailed materials lists to help you price out construction costs.

Is There Anything I Missed?

A typical construction crew consists of a number of skilled professionals. If you plan on doing all or part of the work yourself, or you want to keep tabs on your builder, we offer best-selling building and design books at attractive prices. (See our company Web site at www.creativehomeowner.com.) Our home-building book package covers all phases of home construction, from framing and drywalling to wiring and plumbing. **(See page 352.)**

Our Plans Packages Offer:

All of our home plans are the result of many hours of work by leading architects and professional designers. Most of our home plans include each of the following.

Frontal Sheet

This artist's rendering of the front of the house gives you an idea of how the house will look once it is completed and the property landscaped.

Detailed Floor Plans

These plans show the size and layout of the rooms. They also provide the locations of doors, windows, fireplaces, closets, stairs, and electrical outlets and switches.

Foundation Plan

A foundation plan gives the dimensions of basements, walk-out basements, crawl spaces, pier foundations, and slab construction. Each house design lists the type of foundation included. If the plan you choose does not have the foundation type you require, our customer service department can help you customize the plan to meet your needs.

Roof Plan

In addition to providing the pitch of the roof, these plans also show the locations of dormers, skylights, and other elements.

Exterior Elevations

These drawings show the front, rear, and sides of the house as if you were looking at it head on. Elevations also provide information about architectural features and finish materials.

Interior Elevations and Details

Interior elevations show specific details of such elements as fireplaces, kitchen and bathroom cabinets, built-ins, and other unique features of the design.

Cross Sections

These show the structure as if it were sliced to reveal construction requirements, such as insulation, flooring, and roofing details.

Frontal Sheet

Floor Plan

Foundation Plan

Roof Plan

Cross Sections

Stair Details

Elevation

Illustrations provided by designer/architect

Customize Your Plans in 4 Easy Steps

1 **Select the home plan** that most closely meets your needs. Purchase of a reproducible master is necessary in order to make changes to a plan.

2 **Call 1-800-523-6789 to place your order.** Tell our sales representative you are interested in customizing your plan. To receive your customization cost estimate, we will send you a checklist (via fax or email) for you to complete indicating the changes you would like to make to your plan. There is a $50 nonrefundable consultation fee for this service. If you decide to continue with the custom changes, the $50 fee is credited to the total amount charged.

3 **Fax the completed checklist** to 1-201-760-2431 or email it to us at customize@creativehomeowner.com. Within three business days of receipt of your checklist, a detailed cost estimate will be provided to you.

4 **Once you approve the estimate,** a 75% retainer fee is collected and customization work begins. Preliminary drawings typically take 10 to 15 business days. After approval, we will collect the balance of your customization order cost before shipping the completed plans. You will receive five sets of blueprints or a reproducible master, plus a customized materials list if desired.

Modification Pricing Guide

Categories	Average Cost For Modification
Add or remove living space	Quote required
Bathroom layout redesign	Starting at $120
Kitchen layout redesign	Starting at $120
Garage: add or remove	Starting at $400
Garage: front entry to side load or vice versa	Starting at $300
Foundation changes	Starting at $220
Exterior building materials change	Starting at $200
Exterior openings: add, move, or remove	$65 per opening
Roof line changes	Starting at $360
Ceiling height adjustments	Starting at $280
Fireplace: add or remove	Starting at $90
Screened porch: add	Starting at $280
Wall framing change from 2x4 to 2x6	Starting at $200
Bearing and/or exterior walls changes	Quote required
Non-bearing wall or room changes	$65 per room
Metric conversion of home plan	Starting at $400
Adjust plan for handicapped accessibility	Quote required
Adapt plans for local building code requirements	Quote required
Engineering stamping only	Quote required
Any other engineering services	Quote required
Interactive illustrations (choices of exterior materials)	Quote required

Note: *Any home plan can be customized to accommodate your desired changes. The average prices above are provided only as examples of the most commonly requested changes, and are subject to change without notice. Prices for changes will vary according to the number of modifications requested, plan size, style, and method of design used by the original designer. To obtain a detailed cost estimate, please contact us.*

Architectural Seals

Because of differences in building codes, some cities and states now require an architect or engineer licensed in that state to review and "seal" a blueprint, or officially approve it, prior to construction. Delaware, Nevada, New Jersey, and New York require that all plans for houses built in those states be redrawn by an architect licensed in the state in which the home will be built. We strongly advise you to consult with your local building official for information regarding architectural seals.

Before Customization

After

Decide What Type of Plan Package You Need

How many Plans Should You Order?

Standard 8-Set Package. We've found that our 8-set package is the best value for someone who is ready to start building. Once the process begins, a number of people will require their own set of blueprints. The 8-set package provides plans for you, your builder, the subcontractors, mortgage lender, and the building department.

Minimum 5-Set Package. If you are in the bidding process, you may want to order only five sets for the bidding round and reorder additional sets as needed.

1-Set Study Package. The 1-set package allows you to review your home plan in detail. The plan will be marked as a study print, and it is illegal to build a house from a study print alone. It is a violation of copyright law to reproduce a blueprint without permission.

Buying Additional Sets

If you require additional copies of blueprints for your home construction, you can order additional sets within 60 days of the original order date at a reduced price. The cost is $45.00 for each additional set. For more information, contact customer service.

Reproducible Masters

If you plan to make minor changes to one of our home plans, you can purchase reproducible masters. Printed on vellum paper, an erasable paper that you can reproduce in a copying machine, reproducible masters allow an architect, designer, or builder to alter our plans to give you a customized home design. This package also allows you to print as many copies of the modified plans as you need for construction.

CAD Files

CAD files are the complete set of home plans in an electronic file format. Choose this option if there are multiple changes you wish made to the home plans and you have a local design professional able to make the changes. Not available for all plans. Please contact our order department or visit our website to check the availability of CAD files for your plan.

Mirror-Reverse Sets/Right-Reading Reverse

Plans can be printed in mirror-reverse—we can "flip" plans to create a mirror image of the design. This is useful when the house would fit your site or personal preferences if all the rooms were on the opposite side than shown. As the image is reversed, the lettering and dimensions will also be reversed, meaning they will read backwards. Therefore, when ordering mirror-reverse drawings, you must order at least one set of right-reading plans. A $50.00 fee per plan order will be charged for mirror-reverse (regardless of the number of mirror-reverse sets ordered). Some plans are available in right-reading reverse, this feature will show the plan in reverse, but the writing on the plan will be readable. A $150.00 fee per plan order will be charged for right-reading reverse (regardless of the number of right-reading reverse sets ordered). Please contact our order department at or visit our website to check the availibility of this feature for your chosen plan.

EZ Quote: Home Cost Estimator

EZ Quote is our response to one of the most frequently asked questions we hear from customers: "How much will the house cost me to build?" EZ Quote: Home Cost Estimator will enable you to obtain a calculated building cost to construct your home, based on labor rates and building material costs within your zip code area. This summary is useful for those who want to know the total construction costs before purchasing sets of home plans. It will also provide a level of comfort when you begin soliciting bids. The cost is $29.95 for the first EZ Quote and $14.95 for each additional one. Available only in the U.S. and Canada.

CompleteCost Estimator

CompleteCost Estimator is a valuable tool for use in planning and constructing your new home. It combines the detail of a materials list with line-by-line cost estimating. The result is a complete, detailed estimate—similar to a bid. CompleteCost Estimator is only available for certain plans (please see Plan Index) and may only be ordered with the purchase of at least five sets of home plans. The cost is $125.00 for CompleteCost Estimator.

Materials List

Available for most of our plans, the Materials List provides you an invaluable resource in planning and estimating the cost of your home. Each Materials List outlines the quantity, dimensions, and type of materials needed to build your home (with the exception of mechanical systems). You will get faster, more-accurate bids from your contractors and building suppliers. A Materials List may only be ordered with the purchase of at least five sets of home plans.

Order Toll Free by Phone
1-800-523-6789
By Fax: 201-760-2431

Regular office hours are
8:30AM–7:30PM ET, Mon–Fri
Orders received 3PM ET, will be processed and
shipped within two business days.

Order Online
www.ultimateplans.com

Mail Your Order
Creative Homeowner
Attn: Home Plans
24 Park Way
Upper Saddle River, NJ 07458

Canadian Customers
Order Toll Free 1-800-393-1883

Mail Your Order (Canada)
Creative Homeowner Canada
Attn: Home Plans
113-437 Martin St., Ste. 215
Penticton, BC V2A 5L1

Before You Order

Our Exchange Policy

Blueprints are nonrefundable. However, should you find that the plan you have purchased does not fit your needs, you may exchange that plan for another plan in our collection within 60 days from the date of your original order. The entire content of your original order must be returned before an exchange will be processed. You will be charged a processing fee of 20% of the amount of the original order, the cost difference between the new plan set and the original plan set (if applicable), and all related shipping costs for the new plans. Contact our order department for more information. Please note: reproducible masters may only be exchanged if the package is unopened. CAD files cannot be exchanged and are nonrefundable.

Building Codes and Requirements

At the time of creation, our plans meet the bulding code requirements published by the Building Officials and Code Administrators International, the Southern Building Code Congress International, the International Conference of Building Officials, or the Council of American Building Officials. Because building codes vary from area to area, some drawing modifications and/or the assistance of a professional designer or architect may be necessary to comply with your local codes or to accommodate specific building site conditions. We strongly advise you to consult with your local building official for information regarding codes governing your area.

Blueprint Price Schedule

Price Code	1 Set	5 Sets	8 Sets	Reproducible Masters	CAD	Materials List
A	$300	$345	$395	$530	$950	$85
B	$375	$435	$480	$600	$1,100	$85
C	$435	$500	$550	$650	$1,200	$85
D	$490	$560	$610	$710	$1,300	$95
E	$550	$620	$660	$770	$1,400	$95
F	$610	$680	$720	$830	$1,500	$95
G	$670	$740	$780	$890	$1,600	$95
H	$760	$830	$870	$980	$1,700	$95
I	$860	$930	$970	$1,080	$1,800	$105
J	$960	$1,030	$1,070	$1,190	$1,900	$105
K	$1,070	$1,150	$1,190	$1,320	$2,030	$105
L	$1,180	$1,270	$1,310	$1,460	$2,170	$105

Note: All prices subject to change

Shipping & Handling

	1-4 Sets	5-7 Sets	8+ Sets or Reproducibles	CAD
US Regular (7–10 business days)	$18	$20	$25	$25
US Priority (3–5 business days)	$25	$30	$35	$35
US Express (1–2 business days)	$40	$45	$50	$50
Canada Express (1–2 business days)	$60	$70	$80	$80
Worldwide Express (3–5 business days)	$80	$80	$80	$80

Note: *All delivery times are from date the blueprint package is shipped (typically within 1-2 days of placing order).*

Order Form Please send me the following:

Plan Number: _____ **Price Code:** _____ (See Plan Index.)

Indicate Foundation Type: (Select ONE. See plan page for availability.)

❏ Slab ❏ Crawl space ❏ Basement ❏ Walk-out basement

❏ Optional Foundation for Fee _____ $_____

(Please enter foundation here)

*Please call all our order department or visit our website for optional foundation fee

Basic Blueprint Package

	Cost
❏ CAD File	$_____
❏ Reproducible Masters	$_____
❏ 8-Set Plan Package	$_____
❏ 5-Set Plan Package	$_____
❏ 1-Set Study Package	$_____
❏ Additional plan sets:	
__ sets at $45.00 per set	$_____
❏ Print in mirror-reverse: $50.00 per order	$_____

*Please call all our order department or visit our website for availibility

❏ Print in right-reading reverse: $150.00 per order $_____

*Please call all our order department or visit our website for availibility

Important Extras

❏ Materials List	$_____
❏ CompleteCost Materials Report at $125.00	$_____
Zip Code of Home/Building Site _____	
❏ EZ Quote for Plan #_____at $29.95	$_____
❏ Additional EZ Quotes for Plan #s_____	$_____
at $14.95 each	
Shipping (see chart above)	$_____
SUBTOTAL	$_____
Sales Tax (NJ residents only, add 6%)	$_____
TOTAL	$_____

Order Toll Free: 1-800-523-6789   By Fax: 201-760-2431
Creative Homeowner
24 Park Way
Upper Saddle River, NJ 07458

Name _____
(Please print or type)

Street _____
(Please do not use a P.O. Box)

City _____ State _____

Country _____ Zip _____

Daytime telephone (___)_____

Fax (___)_____
(Required for reproducible orders)

E-Mail _____

Payment ❏ Check/money order *Make checks payable to Creative Homeowner*

❏ VISA   ❏ MasterCard   ❏ AMERICAN EXPRESS Cards   ❏ DISCOVER

Credit card number _____

Expiration date (mm/yy) _____

Signature _____

Please check the appropriate box:
❏ Licensed builder/contractor   ❏ Homeowner   ❏ Renter

SOURCE CODE CE100 www.ultimateplans.com

Copyright Notice

All home plans sold through this publication are protected by copyright. Reproduction of these home plans, either in whole or in part, including any form and/or preparation of derivative works thereof, for any reason without prior written permission is strictly prohibited. The purchase of a set of home plans in no way transfers any copyright or other ownership interest in it to the buyer except for a limited license to use that set of home plans for the construction of one, and only one, dwelling unit. The purchase of additional sets of the home plans at a reduced price from the original set or as a part of a multiple-set package does not convey to the buyer a license to construct more than one dwelling.

Similarly, the purchase of reproducible home plans (sepias, mylars) carries the same copyright protection as mentioned above. It is generally allowed to make up to a maximum of 10 copies for the construction of a single dwelling only. To use any plans more than once, and to avoid any copyright license infringement, it is necessary to contact the plan designer to receive a release and license for any extended use. Whereas a purchaser of reproducible plans is granted a license to make copies, it should be noted that because blueprints are copyrighted, making photocopies from them is illegal.

Copyright and licensing of home plans for construction exist to protect all parties. Copyright respects and supports the intellectual property of the original architect or designer. Copyright law has been reinforced over the past few years. Willful infringement could cause settlements for statutory damages to $150,000.00 plus attorney fees, damages, and loss of profits.

Index

Index

Index

Complete Your Home Plans Library with these Great Books from Creative Homeowner

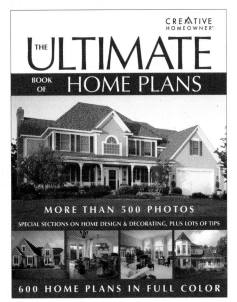

528 pages
Book # 277039

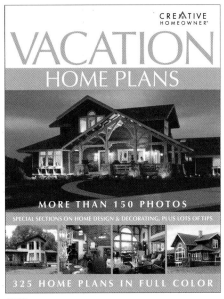

352 pages
Book # 277020

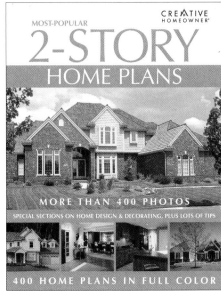

352 pages
Book # 277028

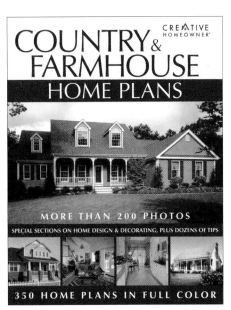

320 pages
Book # 277027

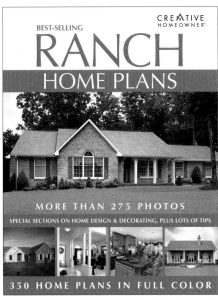

320 pages
Book # 277005

The Best Home Plan Books You Can Find

- Hundreds of home designs from top residential architects and designers

- Hundreds of full-color photographs of actual home that have been built. Many of the homes also include beautiful interior photographs

- Up to 1,000 or more drawings of floor plans, side views and rear views

- Dozens of informative pages containing design and decorating ideas and tips, from working with builders to designing kitchens and installing trimwork and landscaping

---

Books To Help You Build

Creative Homeowner offers an extensive selection of leading how-to books.

Home Building Package

Build and repair your home—inside and out—with these essential titles.

Retail Price: $74.80
Your Price: $65.95
Order #: 267095

Wiring: Complete Projects for the Home
Provides comprehensive information about the home electrical system. Over 750 color photos and 100 illustrations. 288 pages.

Plumbing: Basic, Intermediate & Advanced Projects
An overview of the plumbing system with code-compliant, step-by-step projects. Over 750 full-color photos, illustrations. 272 pages.

House Framing
Walks you through the framing basics, from assembling simple partitions to cutting compound angles for dormers. 650 full-color illustrations and photos. 240 pages.

Drywall: Pro Tips for Hanging and Finishing
Covers tools and materials, estimating, cutting, hanging, and finishing gypsum wallboard. 250 color photos and illustrations. 160 pages.

Look for these and other fine **Creative Homeowner books** wherever books are sold
For more information and to place an order, go to **www.creativehomeowner.com**